CHOOSE **COSTA RICA**
FOR RETIREMENT

HELP US KEEP
THIS GUIDE UP TO DATE

Every effort has been made by the author and editors to make this guide as accurate and useful as possible. However, many things can change after a guide is published—establishments close, phone numbers change, facilities come under new management, etc.

We would love to hear from you concerning your experiences with this guide and how you feel it could be improved and be kept up to date. While we may not be able to respond to all comments and suggestions, we'll take them to heart and we'll also make certain to share them with the author. Please send your comments and suggestions to the following address:

The Globe Pequot Press
Reader Response/Editorial Department
P.O. Box 480
Guilford, CT 06437

Or you may e-mail us at:
editorial@GlobePequot.com

Thanks for your input, and happy travels!

INSIDERS' GUIDE®

CHOOSE RETIREMENT SERIES

SEVENTH EDITION

CHOOSE **COSTA RICA**
FOR RETIREMENT

Information for Retirement, Investment,
and Affordable Living

JOHN HOWELLS

INSIDERS' GUIDE®

GUILFORD, CONNECTICUT
AN IMPRINT OF THE GLOBE PEQUOT PRESS

The prices and rates listed in this book were confirmed at press time. We recommend, however, that you call before traveling to obtain current information.

To buy books in quantity for corporate use or incentives, call **(800) 962–0973, ext. 4551,** or e-mail **premiums@GlobePequot.com.**

INSIDERS' GUIDE ®

Copyright © 1992, 1994, 1996, 1998, 2001, 2003, 2005 by John M. Howells

Text design: Linda R. Loiewski
Map design: Lisa Reneson
Overview map: Stephen Stringall

Spot photography throughout © Photodisc

ISSN 1543-6411
ISBN 0-7627-3431-0

Manufactured in the United States of America
Seventh Edition/Fourth Printing

CONTENTS

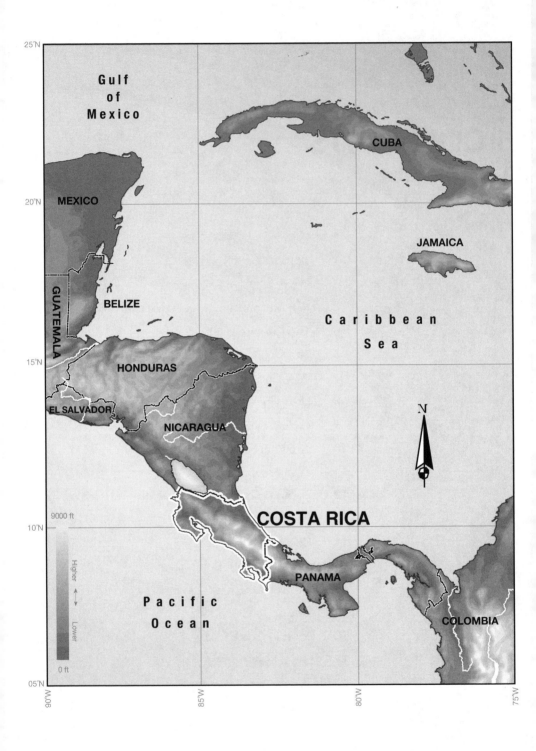

INTRODUCTION

It is much too late to refer to Costa Rica as a *"best kept secret."* The news is out. Costa Rica's rain forests, tropical beaches, and marvelous wildlife are legend. The delights of this small Central American democracy as a place to vacation, retire, or do business have spread worldwide! Eager North Americans and Europeans are arriving in constantly growing numbers—first as tourists, then returning as residents—in search of a new life in a tropical paradise. What's interesting is not only the increasing flow of retirees and business entrepreneurs, but also the younger age of those moving to Costa Rica. Many are retiring at fifty years of age, even younger. The result is an increasing number of families with children who are applying for residency, creating a demand for schools catering to English-speaking students.

My first exposure to Costa Rica came in 1972. While researching Guatemala for a freelance travel article, my wife and I decided to travel a little farther south to see what Costa Rica was all about. We expected it to be nice, but we were stunned by the country's breathtaking beauty. We were captivated by the friendliness of the Costa Rican people and loved the choice between perpetual spring weather in the highlands or perpetual summer along the Pacific and Caribbean Coasts.

Like many other first-time visitors, we wanted to move here immediately! We spoke with many fellow North Americans who were living here—some in business, some retired. Others were seasonal retirees, routinely escaping from frigid winter weather or spending summer breaks from teaching school back home. We made friends with several Costa Rican families as we toured the country—from coast to coast, from top to bottom, and we are still friends to this day. Like many tourists before and since, we resolved that someday we would embark on a new beginning in paradise—if not immediately, then eventually.

This seventh edition of *Choose Costa Rica for Retirement* is the outcome of thirty years of traveling in, living in, and writing about Costa Rica and Latin America in general. My bias toward the country comes through quite clearly, but I try to balance the picture by reminding readers that living in a foreign country is definitely not everyone's cup of tea. It takes a special type of person to enjoy an interesting and challenging life in a foreign country. Hopefully, this book will help you determine if you are that type of person.

Choose Costa Rica for Retirement is intended for not only retirees but also those nearing retirement age who are casting about for ideas for the future. This book is also designed as a guide for those individuals who manage to have part or all of the year free for doing exactly what they feel like doing. It's for the professor on sabbatical, the schoolteacher on a summer vacation, the construction worker with chronic winter unemployment, the executive who can take a leave of absence. This book is also for self-employed individuals who can trust their businesses to others while they enjoy life now instead of waiting for the "someday" that may never come. *Choose Costa Rica for Retirement* is especially oriented toward those who seek a "new start," who might wish to invest time and resources into launching a new business career as well as enjoying a fascinating lifestyle in an exotic foreign country.

Although this is partly a travel book, the emphasis is on "how to do it" rather than "where to stay." A hotel, bed-and-breakfast, or restaurant may be mentioned from time to time but only as an adjunct to the narrative and should not be taken as a personal recommendation.

About prices quoted throughout this book: They are accurate as of the time of writing, based on the current dollar exchange rates in Costa Rica. In fall 2004 the Costa Rican currency, the colón, was worth about 450 colones to the dollar.

After reading through this book, maybe you'll understand why Costa Rica has such a good reputation among North Americans and Europeans. You might even find a niche there for you and your family. A word of caution: Costa Rica isn't for everyone. There are those who can't resist comparing conditions in Costa Rica with those in the United States or Canada. Remember, Costa Rica is still a developing Third World country. There's a world of difference. For those of us who love Costa Rica, we thank our lucky stars for the difference!

NOTE: Unless otherwise stated, all phone and fax numbers in this book are in Costa Rica and to connect, you must dial the proper access and country code.

CHAPTER ONE

SWITZERLAND
OF THE AMERICAS

It's almost impossible to find a guidebook to Costa Rica that doesn't refer to the country as the "Switzerland of the Americas." Costa Ricans themselves like to claim similarities between the two countries. Therefore, even though Costa Rica is as much like Switzerland as a poodle is like a beagle, I suppose this book is obliged to make the same comparison.

At first glance, the only thing the two countries seem to have in common is that they are similar in size (although Switzerland is actually a bit smaller—one of the world's few countries with that distinction). But Costa Rica is lushly tropical and continuously swathed in luxurious green vegetation—a place where coffee, sugarcane, and mangoes thrive and where snow never falls. It's the exact opposite of Switzerland, with its snowcapped peaks and barren, rocky terrain.

Yet the more one travels in Costa Rica, the more apparent are the parallels with Switzerland. Both are peaceful, progressive countries where democracy and stability are hallmarks. Although Costa Rica's tropical beaches are incongruent with the Swiss terrain, the higher mountains rival the rugged beauty of the Alps. The lake area around

the Arenal Volcano could easily pass for parts of Switzerland—during the Swiss summertime, at any rate.

Even closer similarities between the two countries appear in their philosophy of life and economic structures. Both are places of small farms and small businesses, with an air of prosperity and a feeling of equality among citizens. Both countries have renounced aggressive militarism, diverting resources—those that would otherwise be consumed by wars— toward education, medical care, and services for the good of all. In short, both places are affluent, happy, and tranquil. Both are locations where North Americans can feel at home, safe, and welcome.

There are differences, of course. Costa Rica is closer to the United States and Canada, making it somewhat more accessible than Europe. Costa Rica also enjoys a dramatically lower cost of living than Switzerland. And best of all, Costa Rica has a climate that can be enjoyed year-round by those of us who hate wearing snow boots and earmuffs. The higher elevations enjoy springlike temperatures year-round; brightly colored flowers seem to glow in the crystal-clear atmosphere. The countryside is so fertile that fence posts sprout and become trees despite all the farmers' best efforts. Crossing over the mountains, you drop down to tropical lowlands where North Americans own plantations of coffee, macadamia nuts, black pepper, and other exotic crops for export. (Macadamia nut plantations are exceedingly rare in Switzerland.) Beaches flank either side of the country, dotted with small communities where North Americans and Europeans live in communion with surf and jungle.

A UNIQUE **HISTORY**

Costa Rica stands out in this hemisphere in many ways, but its biggest contrast is with its Central American neighbors. When you drive across the border into Costa Rica or when you step off an airplane arriving from another Central American country, you know immediately that you are in a special place. Relative affluence stands out in contrast to the grinding poverty of most other Central American locations. People living in neighboring republics point to Costa Rica as an example of the kind of world they would hope to imitate. "If Costa Rica can be prosperous, democratic, and free," the envious neighbors ask, "why can't we?"

Clearly, there are light-years of difference between Costa Rica and the other Central American countries. How did it get that way? Why does

Costa Rica have so much less poverty and so large a middle class in comparison with neighboring countries? The answers to these questions can be found in a series of historical events—some accidental, some planned.

In 1502, when Columbus happened upon Costa Rica during his last voyage to this hemisphere, he anchored at present-day Limón and dispatched an expedition ashore. Chances are, Columbus himself waited on the ship for a report from his landing party. His explorers returned with news of an inhospitable jungle and impossible swamps, plus ferocious natives who owned but a few paltry ornaments of thinly pounded gold. In short, the Limón Coast offered little to excite the imagination of these avaricious explorers. They quickly moved on without attempting colonization.

According to legend, Columbus gave his new discovery the name Costa Rica or "rich coast." Some historians think the name may have come from another explorer—Fernández de Córdoba—as he charted the Pacific side of the isthmus some thirty years later. Impressed by the magnificent forests, fertile lands, and abundant wildlife of the Nicoya Peninsula, he coined the term *Costa Rica* as he established a settlement in 1539. The Caribbean Coast that Columbus discovered was left virtually untouched and ignored by Europeans for several centuries. Due in part to the isolation of this Pacific Coast settlement, and in contrast with the fast colonization of other parts of the Americas, Costa Rica grew very slowly.

It was the custom for the Spanish Crown to grant huge tracts of land to the conquistadores as a reward for their services. Indians were considered a part of the land, and although not exactly slaves, they essentially belonged to the enormous haciendas—they were forced to work as peons for the aristocratic conquerors. In places like Peru, Mexico, and Guatemala, the Indians meekly accepted their new rulers and continued working the same lands as before, paying tribute to new overlords. However, the Indians of Costa Rica (like their cousins in North America) proved to be determined, fierce fighters who resisted the idea of accepting the intruders as their superiors. Experts in defending their heavily forested lands, the natives simply withdrew farther into the jungle when defeated. They clearly weren't interested in tilling fields for the pink-faced intruders. Archaeological evidence suggests that at least some tribes were headhunters, possibly culturally related to the Jívaros of Ecuador, whose warriors dangled their enemies' shrunken heads around their necks as ornaments. In short, these people were unlikely candidates for being docile field laborers.

This left the newcomers in a position they hadn't counted on. Instead of being lords over huge estates and overseeing gangs of laboring peons, the Spanish conquistadores were forced to work the land for themselves! This required hard manual labor and a marginal existence on small, family-run farms. From the beginning all were equal in their struggle for existence. Even the royal viceroy had to raise chickens and tend his own garden to avoid starvation. Small wonder that many early settlers moved on to easier pickings; others ignored the country completely.

Costa Rica's development got off to an inauspicious start, and the country remained a backwater of Spanish colonization, all but forgotten over the ensuing centuries. It grew in its own way, ignoring the ineffective Spanish governors sent by the royal court of Madrid. Costa Ricans lived quiet lives, isolated and unaffected by events in other colonies. In fact, when Spain granted independence to the Spanish colonies in 1821, Costa Rica was the last to know (and probably cared the least). For all practical purposes, it had always been on its own. Independence was no novelty.

Fortunately, Costa Rica's first president turned out to be a progressive thinker, a visionary who wanted to see the country develop socially and economically. He was convinced that growing coffee for export could be a major economic breakthrough, a key to modernization. Coffee profits could build roads, schools, and cities.

But the country was scantily populated. More people were needed to grow coffee in order to fulfill the president's dream. Consequently, free land was offered to anyone willing to grow coffee plants. Since coffee production in Costa Rica is ideally suited to small farms, European families began immigrating to take advantage of Costa Rica's opportunities. They came from Italy and France as well as from Spain. Instead of huge plantations owned by a few wealthy families, as in other Central American republics, hundreds of small farms sprang up, selling coffee beans to merchants who processed and exported the product. This resulted in a tradition of independence and equality, with a preponderance of middle-class farmers and a few moderately wealthy, coffee-exporting families. The spread between rich, middle class, and poor was much narrower than anywhere else in the hemisphere and remains so to this day.

Troubled times in Europe during the last half of the nineteenth century brought new waves of economic and political refugees to the Americas, seeking a chance to "start over." The standing offer of free land to grow coffee was irresistible. The ranks of small farmers grew even larger. These refugees, often imbued with contemporary Europe's liberal intellectual and political philosophy, contributed substantially to the notions of freedom, democracy, and individual rights that were already in place.

This is not to say that Costa Rica didn't develop a wealthy oligarchy of elite families whose position rested upon their control of coffee exports. But because of their tradition of being "self-made" families and their respect for hard work, their mentality was different from that of the arrogant Spanish conquistadores who worshiped royalty and privilege.

Free and compulsory education was an early development, starting in 1869 and setting a tradition of literacy that ranks Costa Rica higher than most other countries of the world—including the United States. A university was founded in 1844, staffed in part by intellectuals who fled Europe's political and economic maelstrom. These and other modern European traditions developed in Costa Rica in stark contrast with the medieval, feudal heritage of Mexico and other Central American countries.

A PEACEFUL **DEMOCRACY**

Costa Rica is a country where North Americans feel very much at home. It is a country of law-abiding citizens, a place where you don't feel shivers of apprehension at the approach of a policeman or a heavily armed soldier. (You have to have traveled in a police state to appreciate this last statement.) Costa Rica is a country where juvenile gangs and graffiti are the exception, not the rule. It's a place where your conscience isn't continually assaulted by obvious poverty, children begging in the streets, or social injustice. It's a place where North Americans feel comfortable living in just about any neighborhood, not forced to huddle together in enclaves of other expatriates for mutual support. That's not to say Costa Rica is crime-free (is there such a place?), but compared with most other places in this world, the country has a safe feeling.

One reason we North Americans are attracted to Costa Rica is that Costa Ricans are so much like us. They think like us, act like us, and hold much the same values. They are open, friendly, and egalitarian. Most North Americans feel at home in Costa Rica. (The only other Latin country where I feel this way is Argentina.)

Because of these ingrained attitudes, Costa Rica has avoided the problems that have mired its sister Central American republics in a quicksand of turmoil and tragedy. Costa Rica's devotion to democracy and peaceful cooperation with its neighbors has enabled the country to retain its enviable position as a showcase of prosperity, respect for law, and personal freedoms.

More than a century-and-a-half tradition of free and honest elections forms the basis for today's political life. Instead of frequent coups d'état, so common in neighboring countries, Costa Ricans change their government by balloting. Although members of the same affluent families usually win election, they are civilians and intellectuals and for the most part are working for the good of the country as a whole, not just for one particular class. In 1889 a revolution threatened when the defeated incumbents considered not recognizing the election results. But at the last minute, they decided to accept the will of the people, thus reinforcing this tradition of democratic process.

A truly significant event that totally separated Costa Rica from the ranks of other Latin American nations occurred in 1948. The ruling party decided not to recognize the results of an election and refused to give up power, ordering new elections because of the closeness of the vote and accusations of fraud. A crisis of democracy threatened. Pepe Figueres, a charismatic member of one of the wealthy families, stepped forward to lead an uprising against the illegal government and its attempt to use the army to hold on to power. The result of this successful revolution (the first and only in Costa Rican history) was a decision to abolish the army and replace it with the Guardia Civil, a civilian-controlled police force that augments the local police. In some smaller towns the Guardia Civil is the only police force.

This was a brilliant and bold step. Barracks were turned into schools. Ex-soldiers were given jobs building roads. Money that would normally be absorbed by military corruption and graft was devoted to highways, education, and medical care. Today a huge percentage of the national budget goes to education and culture. Public money pays for four universities, three symphony orchestras, and five autonomous state publishing houses. Of the gross national product, about 10 percent is spent on medical care; Costa Rica has an average of one physician for every 700 inhabitants.

Some North Americans shake their heads in dismay at the lack of a standing army. They ask, "Without a military, how can you defend your country from aggression?" The answer is simple. The function of a Central American military has never been to deter aggression; the military's duty is to protect the *rulers* of the country from its *citizens,* to keep the people in line, and to maintain privileges for the military and the country's financial elite. Democracy doesn't stand a chance when armed soldiers can nominate candidates, threaten voters, conduct elections, and then count the ballots. Are we actually surprised when generals are elected president?

Election Day is Costa Rica's most important holiday, a riotous celebration with a joyous spirit that goes far beyond mere politics. Voting is mandatory (nonvoters pay a token fine), but few citizens would think of passing up the fun and excitement of an election. Weeks prior to Election Day, all parties campaign vigorously, with folks everywhere waving their party's flags, cheering enthusiastically when a car displaying a favored flag drives past, or booing good-naturedly when an opposition flag passes by. On the day of an election, all stores, bars, and businesses are closed. All public transportation is free. Buses, taxis, and even private cars are expected to stop when someone indicates he or she wants a ride to a polling booth. In practice, most autos will stop for anyone who waves and asks for a ride in whatever direction the auto is headed. After all, this is a fiesta!

It's interesting to note that many Costa Ricans, when they move from their hometowns to another part of the country, do not change their voting registration to their new address. Because transportation is free, this is an opportunity to return to their hometowns to vote, to visit friends and family, and to party at the same time. Reunions and celebrations are a vital part of Election Day.

Voters must dunk their thumbs into indelible ink to prove they've voted (and cannot vote again), and this purple digit is worn as a proud badge of civic duty. Automobile drivers honk their horns and wave their discolored thumbs in the air as they drive along the streets, to show everyone that they have voted, while shouting, "Have you voted yet?" There are so many horns blowing on Election Day that it sounds like New Year's Eve at midnight.

The result is a country intensely dedicated to notions of democracy. All segments of the political spectrum, from extreme Right to far-out Left, are represented; all are totally legal. The crucial point is this: The electorate has a free choice. Voters can vote Right, Left, or Center—depending on which party presents the best ideas. Because citizens can change their government at will, Costa Rica is virtually revolution-proof.

The end result is a free, prosperous, and peaceful country.

Don't misunderstand—I'm not implying that Costa Rica has no poverty or that Costa Rican workers are highly paid. But compared with the situation in most other Latin American countries, workers here enjoy excellent working conditions, relatively high wages, and government guarantees of fair treatment from employers. Even those living below the poverty level live far better than in most other Third World countries and better, in my opinion, than the millions of people living below the poverty level in the United States. You'll see few if any "street people," panhandlers, or beggars on Costa Rican streets. Children never beg. As a friend observed, "Among the world's poor, Costa Rica's poor are the most affluent."

Welfare is an unknown concept in Costa Rica. Family and friends are always there to help in case of disaster. Jobs are plentiful and unemployment a fraction of that in most highly developed countries. Food is abundant; medical care and education are free. Much agriculture here depends on illegal aliens from Nicaragua to harvest crops and tend banana plantations; Costa Rican workers prefer not to do this kind of backbreaking work. (Does this sound familiar to Californians and Texans

who depend on illegal Mexican immigrants for their crops?) Open-air markets have a tradition of giving food to the poor, with vendors handing out their surplus to those asking. If a family wants land to grow food, the government does its best to set them up with a farm.

Although wages are higher here than in neighboring countries, they appear to be extraordinarily low to us Norteamericanos. How can workers be expected to survive on as little as $50 a week, much less be considered well-off? The answer is that even though the cash salary is small, fringe benefits connected with the job make a big difference. In addition to their cash salary, workers are guaranteed items such as sick leave—at the rate of 50 percent of their salary—from the first day of illness up to a lifetime of disability. Workers receive a month's *aguinaldo,* or Christmas bonus, every year and a minimum of two weeks' paid vacation every year. Medical care is free. Women receive six weeks' maternity leave (at full salary), and all receive a Social Security pension upon retirement. It isn't necessary to put aside money for the children's college tuition, because education is virtually free, a basic right provided by the government. Since medical care is free, a worker can spend his or her entire salary on living expenses without having to put a portion aside for medical emergencies or illnesses.

All these benefits are guaranteed by law, and all Costa Ricans know exactly what their rights are. Since there's usually a chronic shortage of help in many regions of Costa Rica, anyone who really wants to work can find a job. The result is that employers have to pay more than minimum wages in order to attract competent workers. This is in contrast with other Latin American countries, where the minimum wage and the maximum wage are considered the same.

When you measure these benefits and put a cash value on them, you'll find that Costa Rican workers are ahead of many North Americans. In the United States woefully inadequate medical insurance can cost a worker more money than many Costa Ricans' total monthly earnings! Since few low-paid U.S. workers can afford insurance, one short visit to a hospital can push them over the financial edge. Sick leave? In the United States only large, affluent companies can afford such extravagance. Up north, paid vacations are not mandatory; they're granted only at the discretion of an employer. In Costa Rica, paid vacations are the law.

I'm always amused when I hear ultraconservatives point to Costa Rica's health care system as evidence that the government is Socialist. They overlook the point that if universal health care makes a country Socialist, the United States would be one of the few non-Socialist countries in the world! So where does the money come from for health care, pensions, sick leave, and such? It comes out of workers' wages in the form of Social Security contributions and matching funds paid by employers as part of the wage package. Costa Rica's system should be a model for other Third World countries.

EASY **ACCESS**

Entering Costa Rica is very easy; you needn't make a special visit to a consul for a visa before you get on a plane to visit. And the government is very lenient with length of stays; an initial ninety days with a ninety-day extension are available for the asking. This makes a stay of six months possible, allowing plenty of time to investigate and tour all the nooks and corners of Costa Rica to see whether it would be an appropriate place to retire or go into business.

For years Costa Rica granted tourist permits without a passport, tourists simply presented a birth certificate and identification with a current photo, such as a driver's license. This has changed. Now you definitely need a passport to enter the country. Most countries in the world—including Panama, Nicaragua, and all others in Central America—require passports so this should not be considered a hardship for us North Americans. A passport is inexpensive and serves as the ultimate in identification. You'll be surprised how often you'll be asked for your passport or your passport number for occasions such as registering in a hotel or buying a plane ticket. Without a passport, you can't rent a car or cash traveler's checks. You can't even drive a car unless you have a passport showing your entry date.

Your Costa Rican visa is valid for ninety days. It's usually an easy matter to obtain one visa extension for an additional three months; a travel agent can take care of this matter for you. If you don't care to bother with an extension, you can simply exit the country and take a seventy-two-hour break before returning. Many choose to visit Nicaragua, the San Andres Islands (which belong to Colombia), or Panama. Be aware that from time to time, the Ministry of Immigration threatens to tighten the rules on folks who do too many of these in-and-out trips to avoid applying for residency. Occasionally, immigration agents crack down on a few "perpetual tourists," actually deporting two or three who had overstayed their visas. "Perpetual tourists" is a term applied to those who spend years in Costa Rica without applying for legal residency. Theoretically, there is a limit to the number of times one can exit the country for a seventy-two-hour turnaround, but no one seems to know the figure. Overall, enforcement of rules against foreign visitors has been lax and sporadic. That can change, of course.

Speaking of permanent residence, according to a U.S. State Department source, about 40,000 monthly Social Security checks are sent to retirees living in Central America. This doesn't tell us much about North American retirees or investors, since many of these 40,000 are Central American citizens who returned to their country of birth to retire. As best as I can tell, about 20,000 North American citizens live in Costa Rica—some full-time, others making their homes here seasonally. Exact figures are impossible to come by. The percentage of Canadian versus U.S. citizens is difficult to state with precision, but you can be confident that plenty of Canadians are represented. A few North Americans live in other Central American countries—Guatemala, Honduras, Belize, and even El Salvador and Nicaragua—but their ranks are scanty compared with those in Costa Rica.

Because of its small size and economically homogeneous native population, Costa Rica lures a much larger percentage of North Americans (and foreigners in general) who are "starting over" or living part-time in this exotic semiparadise. Furthermore, you'll find these newcomers scattered all around the country—almost every nook and cranny has a few of us living there—instead of concentrated in enclaves or colonies, as is the case in many other foreign countries.

Like Mexico, Costa Rica eagerly welcomes tourists, seasonal residents, and retirees—but Costa Rica places fewer restrictions on newcomers. The government here makes it easy to own property or start a business. You can do either even while holding just a tourist visa. To become a *pensionado* in Costa Rica, you need only to prove $600 a month retirement income. For those who aren't retired but would like to live in the country or manage a business, the requirement is $1,000 a month income. Happily, these amounts can easily cover a couple's basic living expenses, something unthinkable in most other parts of the world. Just consider the living standard you'd maintain in the United States on $600 or even $1,000 a month! In Costa Rica on $1,000 a month, you can afford a maid and a gardener, at least part-time. (Please note: These figures are for *basic* expenses, as will be discussed later on. Basic expenses are rent, food, utilities, and other costs that don't vary significantly with lifestyles. I know people who live well in Costa Rica on $600 a month— and others who spend $2,600 and feel they are economizing.) Be aware that the Costa Rican congress is considering raising the minimum amounts for residency. This has been discussed many times in the past, with no decision ever made. It could happen this time, but one never knows. I will post any news about this on our Update Web site at www.discoverypress.com/update if and when the law becomes effective.

Two other conditions make Costa Rica special as a destination for part-time or full-time living. Most important is the almost perfect weather.

The central plateau is wonderfully temperate, with thermometer readings virtually the same year-round—with highs in the seventies. Beaches are exquisitely tropical yet, like Hawaii, not extremely hot or humid.

The second favorable condition is Costa Rica's exciting investment climate. Instead of placing barriers to prevent foreigners from going into business, as do most other countries in the world, Costa Rica encourages foreign investment. To lure investors, the government offers tax incentives and duty-free imports. Again, you don't have to be a citizen or even a legal resident to own property or conduct a business. You can do it on a tourist visa! Not many desirable countries permit you to do this.

UNLIMITED **GROWTH POTENTIAL**

For the past several years, North American tourism overseas has been on the decline, particularly travel to Europe. Out-of-sight prices abroad discourages many North Americans from traveling or living in Europe. At the time of writing, the dollar has lost 42 cents in value against the Euro over just a few years ago, which *really* makes European travel expensive. It's no surprise that Costa Rica tourism and retirement is gaining momentum with North Americans. For Europeans, the cost differential is even more dramatic. As a consequence, Costa Rica's tourism industry has been on a steady upward curve.

PREPLANNING **FOR COSTA RICA**

One publication I strongly recommend for anyone considering Costa Rica for anything more than a short vacation is San José's English-language newspaper, the *Tico Times*. If you read every issue from front to back, including the advertisements, by the time you actually get to Costa Rica, you will know so much about the place that you will feel as though you are returning home. The classified ads keep you up to date on rental costs, housing prices, and what secondhand furniture and appliances sell for. Display ads tell you what you should pay for a hotel room or a bed-and-breakfast, the best places to dine, or where to go for a beach excursion. The news columns are well written, with complete and unbiased news of what's happening in Costa Rica as well as in neighboring countries—news not available in U.S. or Canadian newspapers. Featured are articles relating to foreign residents, governmental actions, or changes in law that may affect them, as well as news of social activities and club events. An extensive letters-to-the-editor section prints opinions of tourists and residents alike, telling of exceptionally nice places to go and which places are rip-offs, giving opinions about the country, kudos and complaints, political views, and just about anything else you can imagine. By all means, start your subscription several months before you leave.

A second essential publication for your initial trip is a good travel book. U.S. and Canadian bookstores are loaded with excellent travel guidebooks packed with information you need on bus and plane schedules, hotels, and places you'll want to visit—in accurate, nonflowery language. It's best to purchase your guidebooks before leaving home; they are usually overpriced in Costa Rican bookstores. You'll need this additional information because *Choose Costa Rica for Retirement* is not intended to be a comprehensive travel book; it's a guide to retirement, long-term living, and investment in the country.

Choose Costa Rica for Retirement also tries to avoid making recommendations on business services such as real estate agencies, simply because of the impossibility of being able to vouch for reliability or character. Personnel can change; brokerages are sold; and Costa Rican real estate agents aren't bound by the strict rules of ethics common in the United States and Canada. Your job is to investigate, conduct inquiries, and make your own, on-the-spot selections. When business services are mentioned, it isn't as an endorsement of their reliability but simply as a starting place for checking out the field. At the time I interviewed these business representatives, I was impressed by their knowledge—but that says nothing of their competence or honesty. These are judgments you must make for yourself.

RETIREMENT TOURS Although travel in Costa Rica is easy and plans can be very casual, some folks prefer to take a guided tour to the more popular areas for relocation. An organized tour is more efficient and saves time because the tour guide knows exactly where the expatriates prefer to live, and the guide will be able to introduce you to North Americans who have made the move to Costa Rica. One tour that comes highly recommended is conducted by Christopher Howard, a longtime resident of Costa Rica, and author of several guidebooks on living and retiring there. His tours are in-depth and take you all over the country. His Web site is www.liveincostarica.com/pages/retirement_tours.htm.

Another popular Costa Rica tour operator is George Lundquist, who features a retirement tour called "Expose me to life for the Non-Rich in Costa Rica." His four-day tours take guests to some nontraditional retirement locations as well as some of the standard places. He places an emphasis on retiring on Social Security checks. His Web site is: www.costaricaretireonss.com/.

INTERNET RESEARCH Another valuable preplanning tool is the Internet. Allow me to strongly recommend that if you don't already have a computer with a Web connection, get one right away. The amount of Costa Rica information available on the Internet is almost unbelievable, and it grows even more comprehensive by the day. With today's simplified Web browsers, anyone can learn to tap this information with an hour's instruction. Do your research, then take the computer to Costa Rica with you so that you can stay in constant contact with friends and family.

In addition to in-depth descriptions of various sections of Costa Rica as places to live, the Internet brings you Web pages with regional descriptions of Costa Rica, as well as real estate, homes for rent, and on-line expatriate clubs. If you want to correspond directly with folks living in Costa Rica or others who are considering moving there, you'll find forums and bulletin boards where they post their E-mail addresses. You can make some Costa Rica friends before you ever leave for the airport!

One Internet source of information is my own Costa Rica Bulletin Board. This has been on the Internet for five years now and has attracted more than 300,000 visitors. Discussions range from how to find a shipper to take furniture to Costa Rica to where to rent a house, from which is the best bed-and-breakfast in Jacó Beach to how to cook *gallo pinto*. The Web address is www.discoverypress.com/wwwboard.

To keep you informed about important changes in laws or conditions since the publication of this edition of *Choose Costa Rica for Retirement,* I will maintain an update page at www.discoverypress.com/update.

Finally, I emphatically urge that you make no decisions about permanent moves or business investments without spending several months "on location," getting to know the country, meeting the people, and learning what it's all about. Before making any financial moves, find a good lawyer, one recommended by someone in the North American community. Above all, don't hand your money to someone simply because he or she also comes from Omaha or Ottawa and has an honest face. Honest faces and firm handshakes are the mark of successful swindlers! Costa Rica has suffered its fair share of sweet-talking gringos with designs on your pocketbooks. There's something about a foreign country that tends to bring out latent larceny in some people. Later on in this book, we'll discuss ways to protect yourself from theft. ■

CHAPTER TWO

WHAT'S
COSTA RICA LIKE?

Costa Rica is a small country, even though it doesn't appear so from the standpoint of the traveler who is driving a rental car from one end of the country to the other over winding roads, uphill and down. Every turn in the road brings a new vista, something else to contemplate. Actually, the country contains a little less than 20,000 square miles, much of it almost unpopulated.

Travel articles and guidebooks traditionally describe Costa Rica as being "the size of West Virginia," but that's not really accurate. Some travel writer must have said that years ago, and others automatically repeat this misinformation. The truth is, Costa Rica is smaller than West Virginia by 20 percent. To be more accurate, let's say that Costa Rica is about the size of New Hampshire and Maryland, with poor little Rhode Island tossed in for good measure. Would it help to say that Costa Rica is about half the size of Kentucky? If that makes the place sound small and insignificant, we can balance the equation by pointing out that Costa Rica is larger than Albania, Denmark, Belgium, Holland, Israel, or Switzerland (plus many countries you and I have never heard of).

Yet few other countries of any size offer such a diversity of scenery and climate or such a wide variety of flora and fauna. Probably no other

country in the world devotes as large a percentage of its territory to national parks and wildlife refuges. About 27 percent of Costa Rica's land is thus protected. These preserves range from cloud forests to tropical beaches, from volcanic craters to jungle swamps and inland waterways. The national park system is a major attraction for tourism.

Costa Rica's bewildering assortment of wildlife includes 850 species of birds—more than three times as many as in the United States and Canada combined. Representative mammals are monkeys, coatis, jaguars, and ocelots, as well as sloths, tapirs, and agoutis. One evening down on the Pacific Coast, a large anteater ambled in front of my car, its long snout almost touching the ground in front and an equally heavy tail drooping behind, looking very prehistoric. Turtles, colorful frogs, and toads of all descriptions are found, as are crocodiles and iguanas. Snakes? Of course. They range from huge boa constrictors to tiny coral snakes. Experts say there are more varieties of butterflies in Costa Rica than in all the African continent; more than 2,000 species have been collected so far and more are being discovered. The number of orchids and bromeliads confuses the mind. This is truly a naturalist's paradise.

Many tropical countries offer beaches and vacation accommodations, but nowhere else in the world can a tourist find such a combination of beaches, mountains, friendliness, and tropical wonder that's accessible year-round.

The Costa Rican government recognizes these unique assets and actively involves its citizens in both the preservation and the exploitation of nature at the same time. How do you protect as well as exploit the environment? Just one example: By hiring local people to guard and preserve endangered turtle nesting beaches, jobs are created. Beach villages then become tourist attractions, complete with motels, restaurants, and shops, thus creating even more jobs. Visitors from all over the world can now visit cloud forests, turtle nesting beaches, and nature preserves—in comfort. In the process, they leave much-needed foreign currency with Costa Rican businesses and banks.

Many North Americans and Europeans are scrambling to join this bandwagon and, with government encouragement, are investing heavily in tourist businesses, particularly in motels, restaurants, and endeavors of a like nature. Some enterprises become instant successes, with full bookings and plenty of business. One Canadian, who started a motel on the

Caribbean side of the country a few years ago, showed me the registration book for his twelve-unit facility, saying proudly, "This place has an occupancy rate of 98 percent during the tourist season and over 60 percent during the off-season." I asked for a room but was told, "Not until next week. I'm booked solid." Despite occasional slow spells, Costa Rica's commerce and tourism have forged ahead through the past decade and continue healthy and growing into the new century. (Details about starting and operating a business in Costa Rica are presented in Chapter 11.)

A COUNTRY OF **CONTRADICTIONS**

Before readers are left with the impression that things are perfect in paradise, that Costa Rica is the best of all worlds, let's examine some contradictions.

The first contradiction: Even though the Costa Rican government is totally committed to preserving the environment and tries to control illegal deforestation, it also permits foreign companies to bulldoze forests in order to make more banana plantations and tourist resorts. The government puts large tracts of land into biological and wildlife reserves, forest reserves, national parks, and Indian reservations, yet at the same time, farmers and agribusinesses cut down forests on private tracts almost at will. The economy destroys in the name of progress, while the government tries to preserve in the name of conservation. But at least the government does try, and its efforts are improving.

Another contradiction: The growth of ecotourism in Costa Rica brings hundreds of thousands of visitors to enjoy the ecological wonderlands, but large numbers of visitors tramping through delicately balanced wilderness systems threaten to destroy the very ecological treasures that lure them to Costa Rica in the first place. The government raised admission fees to national parks in an effort to cut traffic to some extent. Some say the increase was merely to bring in more revenue—that may well be true—but it did indeed lower the number of visitors and traffic in national parks. The fee increase had a beneficial side effect in directing more business toward private ecological parks and developments. However, the tourist industry raised strenuous objections to the higher fees, claiming they hurt business. So the government offered a deal: "You cut the hotel

rates 15 percent, and we'll reduce national park entrance fees by 60 percent." The result was that entrance fees to national parks, which had ranged from $5.00 to $15.00, were reduced to a fixed price of $6.00, and more than a hundred hotels agreed to lower their room rates.

Entrance fees are the source of complaints from foreign tourists, because Costa Rican citizens and expatriates with legal residency are charged less than foreign tourists are. Some attractions give Tico children free admittance (at a very popular rain forest aerial tram, for example) while charging tourist children $25. Frankly, I see nothing wrong with giving Costa Ricans a break when visiting national parks and scenic areas of their own country. After all, a $10 entrance fee for a Tico equals one day's pay, while most tourists earn more than that in less than an hour. However, foreigners who have residency in Costa Rica pay the same as Costa Rican citizens. Citizens and legal residents also enjoy 50 percent discounts on Sansa, the national airline.

Yet another contradiction in Costa Rica is the high incidence in petty crime among such a peaceful population—particularly in larger cities. In fact, the major criticism this book has received in the past was that it did not place proper emphasis on the crime rates. I have to admit that I've had a propensity to overlook this issue, probably because I feel that the problem is lightweight compared with the situation in other Latin countries and is almost insignificant when matched with the crime rate in most U.S. communities of similar sizes. Any increase in crime rates can be considered a natural phenomenon that parallels the rise of crime back home, although on a more minor scale. We'll discuss crime in more detail in Chapter 8.

Some will disagree, but I feel that Costa Rica's substandard roads, heavy traffic in some areas, and sometimes serious potholes are a bigger annoyance than petty crime. I must admit, the government is trying its best to upgrade the roads and fill in potholes. But ever-increasing traffic, especially heavy trucks, and heavy rainfall make road maintenance difficult. We have to marvel at the progress in road improvement over the past dozen years.

Combine treacherous pavement with too many automobiles on the Meseta Central's street system and you have a situation that encourages taxi rides into congested parts of San José. Fortunately, cab rides are cheap, and more than 7,000 taxis roam the streets, so you don't have a long wait between rides. The problems of potholes and heavy traffic in the city will always be another of those fly-in-the-ointment nuisances you'll have to accept if you want to live in paradise. Nothing's perfect. The farther you get from downtown San José, the less the annoyance. When you are really deep into rural areas, the biggest obstacle to driving might be a herd of cattle being driven down the gravel road or a sow and litter of piglets ambling across the way.

Another situation that could become a problem as the foreign population increases is foreign ownership of most of the coastal lands. Although the Costa Rican people are friendly, gentle, and welcoming, they cannot help but feel some level of resentment as they see foreigners bid up the price of property until it is out of their price range. (The big-money players are heavily represented by German, Swiss, and Italian buyers.) At present this level of resentment is low, and it's balanced by an appreciation for how foreign investment creates jobs and bolsters the economy. Where my wife and I own property, the local people tell us they'd much rather see foreigners own the land, because Ticos tend to clear-cut the forest to make room for cattle. Cattle ranches create few jobs, while businesses and residences bring full employment and prosperity to all.

Visitors and foreign residents can do little to resolve these contradictions, but they need to be aware that problems do exist and may crop up in the future. The best they can do is try to minimize their impact upon the natural resources of the country. None of these problems have gotten out of hand, and solutions are constantly being sought by the Costa Rican government. But as is the way in any democracy, the going is slow and cumbersome. Just be aware that not everything is perfect in paradise—but for my money, it's still paradise!

MENU OF **CLIMATES**

For such a small country, Costa Rica has an astonishing variety of climates. From the misty mountaintops of Talamanca and Monteverde to the dry northern Guanacaste province, from the permanent spring weather of the Arenal area to the jungle lushness of the Caribbean Coast, Costa Rica has every kind of climate one might desire. The exception is frozen snow and bitter cold; but you don't want that anyway. Yes, there are seasons, but the differences between them are minimal, mostly measured in differences in rainfall rather than in temperature variation. Unlike many other world vacation spots, Costa Rica isn't a one-season destination; almost any time of the year can be a perfect time to visit. For those who live here full-time, the seasonal changes add spice to retirement. September and October are probably the least popular months, though, for these are the rainiest ones.

In Costa Rica people transpose the meanings of winter and summer. They call the months of December, January, and February "summer," or the "dry season." These are the months that children take their "summer vacation" from school. To a Costa Rican, "winter" means June, July, and August! Conversations can become very confusing when Costa Ricans and North Americans discuss the seasons, with summer and winter having opposite meanings for each. To avoid misunderstandings, I generally say, "June, July, and August" instead of "winter," or better yet I'll say "dry season" or "rainy season"—then everybody knows what I mean.

The dry season, which actually begins around the end of November and lasts until May, isn't parched and arid, as the name might imply. Occasional showers keep plants and lawns pleasantly green and flowers blooming in the higher parts of the mountains, where most folks live. On the Caribbean Coast and the area around Lake Arenal, the "dry season" is just a figure of speech; rain knows no seasons here. Some Pacific coastal areas are truly dry January through April, very much like California summers, when rain rarely falls.

TEMPERATURES AND RAINFALL
FOR SELECTED COSTA RICAN LOCATIONS

Alajuela

AVG.	JAN.	FEB.	MAR.	APR.	MAY	JUN.	JUL.	AUG.	SEPT.	OCT.	NOV.	DEC.	ANNUAL
					(In degrees Fahrenheit and inches)								
HIGHS	81	83	85	85	82	81	81	81	80	80	80	81	81
LOWS	62	62	63	63	64	64	64	63	63	63	63	63	63
RAIN	0.3	0.5	0.6	3	11	11	7	10	1	14	20	1	92

Golfito

	JAN.	FEB.	MAR.	APR.	MAY	JUN.	JUL.	AUG.	SEPT.	OCT.	NOV.	DEC.	ANNUAL
HIGHS	91	92	92	91	90	89	89	90	89	89	89	90	90
LOWS	71	72	73	73	73	72	71	71	71	71	71	71	72
RAIN	6	6	8	11	19	18	18	22	28	28	23	12	199

Cahuita

	JAN.	FEB.	MAR.	APR.	MAY	JUN.	JUL.	AUG.	SEPT.	OCT.	NOV.	DEC.	ANNUAL
HIGHS	86	86	87	87	87	87	86	86	87	87	86	86	86
LOWS	68	68	69	71	71	71	71	71	71	71	69	69	69
RAIN	13	8	8	11	11	12	17	13	6	8	16	18	141

Nicoya

	JAN.	FEB.	MAR.	APR.	MAY	JUN.	JUL.	AUG.	SEPT.	OCT.	NOV.	DEC.	ANNUAL
HIGHS	91	93	95	96	91	89	89	89	87	87	87	89	87
LOWS	69	71	71	73	73	71	71	71	71	71	69	69	71
RAIN	0.2	0.4	1	3	11	13	10	12	16	16	5	1	89

Manuel Antonio

	JAN.	FEB.	MAR.	APR.	MAY	JUN.	JUL.	AUG.	SEPT.	OCT.	NOV.	DEC.	ANNUAL
HIGHS	87	87	89	89	89	87	87	87	86	86	86	86	87
LOWS	69	69	71	71	71	71	69	69	71	71	71	69	71
RAIN	3	1	2	7	16	17	18	19	21	26	16	7	153

San José

	JAN.	FEB.	MAR.	APR.	MAY	JUN.	JUL.	AUG.	SEPT.	OCT.	NOV.	DEC.	ANNUAL
HIGHS	73	75	77	78	78	78	77	77	78	77	75	77	77
LOWS	59	59	60	60	62	62	67	62	60	60	60	59	62
RAIN	0.4	0.2	0.5	2	9	12	9	10	13	13	6	2	77

The "winter" months of June, July, and August—also referred to as the "green season"—are cooler than the "summer" months. This is because of frequent rains and almost daily afternoon cloud cover.

A common misconception is that "rainy season" means continuous downpours. Typically, even in the most rainy parts of the country, the day begins with glorious sunshine, with blossoms glowing in the sparkling clean air and birds singing happily. Then clouds roll in after lunch, and rain starts falling between 2:00 and 4:00 P.M. (In some places you can almost set your clock by it.) A heavy downpour sends people indoors for a couple of hours (an ideal time for a nap!). Then sunshine returns, and the world is once again refreshed. Other sections of the country enjoy sunshine all day, with the rain falling mostly at night. This is the "best" rain, for falling asleep to the drumming sound of raindrops on a metal roof is a delight. Seldom does it rain every day; several days in a row can be perfectly dry.

Because most North Americans customarily think of the tropics as a place to visit in their winter season—to escape the snow and ice of their homelands—they are often surprised to find that the rainy months of June, July, and August are the favorite time of year for many who live in Costa Rica. "You can't really appreciate this country until you've experienced our winter months," says Graham Henshaw, an expatriate from England. "Everything is green now in January, but when the rains start in May, the grass changes to an even brighter emerald color. Flowers that bloom only in July and August are absolutely stunning. Winter is my favorite time of year."

To further complicate matters, what is true of the mountain valley environment around San José isn't necessarily true on the Caribbean side, which can be flooded with sunshine while the capital is awash in *aguaceros* (rainstorms) and vice versa. The truth is, no matter what time of year you choose to visit, you're guaranteed a serving of nice sunny weather—and probably some rain as well.

Seasons in the tropics are largely determined by altitude. At ocean level the climate is a year-round summer; at moderate elevations year-round spring is a better description. The higher you go, the cooler it gets. A sweater or jacket can be worn almost every evening of the year in higher elevations. Your travel wardrobe should include shirts, sweaters, and jackets you can peel off or pile on, depending on whether you're dining at a beach restaurant, visiting a volcano, or traveling somewhere in between. Be sure to bring rain gear and sturdy shoes if you plan any jungle exploring, plus sunscreen for visits to mountains or beaches; the tropical sun is persistent at all altitudes.

On the northwestern Pacific side, the dry season is exactly that, with very little rain falling from early December until the beginning of May. The grass turns brown, and many trees lose their leaves, just as they do in North America in the winter. But the reason for leaf loss is to conserve water, not because of frost and freezing weather. Most trees are evergreen, but even some of these lose a portion of their leaves. It isn't as bleak as it sounds, for many of these trees replace leaves with brilliantly colored blossoms, as this is the time of year to attract bees, butterflies, and other pollinating insects.

Even on the dry Guanacaste Coast, you'll find microcosms of green environments tucked away in the interior valleys, where sporadic rains are coaxed from the westerly Pacific winds. Farther south along the Pacific Coast, the dry-season rainfall is even more frequent, keeping things pleasantly green during the driest months. (The weather chart on page 27 provides statistics on the microclimates of Costa Rica.)

INSECTS AND THE **TROPICS**

An odd thing about the weather checkerboard of Costa Rica is that, contrary to what one might think, the more humid areas are not necessarily the most insect-plagued. Of course, bring your insect repellent, but I'm convinced that you need it less in most places in Costa Rica than you do in the American Midwest or places in Canada. Along the forested Pacific Coast and the Nicoya Peninsula—where the insect varieties are amazingly abundant—mosquitoes and flies pester you far less than in the dry, almost desertlike parts of Guanacaste. On the humid Caribbean Coast, where rain can fall almost any time of the year and where bugs can get so large you'd think they've been taking hormones, household cockroaches and flies are not nearly as plentiful as I've seen in Houston or New Orleans. (I've seen many kinds of beetles but surprisingly few ordinary cockroaches in my Costa Rican travels.)

In parts of Costa Rica, even in the most tropical locations, insects are so benign that many natives don't bother with screens on their windows.

Of course, the rainy season in some areas will make a liar of me, so it would be best to carry repellent. This is particularly advisable when staying in one of the areas where dengue fever has been reported (mostly around the outskirts of Puntarenas and near Liberia). There's a vigorous campaign continually under way to eliminate the mosquito that spreads the flulike ailment.

That flies and mosquitoes are relatively scarce might seem puzzling. But I believe the answer is that the physical environment in Costa Rica is largely intact. The natural enemies of pests like flies and mosquitoes haven't been eliminated by pesticides, chemicals, and other methods, as they have back home. By day, birds of all descriptions flit back and forth, snacking on insects, keeping them in balance with nature. Many birds consider houseflies to be special treats. By night, squadrons of bats keep up the good work, finishing off mosquitoes before they get a chance to do much damage. According to one naturalist, a small bat can catch about 600 mosquito-size insects per hour, and a large colony of bats will consume thousands of pounds of insects every night! (There are more than thirty species of bats in Costa Rica, thank you very much.)

Meanwhile, lizards, geckos, and chameleons patrol the walls and corners of houses, cleaning up cockroaches and water bugs before they have a chance to infest the kitchen or make a condominium out of your bathroom. The fearsome-looking praying mantis sometimes prowls about the edges of rooms, snapping up bugs that the lizards miss. Ugly as the mantis is, we love 'em!

ATTACK OF THE ARMY ANTS Folks living in the tropical lowlands have additional help in keeping their homes bug-free. From time to time our Costa Rica house is invaded by army ants. They march in broad formation up a concrete column to the veranda and spill over the floors in a busy wave of housecleaning. They remove moths and other night-flying insects that committed suicide against the porch lights the previous night, and they scour the baseboards, corners, and ceilings in search of bugs, beetles, and insect eggs. Scorpions flee in terror; they have no defense against army ants—if they tarry, they are dismantled and served as snacks. Even snakes fear the ants. We simply stay out of their way or prop our feet out of range on a footstool while we read a novel, until their twenty-minute cleaning expedition is finished. We say good-bye and thank them as they continue on their way to their next housecleaning duties.

To our dismay, when our housekeeper sees army ants coming, she runs for the insecticide can and sprays profusely. This stops the wave of ants immediately, and they retreat. She is totally deaf to our protests and won't stop spraying until the ants completely disappear.

I have to admit that at times, the army ant visits are neither so brief nor so charming. During the middle of the dry season in the coastal lowlands, an insect that looks like a large winged termite (although it isn't that at all) hatches in profusion all at once. They stick around for a week or so and then mysteriously disappear. These critters only fly at night and are difficult to see, so you would never be aware of them if the army ants didn't show up for the harvest. The insects are aware of their danger, so they search out any crevice or crack to hide from predators during daylight. (Army ants hunt by sight rather than smell, so they don't work efficiently on the night shift.) The swarming insects soon discover that the hollow space inside your wooden walls makes a great hiding place, and they pack in by the millions.

When army ant scouts discover their hideouts, they send the news to the columns of marching soldiers. They show up for dinner in droves. That's not so bad, but there are so many insects hidden that it can take hours for the ants to clean them out. Afterward they leave your floors littered with wings and cast-off body parts. The sight of this battle is awe inspiring to us but totally disgusting to our maid. We can't decide which is worse—the inconvenience of having our walls covered with army ants or the knowledge that we have bugs in our walls. When the housekeeper's around we have no choice; it's the spray can. Our contractor says it's all our fault. "I told you that cement walls are better than wood!" But we love our pochote redwood living room and figure it's worth having to deal with an occasional invasion.

Not that insects can't make one suffer. Some very small creatures made my last trip to the Pacific beaches memorable for several weeks. These were the dreaded "no-see-ums," a generic name given to any tiny bug that bites without your knowing you are being attacked but makes you suffer afterward. In this case, they were probably some kind of miniature sand flea because they got me on the ankles and lower legs. However, it was my own fault; I should know better than to stroll along the beach at dusk without repellent on my bare legs.

Now I'm going to reveal a personal discovery concerning these bites: It's a salve called Panalog. This is an all-purpose antibiotic and fungicide

that veterinarians routinely prescribe when treating cats and dogs for infections, rashes, and general skin problems. If you have a dog or cat, you'll probably have some of this medication at home. I've found that a dab of Panalog on a mosquito or no-see-um bite not only stops my itching but heals the puncture almost immediately. According to my brother, who is a veterinarian, the only known side effects of Panalog are an occasional urge to chase Pontiacs and a tendency to scratch behind your ear with your hind foot.

It's claimed that Costa Rica has more species of insects than anywhere else in the world, and I believe it. Once in Cahuita—on the Caribbean Coast—I was about to enter my cabin when I encountered an enormous beetle. It was about the size of a teacup, shaped like a giant ladybug, and the color of an olive drab army helmet. Feeling brave, I gingerly picked it up by its back, correctly figuring that its wicked-looking legs couldn't reach around the shell. I carried it to a nearby restaurant and proudly displayed my beetle to the people sitting at the bar, figuring that I'd raise a few eyebrows. The bartender looked at my discovery with a bored expression as he remarked, "Yes, those little ones are females." It turned out that I was holding a rhinoceros beetle, possibly the largest bug of the entire insect world. They tell me the male, which fortunately I never happened to confront, grows to a length of 10 inches, sports enormous horns, and is colored in brilliant metallic hues. Harmless, though.

EARTHQUAKES

All along the mountain chains that stretch from the tip of South America to Alaska, you will feel earthquakes. As a Californian, I've become accustomed to them and seldom experience more than a slight feeling of excitement when windows start rattling and my desk sways a bit. We Californians expect to have several minor quakes a year and a big one every twenty-five years or so.

So it should come as no surprise that Costa Rica has its share of shakes and tremors—actually, more than its share. The really big ones here are spaced by decades instead of generations. Yet Costa Ricans are just as calm about earthquakes as most Californians are. After all, compared with the 700 or so tornadoes that slam the midwestern and eastern parts of North America, claiming eighty to a hundred victims each season, an occasional shaker seems relatively mild.

The last big tremor—a whopping 7.4 on the Richter scale—hit the Caribbean Coast near the city of Limón in April 1991. Older structures suffered the most damage, particularly those not constructed to modern-day standards. However, by the beginning of the next tourist season, much of the damage had been repaired, hotels were operating, roads were open to traffic, and tourism was going full blast.

A few months after the quake, I visited Cahuita, not too far from the epicenter. Expecting to see a lot of damage and hear horror stories, I was delighted to learn that there were no fatalities in the village and that, except for one major building (which had been made of nonreinforced cement) and a few other smaller structures, the town came through relatively unscathed. Cahuita construction is of wood, which may shake, rattle, and twist but doesn't usually tumble down.

Costa Rica's 7.4 shaker claimed about forty lives, one of the worst ever. But compare this earthquake with the one in Iran the year before; it was 7.5 on the Richter scale and claimed more than 50,000 victims. A horrible 6.9 quake in Armenia in 1989 killed 25,000 people; one in Costa Rica the following year was just as strong yet nobody was killed. Why the difference?

One answer to this question, besides lower population density, is sensible construction methods. Costa Rican homes and businesses are designed with earthquakes in mind. Costa Rica has prohibited the use of adobe in constructing homes for more than eighty years. This is the only nation in the hemisphere with a ban on adobe, a material that has a tendency to collapse and bury earthquake victims. Wood, reinforced concrete block, or stressed cement is infinitely safer. Instead of picturesque tile roofs, which can crush inhabitants under tons of heavy beams and broken tile, most Costa Rican roofs are of ordinary-looking corrugated aluminum, plastic, or sheet metal. These lightweight roofs may slide about during a quake, but they won't collapse and kill people by burying them.

An interesting feature of the 1991 quake was an uplifting of the coastline. The force raised the land as much as 5 feet near the town of Puerto Limón and 1½ feet at Puerto Viejo. What once were coral reefs are now dry land at the edge of surf where fishermen once hauled in crab, shrimp, and red snapper. This lifting of the land from the sea is a wonderful example of how the Central American land bridge was formed some two or three million years ago when quake activity began pushing the land ever higher. Geologists find coral fossils on mountaintops now 9,000 feet above sea level. ■

CHAPTER THREE

WHAT ARE
COSTA RICANS LIKE?

Most travelers will agree that every country has its own distinct personality. This is illustrated in a story describing the difference between
Travelers' Heaven and *Travelers' Hell*. Heaven is when you are greeted
by the British, the French do the cooking, Italians plan the fun and
games, and Germans keep order. But Travelers' Hell is when you are
greeted by the French, the British do the cooking, Italians keep order,
and Germans plan the fun and games.

Americans and New Zealanders, for example, are stereotypically
outgoing, friendly, and loud talkers. Russians are pictured as dour and
morose, with no sense of humor. British are said to be terrible cooks.
These are stereotypes of course, and we all agree that it's unfair to
apply stereotypes (except in the case of the Brits, who tend to boil
everything they can't fry). Yet there is more than a kernel of truth here.
The reasons for a nation's personality difference often can be explained
by the historical development of each country.

In South America, for example, Argentina has a personality that
reflects the heritage of its large Italian immigration, while next-door
Chile was influenced by English and German newcomers who joined

the original Spanish settlers. The result is an outgoing, vivacious, and self-confident Argentine personality compared with Chile's more reserved, polite, and introverted temperament.

Costa Rica's distinct personality also is a product of history. In Chapter 1 we discussed Costa Rica's isolation during the early Spanish years and how, during the early days of the republic, Costa Rica invited Europeans from all nations to immigrate and start coffee farms. Italian and French refugees from a severe European economic recession joined Spaniards in the land rush, each nationality bringing its customs and personalities to blend together into Costa Rica's unique way of European–Central American life and creating the Tico personality of today.

One way Ticos differ from residents of some other Latin-American countries is tolerance toward other religions and other points of view. Costa Ricans are predominantly Catholic but without the zeal and rigidity sometimes found in other countries. This, too, has an historical explanation. In the early days, small villages were so isolated that the Church either couldn't or didn't bother to install chapels or send priests. The result was an informal observance of religion as something remote and almost irrelevant (except for the celebration of village saints' days). Even today, the Catholic churches in many villages are often attended by visiting priests. This situation creates fertile ground for evangelical denominations to establish churches. Numerous small villages have evangelical Protestant churches only.

Yet curiously, one of the country's most important events is on August 2, when thousands of Costa Ricans end a pilgrimage walk of several days to pay homage to the Virgen de los Angeles in Cartago. And everyone—

Catholics and Protestants alike—enthusiastically celebrates their village's religious fiestas with dances, bullfights, parades and fund-raising events. Don't miss attending these celebrations—all the gringos living in the community will be there, too; you'll have a great time.

WHY **"TICOS"?**

Throughout this book you'll see the term *Tico* used when speaking of Costa Ricans. This is the appropriate nickname for a Costa Rican citizen, just as *gringo* is used for North Americans in general, and *Yankee* for a citizen of the United States. The term *gringo* is an accepted nickname for both Canadian and U.S. citizens—no one takes umbrage by it, because Ticos mean it in an almost affectionate way. And Costa Ricans call themselves Ticos when distinguishing themselves from foreigners, instead of the more cumbersome *Costariquense*.

The name *Tico* comes from an archaic practice of using the sound *-tico* on the end of a word as a diminutive instead of the normal *-tito*. For example, whereas a Mexican would say *momentito* for "just a tiny moment," some Costa Ricans (not all) might say *momentico*. Thus, a kitten would be a *gatico* in Costa Rica but a *gatito* in Mexico. Not all Costa Ricans use this ending, but enough do to keep the tradition alive.

THE TICO **PSYCHE**

An outstanding difference in the psyche of Costa Ricans and other Latinos is the way they view the world and their place in it. Because of a long tradition of democracy and equality, the country has developed an egalitarian society that reminds one of the U.S. and Canadian ideals of social equality. Unlike many other Latin American countries, the spread between Costa Rica's rich, poor, and middle classes is narrow. The middle class is large and relatively prosperous; the upper class is small and only moderately wealthy. People here do not bow to anyone, regardless of who they are. This is a country where you can see the country's president and his wife pushing a grocery cart in a supermarket. People look you in the eye and shake your hand, fully convinced that everyone is equal.

Because Tico attitudes are so similar to North Americans', we feel perfectly comfortable when socializing with them. However, there are some subtle differences in the Tico psyche that need to be understood. First of all, it is considered ill mannered to be loud, brash, argumentative, and overly competitive, as Americans tend to be. (The exception of course, is when playing soccer or driving a car.) In fact, they hate confrontation so much that they'll do anything to avoid giving you bad news. When your contractor tells you that the transformer for your new home didn't arrive today but is coming *mañana,* he may be avoiding the bad news that it might be a week or a month before you have electricity. Costa Ricans want to tell you what you would like to hear if at all possible. If it's not possible, they avoid talking about it so that you won't feel bad.

In line with the hesitation to give bad news is a tendency to avoid saying "No" to a request or business proposal, if they think that saying "No" will make you feel bad. So when doing business, remember that you can only count on a "no" as being definitive; a "yes" or "maybe" could mean anything. I've often heard that Ticos won't admit that they don't know something. For example, when asked directions they'll give any response, pointing whichever direction they think you might like. I've often wondered where that notion came from. I have never, in all my years of traveling in Latin America, had someone do that. (I ought to know, because without street signs, I have to ask directions frequently.) If Ticos don't know the answer to a question, they simply say so, like anywhere else. They might even flag down a passing car to ask. Giving misleading directions would be the height of rudeness and a violation of Tico etiquette.

Another interesting trait is reluctance to accept blame. When our maid drops a plate on the floor, she says, *"Se quebró el plato."* The plate broke itself (it's important to save face). I once tried to convince my electrician that he had installed my telephone wrong. (The problem was obvious; he had shorted the wires by pounding a staple across the cable shroud.) He insisted that the problem was a temporary glitch at the telephone exchange. "Pretty soon they'll find their mistake and fix it." He installed a new cable at my insistence and according to my directions, after which, the phone worked. "You see?" he crowed in triumph, "While I was putting in the new cable, the telephone company found their mistake and fixed it!" I agreed with him. He had to save face.

The well-known *mañana* attitude of Latin America is present in Costa Rica, but not nearly to the extent as in some other Latino countries—at least in my experience. Our workers are usually always at the job on time and work hard while they are there. (They also quit exactly on time.) The exceptions to this rule are Mondays after a local fiesta, when the entire village celebrates on Saturday and Sunday. Nobody expects all of their workers to show up on Monday or any to be really capable of work. Guests to your dinner party will be late anywhere from fifteen minutes to an hour. Your auto mechanic will be an hour late changing your oil, but seldom a day late.

In several ways, Ticos are very much like us, except that Ticos speak more softly and seem just a little more stoic about the world's problems than their Latin American counterparts. They laugh just as much as we do and share the same sense of humor. The best part of all: They really like North Americans, probably because our personalities mesh. Most of us who live in Costa Rica reciprocate this instant friendship; we like Ticos, too.

TICO **SPANISH**

Because of Costa Rica's early isolation, the country developed some unique linguistic differences from other Spanish-speaking countries. Furthermore, within Costa Rica itself, local accents developed in isolated parts of the country back when communication was extremely difficult. For example: An oxcart journey from San José to Limón used to take nearly two weeks.

These accents vary from being so slight that it takes an expert to distinguish them, to being all but unintelligible to those not fluent in Spanish. The differences are similar to the way words are pronounced in Minneapolis, Minnesota, and the way they're pronounced in Montgomery, Alabama. This is most noticeable in Guanacaste (northwestern Costa Rica). Like English in Montgomery, the Guanacaste accent is caused by dropping some consonants and slurring vowels together. This lingo is similar to that spoken in Nicaragua (not surprising since Guanacaste originally was part of Nicaragua). Once you get used to this blending of sounds, it becomes clear.

Don't worry too much if you are just learning Spanish. Almost all people can, and will, speak "proper Spanish" when they see that you don't understand. They simply repeat their words with a more careful pronunciation and avoid using local slang—just as they learned to do in school.

There is one outstanding difference between Tico Spanish and standard Spanish grammar that could puzzle those who have studied the language in high school or college. Instead of hearing the polite *usted* and informal *tu* forms of Spanish that are normally taught in our high schools and universities, Costa Ricans use the archaic Spanish *vos* instead of *tu* for the familiar first person singular. Originally, *vos* was the polite form of Spanish first person singular, and *tu* was familiar. Then somewhere in the late sixteenth century, the use of *vuestra merced* (your grace) became the polite form, later shortened to usted. This downgraded the formal pronoun *vos* from formal to informal use and the pronoun *tu* was used only when speaking to inferiors or animals. Later, the use of *vos* was totally dropped and *tu* once again became standard for informal speech in Spain. However, the first Costa Rican immigrants from Spain came *before* that switch in grammar occurred and therefore retained the old customs. To make things more confusing, the *tu* form is sometimes used as a form of intimacy between lovers.

Verbs have a different declension or word ending when using *vos*. Unfortunately this construction isn't usually taught in U.S. schools, even though this mode is used by several million people in the Western Hemisphere. (Yes, they teach the *vosotros* form, but that is plural and is used mostly by Spanish priests when addressing a congregation.) It takes some time to become comfortable with the *vos* form; in the meantime play it safe by using *usted*. Look at the chart and note the differences.

	Usted form	**Tu** form	**Vos** form
Do you want?	¿Quiere Ud?	¿Quieres tu?	¿Queréis vos?
You speak . . .	Usted habla	Tu hablas	Vos hablá
You are . . .	Usted es	Tu eres	Vos sos

Earlier we discussed how the word *Tico* came about: using a *tico* at the end of an adjective to express "small" or "tiny." You'll encounter some other interesting differences between Tico expressions and the way they are said in other countries. Some are quite charming. For example: In most Spanish-speaking countries, the term for "you're welcome," is *por nada*, "it's nothing" or *no hay de que*, "don't mention it." Costa Ricans feel those expressions somewhat impolite. To say "you're wel-

come" they say *con mucho gusto*, which translates "with much pleasure."
(Is that polite or what?) Instead of greeting acquaintances with *¿Como está
usted?* ("How are you?") they prefer to ask, *¿Como amaneció?* ("How did
you wake up this morning?").

They also feel that asking for something using the word *dar* ("to
give") is impolite. Instead of *Dame una coca, por favor,* meaning "Give
me a Coca-Cola, please," they consider it more polite to use the verb
regalarse (which actually means, "make me a gift of . . ."). So properly it
would be *"Regálame una coca, por fa."* (Note dropping the syllable *vor*
from *favor.*) Of course they're used to hearing gringos use the other
expressions, so they won't be surprised when you say *"de nada."*

One uniquely Costa Rican term, solidly ingrained into the language,
is *pura vida.* I suppose this would translate as "it's a great life," but in
effect it means "okay," "cool," "all right," sometimes as an emphatic
"aw-right!" A clerk in a store, instead of asking, "Would you like anything
else?" might say, *"¿Pura vida?"* A gas station attendant may ask, "Is your
oil *pura vida,* or should I check it for you?"

A couple of strictly Costa Rican expressions puzzled me—until I finally
figured them out—and could be puzzling to those learning the language.
This is a tendency to begin sentences with the words *"vieras que . . ."* or
simply *"vieras . . ."* Literally it means something like "You see . . ." or "You
know." Also used in the same way is *"digamos que"* or *"digamos"* ("let's

say . . ."), but since the sound *d* is often softened or dropped entirely, it comes out *"igamos."*

You should be careful not to use sayings with obscene implications, and also realize that slang changes over time. About thirty years ago I ran across a series of tapes with Tico slang expressions; I bought them and put them away, vowing some day to master Tico slang. Twenty-five years later I actually began to study those tapes. Armed with this knowledge I ventured forth to display my proficiency with slang—and was shocked to see smiles and laughter. Then I realized that over the years, this slang had fallen from favor. I was saying things like "twenty-three skiddo!" or "groovy!" and "oh, you kid!" ■

CHAPTER FOUR

THE MESETA
CENTRAL & BEYOND

Those North Americans who make Costa Rica their home—part-time or full-time—fall into one of two categories. They either insist on living in the temperate zone or choose the more romantic, although warmer, tropical zone. Each group can't understand why the other group wants to live where they do. Costa Ricans themselves are also divided about which is best, tropical or temperate. As proof of this division, half of the entire Tico population chooses to live in the higher reaches of the country, more or less in the middle, in an area known as the Meseta Central. Roughly half of the expatriates from the United States and Canada also prefer living here.

The Meseta Central is surrounded by the mountain range that starts near Costa Rica's border with Nicaragua and marches south until it crosses the border of Panama. This range is known as the "Cordillera," a picturesque complex of high ridges, valleys, peaks, and tablelands—perpetually covered with green vegetation and teeming with wildlife. The mountains vary from rounded promontories to the rugged peaks of the Talamanca Range, dominated by 12,600-foot Cerro Chirripó. Valleys and rolling tablelands are interspersed between

MESETA **CENTRAL**

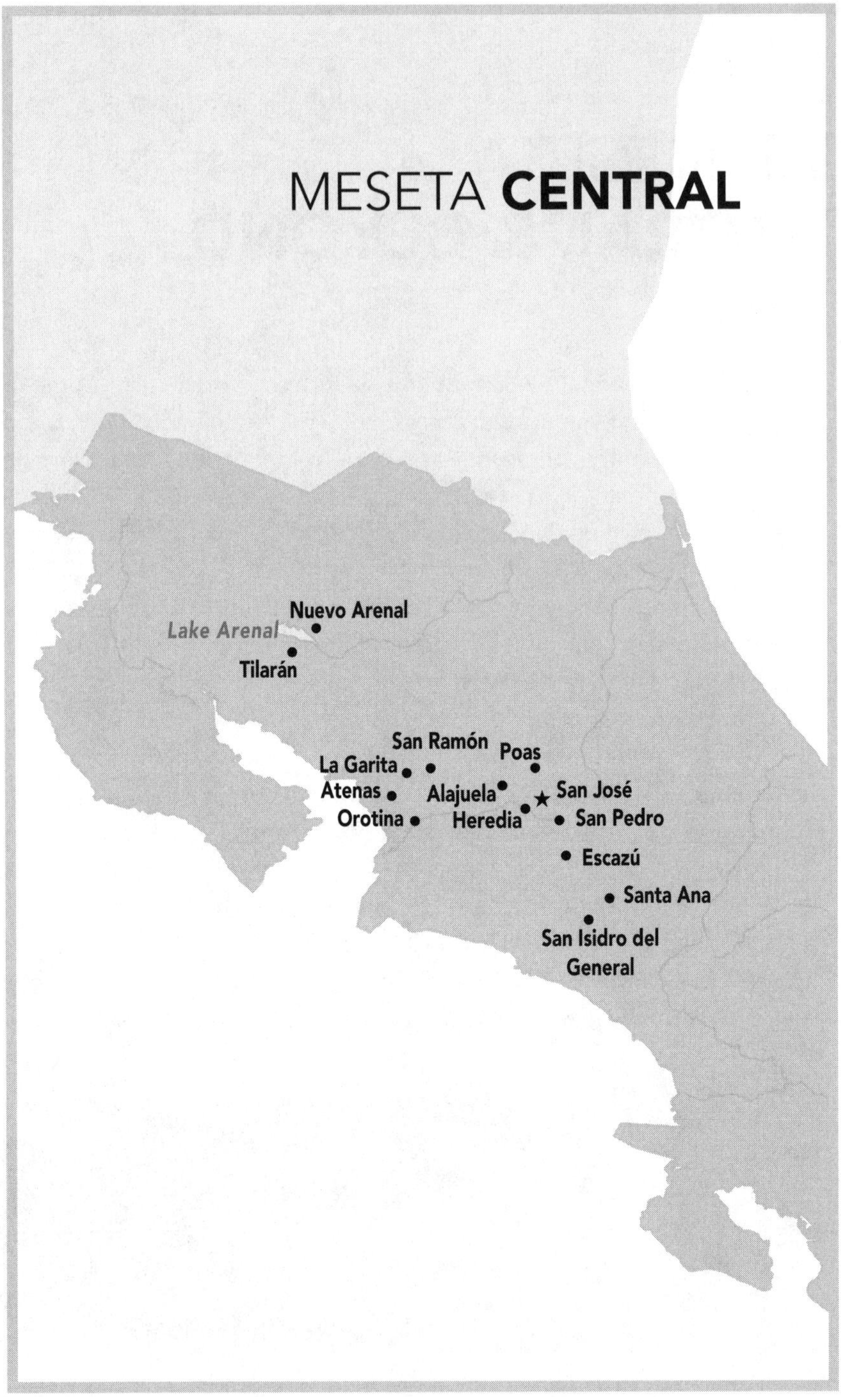

Lake Arenal ● Nuevo Arenal

● Tilarán

San Ramón ● Poas

La Garita ● ●

Atenas ● Alajuela ● ★ San José

Orotina ● Heredia ● ● San Pedro

● Escazú

● Santa Ana

● San Isidro del
General

steep mountains and volcanic formations, providing fertile agricultural space. The largest complex of valleys is the Meseta Central.

San José, the largest city in Costa Rica, nestles in a wide depression about halfway down the Cordillera, at an altitude of 3,750 feet above sea level. The city of about 300,000 inhabitants is surrounded by dozens of satellite towns and villages and by small cities such as Heredia, Alajuela, Escazú, and Cartago perched at various elevations on the uneven plateau. About 15 miles wide by 40 miles long, this break in the mountains is called the "Valle Central" (Central Valley) or the "Meseta Central" (Central Plateau), depending on who is speaking. From just about any point in this area, you are treated to views of the high mountains that form a half-bowl around the Meseta Central. This is not only where most Ticos live but also the most heavily populated area in Central America.

Towns and villages surrounding the capital have grown to the point that it is sometimes difficult to tell exactly where one ends and another begins. Although greenery and small farms are abundant, much of the Meseta Central blurs into a loose suburban complex.

Why so many prefer the Meseta Central is a question answered in two words: superb climate. This is the land of perpetual spring. Daily high temperatures are almost always in the seventies—creating newspaper headlines on occasions when the thermometer climbs into the high eighties. Low temperatures are always in the sixties. Understand, these aren't average temperatures, which can give a distorted picture, but average high and low readings. Because Costa Rica is so close to the equator, temperatures vary little between summer and winter.

Even this weather doesn't please everyone; some prefer temperatures in the eighties and even nineties, while others feel more comfortable in the sixties and low seventies. Fortunately, in Costa Rica it's possible to "fine-tune" your weather simply by moving a few kilometers in one direction or another. Since temperatures and weather patterns are determined by altitude in the tropics, just a few meters higher or lower elevation make a difference. A fifteen-minute drive from anywhere on the Meseta Central brings you to a slightly different climate, with more or less rainfall and warmer or cooler temperatures.

It seems as if each town or community here brags of having the "best climate in the world." Each is perfect for at least some folks. Alajuela is proud of being a few degrees warmer than San José, while Escazú is happy about being a few degrees cooler. Poas boasts about being even cooler than Escazú, and La Garita brags about its rating by *National Geographic* of having one of the three best climates in the world. The wonderful thing is that all these choices, however slight, are freely available to you. (The weather chart on page 27 in Chapter 2 illustrates this diversity of weather.)

SAN **JOSÉ**

When their airplane approaches the country's international airport, visitors are treated to the sight of a broad green valley flanked by steep, volcanic mountains that seem to be forever topped with fluffy clouds. The city of San José spreads out below, thinning to a scattering of towns and villages that eventually merge into a lush green countryside. From the air one can see homes and tidy farms lining roads and highways, showing patches of cultivated fields intermixed with wild tropical vegetation.

After passing through the easy customs booths in the modern terminal of Juan Santamaría Airport, travelers make their way toward the city of San José along a modern divided four-lane highway. Those expecting to see the usual Central American panorama of dingy buildings, shacks, and junkyards will be surprised by tastefully landscaped grounds of light manufacturing facilities, fancy hotel complexes, offices of international corporations, and other evidence of business prosperity. A large Intel computer chip facility is one of the latest additions to San José's high-tech ambience. I've heard people proclaim in surprise, "Why, it almost looks as if it could be Europe!"

The closer one gets to the center of San José the denser the population becomes, and the less it looks like Europe. Suddenly, as the highway becomes a boulevard when it curves toward downtown and past Sabana Park, the city starts appearing more as you might expect of Central America. By the time the average newcomer reaches the heart of downtown San José, entirely too many vehicles creep along narrow streets, past hundred-year-old buildings mixed with a few modern ones. Dense crowds of pedestrians swarm past a confusing agglomeration of small shops, vendors, and street stands with blaring music. Typically, a feeling of disappointment sets in as the newcomer thinks, "Is this the beautiful Costa Rica I've heard so much about?"

This first impression of Costa Rica can be a lasting one for those with limited vacation time—those who spend most of it in San José with an occasional day trip to nearby tourist attractions. When you hear people remark that they were *extremely* disappointed in Costa Rica, that they consider the country ugly, you can pretty much bet that their visit was a one-day stopover on a cruise ship. Cruise ships here disembark at a shipping port where the scenic attractions are industrial warehouses, tank trucks, and storage sheds. This doesn't create a terribly nice impression, so the cruise director quickly loads passengers onto buses and zips them away to San José for a four-hour visit and then back to the ship in time for dinner. It's little wonder that cruise ship visitors can't understand why people praise Costa Rica.

However, it's all in the eyes of the beholder. I for one absolutely adore visiting San José. The city becomes more attractive to me with each visit. We who live hours away from the city get excited when we find an excuse for a shopping excursion to San José. We look for reasons to drive or fly to "San Chepe"—as Ticos humorously refer to San José—to schedule an appointment with our lawyer when the business could just have well be done by telephone. (By the way, *Chepe* is a child's way of pronouncing José and, thus, a nickname.)

Those who live here soon learn to appreciate San José for its many cool cultural events. No other place in Central America—or even most cities in the United States—offers as many opportunities for opera, plays, museums, art galleries, symphonies, and foreign artists of all kinds. Once you learn where the good restaurants are found, you'll look forward to visiting often. Those who only know downtown San José can never appreciate San José's suburbs—places like Escazú, Santa Ana, Rohrmoser, Heredia, San Pedro, and all the delightful neighborhoods nearby.

San José, the capital and business center of Costa Rica, is a comfortable place to live despite its large population. Although downtown streets throng with shoppers and automobiles, neighborhoods a dozen blocks away can be tranquil residential areas. San José doesn't suffer from the widespread slum zones that plague many U.S. cities. You'll find modest neighborhoods, to be sure, and a few run-down areas but not the starkly depressing ghettos so apparent in some large U.S. cities. Truthfully, I've found few residential neighborhoods in San José where I would feel uncomfortable or ashamed to live. There is a slight smog problem in the downtown streets—mostly caused by belching diesel trucks, buses, and taxis. Continuous cross-breezes keep the atmosphere superclean, except in the immediate vicinity of a bus or truck. Some residents disagree with my denial of San José smog. But having lived in Los Angeles and visited places like Athens and Rome, I just don't trust air I cannot see.

As you might expect, the farther from the business center, the better the housing. However, this isn't because of a decaying city core, as is the case with some U.S. cities; it's because the center is taken up with businesses, hotels, restaurants, and uncountable shops and stores. For some reason, people from all over the valley feel a compulsion to do their shopping in downtown San José. This is partly from habit and the fact that shopping is something of a social event. By the thousands, crowds of shoppers amble along the streets and avenues, checking out window displays, making purchases, and gossiping with friends. Most could shop in their own neighborhoods, but it's more fun this way, and here is where you will find those scarce items you need. So many pedestrians pack the main downtown avenue (Avenida Central) that the city has been forced to turn part of it into a pedestrian mall. During peak periods pedestrians turn the rest of the downtown section into a virtual mall by filling the streets, forcing drivers to detour around Avenida Central.

Although just about any neighborhood in San José is comfortable, North Americans are predisposed to congregate in some of the more costly areas. This is understandable, since they tend to be more affluent than Costa Ricans and can better afford upscale neighborhoods. The western edge of San José attracts a large number of foreign residents, particularly around the Sábana Park area (Sábana Sur and Sábana Norte), the upscale neighborhood of Rohrmoser, and some areas of Pavas. Better supermarkets, nicer restaurants, and amenities such as tennis clubs and attractive parks make this a very livable part of the city. The *Tico Times* classified section frequently lists homes and condos for sale or rent in Pavas and Rohrmoser. Typically, rents for condos start around $400, and homes can go as high as $1,500 a month for a super-nice place. Still farther out, toward the airport, is Cariari, a luxury area with a golf course and country club.

Directly across the valley, the towns of Escazú and Bello Horizonte match Rohrmoser for elegance and expensive housing. Just to the east of downtown San José, Barrio Escalante is an affordable neighborhood of stately older homes. This was the "in" place for wealthy Ticos years ago and is now in the process of adapting to middle-class families. Still farther out on the eastern edge of the city, Los Yoses and San Pedro supply moderate to expensive housing, with some of San José's most exclusive neighborhoods. San Pedro provides a university atmosphere, with many rentals available at student-budget levels. For the height of luxury housing and opulence, some neighborhoods around Curridabat cannot be topped. One area, known as "Embassy Row," has some stunning homes. This is where the infamous Robert Vesco had his mansion.

By shopping around you can usually find housing that will fit your pocketbook and lifestyle. Remember that ads in the *Tico Times* are directed toward North Americans who can afford to pay more. For less expensive places, check the classified ads in *La Nación;* that's where Ticos find their rentals. San José has several apartment complexes renting furnished places by the day or week that make excellent "base camps" while one is looking for permanent quarters or trying out Costa Rica as a place to live.

FINDING YOUR WAY Searching for an address in and around San José and its suburbs can be an exercise in frustration; few buildings have street numbers, and no one pays attention to them when they do. Even worse, many streets have no names, or at least no street names posted on the corners. Suppose you are looking for the García residence, whose address is listed as "From Caballo Blanco 250 meters west, 300 south." To understand where this house is located, you need to know the location of a store called Caballo Blanco, then go 2 ½ blocks (250 meters) to the west and then 3 blocks (300 meters) south. At that point, you need to ask someone which house belongs to the García family.

This confusion isn't restricted to residences; businesses use the same system. On maps, advertisements, and business cards, the word *calle* is often abbreviated as *c, avenida* as *a,* and *central* as *ctl.* The distance from a point is given in meters (abbreviated with an *m*), although sometimes people give it in *varas* instead of meters, both meaning a long pace or step about a yard long. (A *vara* is a bit shorter than a yard, about 33 inches, an ancient measurement in use before the introduction of the metric system.)

Examples of address insanity: The address of the Hotel Presidente would be "c ctl, av 7–9," which translates "on Calle Central between Avenidas 7 and 9." The address of the bus terminal for Alajuela is "a 2, c 12–14," meaning "facing Avenida 2, between Calles 12 and 14."

Directions and addresses can be vague to the point of impossibility. This is particularly true away from the orderly grid of north-south, east-west streets. An address might be described thus: "From the gasoline station, go 100 meters north and 75 *varas* to the east." Which gasoline station? My favorite address is on a real estate agent's business card. It says "50 *varas* south from where the Mas Por Menos supermarket used to be."

It doesn't do any good to complain; Ticos understand the system perfectly and actually become confused when you use logical addresses. Often when I take a cab downtown, asking to go to "Avenida Segundo and Calle Primera," the driver responds with a puzzled frown. When I add "Teatro Nacional," his face lights up with understanding and away we go.

AWAY FROM THE **CITY**

Although many foreigners live in the city of San José, the majority prefer one of the smaller communities surrounding the city. These towns range from expensive to moderately priced places to live. For some mysterious reason, at least six of these towns have the same name—San Isidro—which adds to the confusion of finding your way around! San Antonio is another favorite place-name that is scattered about like leaves in the wind.

As explained elsewhere, the explanation for identical names is that during colonization, communication was extremely difficult between communities even though the actual distances might not be far with today's transportation. People couldn't possibly confuse *their* San Antonio with another when it took a dozen days' travel by oxcart to get to the other San Antonio.

ALAJUELA One of the less expensive yet pleasant places for foreigners to live is Alajuela. Situated on the western edge of San José, this small city is convenient to the airport and a twenty-minute bus ride from downtown San José. Clean, modern buses run every few minutes during the day, stopping at the airport on the way to and from San José. (If you have a small amount of luggage, this is an inexpensive way to get downtown from the airport.)

Your first approach to Alajuela can give a misleading impression. The highway comes in on a higher level than the town, providing an unfortunate panorama of tin roofs in every direction—some new, some rusted, some painted red to resemble tile, but mostly of corrugated iron or aluminum. Now, in the United States a tin roof usually implies cheap construction, structures such as storage sheds or temporary buildings. But as explained in Chapter 2, this is earthquake country; those picturesque tile roofs can be deadly when they collapse. You may see occasional tile roofs, but you can be reassured that underneath all that pretty tile is a steel-reinforced cement roof. Since the temperature never gets hot or cold, the insulation value of a heavy tile roof is beside the point.

Alajuela's focal point is a large park in the center of town (called the Parque Central, of course), a pleasant place shaded by tall trees, with chessboards built into some of the cement benches that surround the park. If you would like to meet North American retirees to ask for information about Alajuela, this is the place to come; sometimes there seems as much English spoken here as Spanish. This is the place to find out about housing rentals, who is leaving for the States, who has a car for sale, and who can recommend a gardener or a maid. In the evenings a mixture of classical and pop music can be heard by the park's bandstand, where professional musicians entertain a couple of times a week.

Alajuela was the home of Juan Santamaria, the young hero of the final battle against the American buccaneers under General William Walker. Every year on April 11 the town celebrates Juan Santamaria Day with a jubilant parade through town, a public fiesta, and dancing in and around the Parque Central. On one corner of the square, a museum dedicated to the hero is located in what used to be a jail. Two hundred meters west of the park is the Public Market, the perfect place to find the freshest veggies and choicest cuts of meat.

A good way to become acquainted with the expatriate scene in Alajuela is to visit restaurants and cafes in and around Alajuela center that are frequented by gringos, who drop in for an afternoon snack or a cold drink. If you spend enough time drinking coffee in one of Alajuela's more popular cafes, or sunning yourself on a park bench, you'll eventually meet every gringo in Alajuela.

Alajuela is an excellent example of moderate housing costs, for both sales and rentals, in the Meseta Central region. Prices are neither as elevated as they can be in upscale areas of Rohrmoser or Escazú, nor are they depressed as in poorer working-class neighborhoods. Neighborhoods here are middle class—where newcomers will feel comfortable, where neighbors can tell you exactly who lives in which house on the street.

Within a ten-minute walk from the Parque Central, homes can be purchased for less than $40,000 and rented for $250 to $500 a month. A friend recently bought a very nice two-bedroom, one-and-a-half-bath home—small but super nice, with a huge kitchen, built-in dishwasher, and Italian-tile floors—for $30,000. A similar house should rent for $300 to $400 unfurnished.

José Pelleya, from Miami, Florida, rents a huge five-bedroom place here for $650 a month and has turned it into a rather successful bed-and-breakfast. (I often stay there when in San José.) One of our favorite neighborhoods in Alajuela is Trinidad, about a fifteen-minute walk from the town center. Most homes have nice landscaping and attractive wrought-iron fences around the front yards. The price of a three-bedroom home starts around $55,000. A nice place rents for $450.

Land and construction costs in Alajuela are typical of middle-class residential areas. You can use them for comparison with other places around San José. Building lots in a nice neighborhood sell for around $30,000 (in fall 2004). Building costs can be as little as $30 a square foot. Typically, lots in town are small, between 3,000 and 4,000 square feet, but if you drive five to ten minutes from the town center, you can buy twice as much land for the same price. A thirty-minute drive and you can have a small *finca* of a couple of acres for your $30,000.

HEREDIA When I first visited Costa Rica, Heredia was a small provincial capital of about 10,000 persons. Today the population is closer to 30,000, and Heredia has expanded to meet Alajuela's growing sprawl until they've essentially joined into one large town, with nothing but a CITY LIMITS sign to indicate where one ends and the other begins. Situated Northwest of San José on the sloping hills of the Barva and Poás Volcanoes (extinct of course), Heredia's higher elevation means a cooler climate and more rainfall, which keeps things looking green and fresh even in the dry season. The rural areas farther up the sloping hills toward

Barva are renowned for quality coffee production. Small and medium-size coffee farms are scattered here and there, a few owned by foreign residents. Others own homes with orchards of citrus, avocados, and tropical fruit instead of coffee. Most places enjoy breathtaking views of the valley below.

The center of Heredia, like Alajuela, features a large, friendly Parque Central complete with weekly band concerts. This park is shaded by stands of enormous mango trees and has the usual park benches for informal meetings and gossiping. Like the Parque Central in Alajuela, Heredia's Parque Central has a large church at one end—a cathedral, actually—that has watched over the quietness of the square for more than 200 years.

The center of town is somewhat congested, but that doesn't stop expatriates from meeting at their special restaurant on a corner of the square, browsing an English-language bookstore (called "The Literate Cat"), or taking care of banking and other errands on the plaza. One resident points out that "Heredia isn't exactly a 'culinary mecca,' yet you can find some nice restaurants nearby besides the McDonalds, Taco Bell, and Kentucky Fried Chicken that cluster around the plaza."

La Universidad Nacional, the country's second largest university, is located not far from the plaza. A private school, *Universidad Interamericana,* and several language schools that teach Spanish to North Americans also exert an influence on the life and commerce. Many exchange students from the United States and Canada take classes here and become part of the expatriate scene in Heredia.

Heredia's famous market is large, featuring quality meats and exceptionally fresh vegetables, fruits, and greens of all descriptions. Much of the market's exotic produce is grown by local residents in their backyards. Saturday is market day, and selections are bountiful as well as fresh-picked. People from all over the valley come here for their weekend shopping. The market is near the Parque Central and dates back one hundred years. Like most other cities on the Meseta Central, Heredia homes don't have street numbers. But instead of saying "150 meters north," it's customary to say "150 meters *arriba*," for the town slopes uphill toward the north. "Two hundred meters *abajo*" would, of course, mean 200 meters to the south.

Continuing *arriba* is the town of Barva, location of the large coffee producer Café, where many tourists visit for a tour of a coffee plantation. Up the slope toward the extinct Barva Volcano, many lovely homes are tucked away among the tropical vegetation that crowds the side of the narrow highways.

From Heredia's northern edge, hills and mountains rise steadily toward the Poás Volcano. All along these foothills are winding roads that travel past beautifully maintained homes, alternating with evergreen forests, small farms, and verdant pastures. This is one of my favorite parts of the Meseta Central (I almost bought a coffee farm here a few years ago). As the roads climb higher into the mountains, temperatures become progressively cooler, allowing prospective home buyers and renters precise adjustment in their environment.

An interesting place to check out is nearby San Isidro, a small village to the east of Heredia. A number of foreigners have made their homes here. They point out that the village is small enough that they can interact with villagers and get to know everyone in town. They enjoy the rustic, rural ambience—a place where oxcarts are still used for everyday farm chores.

Incidentally, those foreigners who own rural parcels and who spend half the year in Costa Rica and the rest of their time in their home country are sometimes willing to rent their property in their absence to ensure that someone will keep an eye on their place and protect it from vandalism. Some attractive rental deals can be worked out in these instances.

ESCAZÚ For North Americans who prefer the higher elevations, Escazú is the premier retirement and residential location. Only 8 kilometers from San José and fifteen minutes or less driving time, depending on traffic, the town of Escazú is somewhat removed from the city hustle and bustle. Nestled at the base of magnificent ancient volcanic mountains, Escazú has always drawn the affluent and those seeking tranquillity away from the city. Somehow this area has managed to preserve remnants of the peace and beauty of its agricultural past yet provide a modern backdrop for suburban living. As one hotel advertises, "Close to the capital, but worlds away." Of all the suburbs where foreigners choose to live, Escazú is the most popular and is well stocked with English-speaking expatriates.

Three mountains hover over Escazú. The tallest is Cerro Rabo de Mico, at 7,770 feet; the most spectacular is Pico Blanco, at 7,250 feet, with a dramatic, sheer rock face that has challenged the skill of many a mountain climber. Residential streets on the edge of town ascend the mountainside bravely, presenting an even better view with each gain in altitude.

The total population of the Escazú area is said to be 40,000, but it doesn't appear nearly that large. It looks more like a cluster of sprawling villages, with quaint old adobe buildings painted in a traditional two-color motif. Incidentally, the 3-foot colored stripe you'll see painted along the bottom of a house is believed to ward off evil spirits and witches. It must work, because I've encountered few evil spirits or witches during any of my visits.

Escazú is actually divided into three separate towns: San Miguel de Escazú, San Rafael de Escazú, and San Antonio de Escazú, each having its own church and patron saint. The red-domed church in San Miguel de Escazú was constructed in 1799 and has survived numerous earthquakes since.

As San José grew and spread out, artists and those in search of serenity began moving to Escazú. No longer the peaceful retreat of yesterday, the area retains a reputation as an artists' colony as well as a retirement center. Escazú's higher elevations are ideally suited for those who think that San José's climate is too warm. It is also high enough that the occasional light smog that sometimes touches San José remains far below. For these reasons, a large number of North Americans choose Escazú and surrounding towns as their place of residence. Here is where the U.S ambassador's residence is located. Two famous country clubs provide the area with golf, tennis, and a focal point for the society set. Escazú is the center of much of Costa Rica's expatriate social life.

Escazú (and its environs) has a sophistication that makes it stand out among San José's suburbs as a prestige address. Although it admittedly has some of the more expensive places to live, modestly priced homes and apartments are also available throughout the community. Those who choose to live here say they wouldn't think of settling anywhere else. "We have the

best of all worlds," explained a couple who owns a small house on the slope of Pico Blanco. "We live in the country, with a gorgeous view of the city below, yet we are just five minutes away from stores, restaurants, or whatever we need." They pointed out that although they are close to San José, they rarely go there on other than essential business. Well-stocked supermarkets, shops, doctors, dentists, and a first-class health clinic serve the community's needs quite well. Restaurants of all descriptions abound, including European, barbecue, Chinese, and even a Cajun restaurant for the yuppie trade.

Although new homes are sprouting on the fringes of Escazú, the municipality requires that construction near the town's center conform to colonial or traditional style. Most buildings are one-story, two-story at most, fulfilling a sense of rural, Costa Rican countryside living.

"Property here is probably the most expensive of anywhere in the valley," explained one of Escazú's many real estate agents. "Everyone wants to live here. You can pay $150,000 and more for a nice three-bedroom home that you could buy for $95,000 elsewhere, but this is a quality area." He pointed out that there is no real "foreign colony" in Escazú, because gringos tend to spread throughout the community, interspersed with Ticos and other foreigners. Although some prefer to live in "sealed-in" developments—compounds with high walls and twenty-four-hour guards—more folks live in ordinary homes or town houses. Those who choose to pay more for the security feel it is worth it, since they can comfortably leave their places unoccupied for months at a time while they return home for visits. Others rely on neighbors and friends to take care of things while they are gone.

ROHRMOSER Rohrmoser is at the upper end of the housing market in the immediate San José area, and it is Escazú's main competition for upscale residences. For some folks there is no competition; Rohrmoser wins hands-down. Here homes and condos consistently command rents and sale prices higher than elsewhere in the metropolitan area. Unlike Escazú, Rohrmoser looks more like a modern city suburb; it has sidewalks and boulevards instead of mostly narrow roads and streets with dirt shoulders. (For some that's an advantage; for others it's not charming enough.)

Homes and apartment buildings here are much newer, with some condo development and home building still under way. Started by a German developer, Rohrmoser begins at the end of Sábana Park and runs along both sides of Rohrmoser Boulevard until it reaches the ultramodern shopping center of Plaza Mayor. From that point west Rohrmoser is on the northern side of the boulevard, and Pavas is on the eastern side. The U.S. Embassy, incidentally, is in Pavas, on Pavas Highway.

Not long ago, a friend moved to Rohrmoser with her teenage daughter in order to work full-time doing medical transcriptions via the Internet for a U.S. company. She chose to live in Rohrmoser because of the availability of high-speed Internet access. Fast connections were not available just anywhere in Costa Rica, and it is the lifeline to her profession. She says, "This is an expensive neighborhood, but since I need the two-way cable access and we want to 'feel safe' while we learn about this country, it works out fine. Hopefully, high-speed access will someday be available at a reasonable cost throughout the country, and we can venture out a little more! Here in Rohrmoser we have two-way cable through Amnet. I simply connect through the Amnet connection directly to AOL, which is basically the same way I connected in the States through a DSL line."

Many North Americans live in Rohrmoser, but the largest percentage of your neighbors will be Tico professionals who like the convenience of being close to the business center of the city. A big advantage of locating here is that it is just a ten-minute drive to downtown San José (five minutes by taxi) yet has a quiet and safe feeling. Adding to the security is the presence of private guards who are hired by homeowners on the block. With everyone contributing, the cost of twenty-four-hour security is affordable and comforting.

My wife and I used to live in Rohrmoser and enjoyed the peaceful ambience. We would stroll from Rohrmoser Boulevard to Pavas (some 4 or 5 blocks) to dine at one of the many great restaurants and return late at night, with absolutely no feelings of insecurity. One reason we felt okay about this was the presence of watchmen on almost every block. We had full confidence in the integrity of our neighbors because most were doctors, professors, attorneys, and the like.

Then one day we saw on television that a very nice home a couple of houses away from us had been rented to a gang of professional bank robbers from Venezuela. The bandits had been living there for some time while they committed a string of robberies, a couple of them rather violent. They were on the "most wanted" list of the OIJ (equivalent to the FBI). The culprits dressed well, they kept their front yard tidy, and they probably paid their rent on time, so they couldn't have been all bad.

SANTA **ANA**

Another part of the Meseta Central that attracts North Americans to become residents is Santa Ana, a sunny mountain valley just another 6 kilometers to the west of Escazú. The altitude here is lower than at either Escazú or San José, making it slightly warmer and drier. A number of small rivers cross the rolling valley, and rounded mountains provide a scenic backdrop.

Santa Ana's setting is also more rural than Escazú's, with crops such as sugarcane, rice, beans, and coffee growing all around this town of 20,000 residents. Roadside stands sell braids of garlic and onions, garden-fresh vegetables, and jars of rich local honey. (Despite Africanized bees' nasty reputations, they produce high-quality honey and more of it than ordinary bees.) All roads converge upon a central area, giving Santa Ana the feeling of a downtown center, rural yet sophisticated. High above the town, on the mountain Cerro Pacacua, is a 20,000-acre forest preserve and bird sanctuary, keeping nature ever present in the local ambience.

A few generations ago—before it became an easy thing to drive to the beach for vacations—San José's wealthy families maintained summer homes in Santa Ana. This was the place to spend weekends and school vacations, a place for the upper crust to host parties and entertain lavishly. This old tradition left its traces on today's community, with nice homes scattered about the area. Some rather attractive developments, complete with swimming pools, gardens, and twenty-four-hour security, are found here. This is the place for polo matches and international equestrian competitions. Seasonal festivals bring an impressive parade of horseback riders, who ride their high-stepping steeds along the streets to the central plaza where the main celebration is under way. (Don't try to drive along the parade route on festival day; horses have the right-of-way.)

Santa Ana has a deserved reputation as a working artists' colony, with a number of writers and amateur artists present as well. The town is famous for ceramics, and production of excellent pieces is a major industry, with almost thirty workshops and 150 local people engaged in the art. Excellent restaurants, a first-class supermarket, and shopping of all descriptions are at hand, eliminating the need to go to the crowded world of downtown San José for odds and ends. Yet when such travel is necessary, it's but an easy 10-mile drive along one of the country's few stretches of superhighway. One of the largest and most elegant shopping malls in the country is found between Santa Ana and Escazú on this highway: the Multi-Plaza. It's worth a visit.

Every community seems to have an especially popular hangout where expats gather to socialize over a few drinks, lunch, and dinner. The Tex-Mex restaurant in Santa Ana seems to be the place for this. English is spoken here by a ratio of 10 to 1, and the place always seems to be crowded. I believe there is also a Tex-Mex restaurant in Ciudad Colón, as well.

Of all the Meseta Central retirement locations, I suspect that communities from Santa Ana west to the town of Ciudad Colón may have a great potential for development and property appreciation. The reason for my belief is planned extension of the divided highway from San José through Ciudad Colón that will someday hook up with the Pacific Coast Highway 34. This highway, by the way, is one of the few made of cement instead of the usual mixture of asphalt, gravel, and brown sugar (or whatever they mix with asphalt to make a dissolvable road surface). It's lasted without damage—not even a tiny pothole—for about fifteen years. Surely, the government transportation bosses will someday realize the value of cement highway construction as opposed to disappearing asphalt surfaces.

Anyway, traffic moves right along on this highway, zipping back and forth to San José with surprising ease (surprising for Costa Rica). When the highway is extended to the Pacific, this will dramatically cut the driving time to the popular beach communities of Jacó and Quepos. With Pacific beaches just an hour's drive from Santa Ana, the convenience will make the area even more attractive as a place to live, and real estate could become a good investment. When I mention this possibility to my Tico friends, they shrug their shoulders and say, "Don't count on that highway in the near future. We'd be delighted if they'd just fill the potholes on the roads we have!"

OTHER TOWNS **AND VILLAGES**

To the south of Heredia and Alajuela, several smaller towns and open countryside sprinkled with small farms and beautiful homes draw Ticos and foreigners wanting to escape the city's crush.

The road from Heredia to Turrucares is particularly striking, with lovely, high-quality homes interspersed with small, neatly kept farms and residences. Our taxi driver, who was renting his cab and services by the day, drove us there and pointed out some of the prettier homes along the way. "I was born in this area," he said proudly. And then, with a hint of sadness in his voice, he added, "Of course, it is too expensive for me to live here now."

More to the west, Atenas and La Garita are pleasant places that are gaining in popularity, particularly with foreigners who prefer slightly cooler weather. (Some folks are hard to please!) These towns sit along the alternate highway that winds down through Orotina, toward the Pacific beaches. Right now the traffic through this area is often snarled and frustrating (frightening on Sunday evening, when everybody's returning from Jacó Beach), but when (and if) the superhighway past Ciudad Colón is completed, coast-bound traffic will bypass the Atenas–La Garita area and make it an exceptionally desirable place to live. It's nice here now—even with traffic—lightly settled, with luxury properties interspersed with modest-priced, livable homes. The commercial centers of both towns are particularly neat and attractive. Some friends considered buying a wonderful three-bedroom house on a large lot on the outskirts of Atenas for $46,000; had we not already owned more property than we needed, we'd have bought it ourselves.

GRECIA Grecia (population 50,000) is about a thirty-minute drive northeast from the airport and has been attracting a growing number of expatriates. The turnoff from the Pan-American Highway is marked by a monument that tries to look like the ruins of a Greek temple. The town is reached via a picturesque road that traverses sugarcane fields, high-quality coffee plantations, and small farms. The views are spectacular, overlooking deep valleys and lofty mountains in the distance.

The center of town features a lovely square in front of one of the country's most interesting churches. It's made of sheet iron, probably manufactured by the Eiffel company of France during the period when they were prefabbing churches for export around the world. Grecia is noted for its wide streets and prosperous-looking middle-class neighborhoods and has been voted the "cleanest town in Latin America" on several occasions. A good place to meet local expats is at the central square where they meet most weekday mornings for coffee and gossip. Near the plaza is a large central market that, in addition to the usual collection of veggie and meat vendors, has a wonderful Tico restaurant serving some of the best *comida typica* we've ever tasted.

English-speaking residents here vow that this is one of the friendliest and safest places in the country, and I tend to believe it. As I've driven the roads in the area, I've noticed a surprising exception to the rule of bars on windows; many homes do not have bars! There doesn't appear to be any one particular place here where gringos congregate; they are dispersed about the landscape, sometimes on small plots of land near town or in Grecia itself. Some prefer one of the nearby villages such as San Rafael, San Roque, Tacares, or any number of similar locations.

CARTAGO This quiet, exceptionally clean city is about 25 kilometers southwest of San José, in the center of a rich agricultural region. Costa Rica guidebooks seldom mention Cartago except to note the ruins of an ancient cathedral and the slightly newer cathedral that houses Costa

Rica's religious icon, the Black Virgin, and the fact that Cartago was once Costa Rica's capital city.

Cartago used to be a major station on the now-defunct San José–Limón railroad line. While waiting for the train to resume its slow crawl to the coast, we would stroll around the nearby market and buy steaming empanadas as we waited for the train's whistle to announce the continuance of its journey. I liked the town at that time, often wondering why it wasn't being "discovered" by gringos looking for an "authentic" Costa Rican relocation haven. Cartago was also one of the obligatory places to take visitors—close enough to San José's suburbs for an afternoon's visit to the historic monuments, a lunch at a Tico restaurant, and then home before nightfall.

Things are starting to change. Bearing out my observation that North Americans feel at home almost anywhere in Costa Rica, the city of Cartago and its surrounding communities are attracting more newcomers. This idea isn't exactly new; some expat residents have lived here for more than twenty-five years. Only ten or so expatriates live in Cartago itself, while at least fifty live in or around the nearby suburb of Paraiso. There you'll find one of those new Mega Supers, as well as a newly constructed shopping mall.

An expat resident from Ohio who lives with his wife in Taras (at the beginning of the road to Irazu Volcano) said, "I was surprised that so many expats say that they live here mainly because of the climate. I always considered it to be cool, and my Tica wife says it's cold. Also the rainy season here is probably a little wetter than in San José."

Cartago doesn't seem to have a "hangout" where gringos go for morning coffee like some other towns do. For the most part you run into them in the various shopping centers or on the downtown streets. They will tell you that they enjoy the quality of life in Cartago and that the people "really do accept expats and make you feel good about where you live."

POAS For those who are so fussy that even Escazú temperatures are too warm, there is a cooler alternative where living is pleasant and heavy exhaust fumes from diesel buses seldom foul the air. This is the Poas area, partway up the side of the mountain and volcanic crater of the same name.

To get to Poas, a winding, scenic road takes you past fields of produce and coffee, past comfortable houses with spectacular views. Along the way are roadside stands vending the specialties of the mountainside farms. Strawberries, enormous and sugar-sweet, are year-round treats here, displayed on stands along with homemade cheeses, candies, and fresh veggies from backyard gardens. As you gain altitude, the air becomes cooler and slightly crisp. The panorama of the valley in the distance looks impressive indeed. The vegetation becomes even more lush; enormous plants with leaves 6 feet across hang over the roadside, and flowering trees filter the sunshine overhead.

Finally, the road tops a grade and enters the town of Poas. This is a quiet, middle-class town of workers, farmers, and, lately, North American *pensionados* and *rentistas*. Its unimposing, no-nonsense business center lacks spiffy boutiques and gourmet restaurants yet maintains a folksy, neighborly atmosphere, with adequate commercial conveniences.

The Poas area isn't for everyone, only those who view temperatures over 70 degrees as beastly hot. If any place in the Meseta Central can be described as "the place of eternal spring," it would have to be the area around Poas. I've been told that temperatures almost never rise above 75 degrees; neither do they drop below 60, day or night, summer or winter.

OTHER TEMPERATE ZONE **LOCATIONS**

The following locations do not exactly lie within the Meseta Central, but they do have similar climates. These are places for those who don't care to put up with the heat and insects of the jungle, yet they are close enough to salt water that you can usually drive down to the beach for the day and return to sleep under a blanket that same night. Temperatures here have a wide range, with places like Arenal being very cool and San Isidro del General being rather balmy.

SAN ISIDRO DEL GENERAL At first glance, this town would seem to be a rather unusual place for North Americans to choose as a place for residence or retirement. There is nothing spectacular about San Isidro del General; it is an ordinary, small Costa Rican city. It's neat and orderly, with the ubiquitous mountain views common to most other parts of the country. Few vacationers visit San Isidro, and those who have passed through the town may get it mixed up with one of the half-dozen other San Isidros in the mountains. But those North Americans who have discovered San Isidro's secrets love living here. The climate is considerably warmer than that of San José, which suits some folks just fine, and the pace far slower.

Located on a wide ridge, not far from the high peak of Cerro Chirripó, the town enjoys a continuous breeze that keeps the air clear and aromatic with flower-blossom perfume. Daytime temperatures are pleasantly warm for my taste (maybe hot for some folks), and evenings are tempered by cool air flowing down from Chirripó Peak. Although San Isidro is not as serene and idyllic as some other Costa Rican towns, once you are away from the main square—and the inevitable cars, motorcycles, and trucks circling in search of a parking space—the pace slackens to a very peaceful stride.

Like most older Costa Rican towns, San Isidro features a main square in its center, the usual well-kept park. Since the park is the social gathering place for local residents, it isn't surprising that the members of the North American community use it as their social focal point as well. The open-air restaurant of Hotel Chirripó faces the park, and at any given time you can count on at least some of the tables being occupied by English-speaking patrons.

Real estate and rentals are exceptionally inexpensive here. Since it is off the ordinary tourist routes, with no beaches and lacking in discos and other flashy attractions, San Isidro is likely to remain inexpensive. On one visit I talked with an American who had just completed building a small, two-bedroom home and was eager to find a tenant. He was offering to rent it for almost nothing just to have someone to take care of it while he returned home.

Several North Americans have taken advantage of the climate and low-cost real estate, living on small farms on the outskirts of town or along the highway toward the beach at Dominical. The views along this road are absolutely spectacular, with neat, prosperous-looking farms and picturesque homes in the mountain valleys below looking like toys along a model train set. At the time of a recent visit, one American from Texas, who was married to a Tica woman, operated a motel, restaurant, and bar on the highway, midway between San Isidro and the ocean.

LAKE ARENAL DISTRICT The northern portion of the Cordillera mountain chain, until recently ignored by North Americans, has one of the best potentials for growth of any place in Costa Rica. Certainly that's my opinion and one shared by many other North Americans who are buying property around Lake Arenal as quickly (and quietly) as they can. Those who know about Lake Arenal would love to keep it a secret, but truth will out! The character of this region is so different from that of other parts of Costa Rica that it's difficult to believe you are in the same country.

The Lake Arenal district is in the upper end of the same mountain chain, but that's as far as the similarity with other highland areas goes. As I understand it, the mountains dip lower at this position in the chain to form a low break or window in the Cordillera. This interruption in the mountain ridges permits a reversal of wind patterns, allowing strong easterly winds to bring moist air off the Caribbean with an abundance of rain. There is no such thing as a dry season in the Arenal area; it's a year-round wonderland of greenness and lush vegetation. When I asked one long-time resident how much it rained, she replied, "On average, about fourteen months out of the year."

Before the government started building a dam to create the wonderfully scenic lake, few people lived here. The project required several thousand workers and support people and sixteen years to complete. Roads were cut into the area, opening it up to Costa Rican settlers who started farms and small villages. After the lake was created, many workers elected to stay on in the company housing that was built during the construction stages. The population here is still scanty, but it is growing daily, particularly in the numbers of foreigners who have "discovered" Lake Arenal.

To get there via paved road, the quickest way is by turning off the Pan-American Highway at Cañas, an extremely hot and dusty place during the dry season. Were it not for the ample irrigation water coming from Lake Arenal, Cañas would be more like a desert than a rich agricultural region. An air-conditioned auto and lightweight clothing are necessities here. Yet just 18 kilometers away by a tortuously winding road, the air conditioner is shut off and car windows rolled down to take advantage of the delightful fresh air.

TILARÁN By the time you reach the little town of Tilarán, only 23 kilometers from Cañas, a sweater might feel comfortable when the sky happens to be overcast. The countryside changes from pool-table-flat to steep-sided hills; colors change from dusty dry to emerald green. The road climbs gently now, as vegetation seems to become fresher with every curve, past fat cattle grazing fetlock-deep in richly grassed pastures and—where land hasn't been cleared for cattle or agriculture—some astonishingly heavy stands of tropical forest. Just about every imaginable kind of tropical tree or crop thrives here, from bananas to macadamia nuts.

A surprisingly nontropical-looking town—with wide streets, neatly maintained homes, and prosperous businesses—Tilarán has become the home base of a number of expatriates. The climate is temperate and springlike due to a continuous eastern wind that drops moisture on Tilarán even during the dry season. This keeps the town green year-round but with less moisture and wind velocity than are found at nearby Arenal. Local residents publish their own newspaper, partly in English, which promotes ecology and recycling projects for the nation.

A few miles east of Tilarán, the view of Lake Arenal bursts upon you, one of the prettiest lakes in the world. The fact that it is artificial fades in importance when the overall effect is considered. Windsurfers claim this is the second best place in all the world to enjoy their sport. What the first place is for windsurfers, I don't know, but it surely can't be any more beautiful than Lake Arenal.

Almost all residents in this area live on or near the drive that skirts Lake Arenal. The paved portion of the road has a scattering of European-type homes, chalets, and an occasional commercial unit such as a *pulpería*, those community store-tavern combinations so common in rural Costa Rica. Many homes are obviously recently constructed, giving evidence of their newness in a developing region.

This area somehow doesn't seem like Costa Rica. Were it not for the colorful bougainvilleas, flowering oaks, and luscious yellow Cortez trees, this countryside would look like an exaggerated version of the Tennessee or Kentucky hill country, or perhaps the lower elevations of Switzerland in the summer. Of course, the banana plants and broad-leaved philodendrons quickly dispel this notion.

Several charming little villages and occasional inns or small hotels are spaced along the highway between Tilarán and Arenal. The road is paved

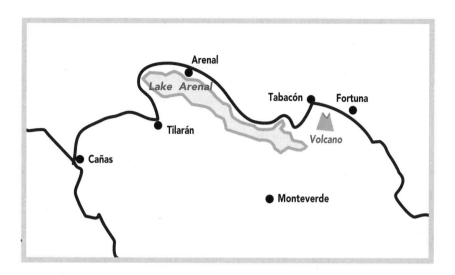

and is usually in pretty good condition. A few miles east of the town of Nuevo Arenal, the road turns into graded clay and occasional stretches of blacktop. The condition of the road is never predictable. At the beginning of the dry season—after bulldozers scrape the road into a smooth surface, fill in the gigantic potholes, and sometimes cover it with a bit of gravel—the route feels like a superhighway to drive. The distance from Nuevo Arenal to Arenal Volcano seems like nothing, with a wonderful view of the lake and thick tropical vegetation lining the road. But at other times the road is an absolute nightmare, with sections missing, water and mud that can bury a four-wheel-drive up to its windshield, and other horrors. I believe the problem is that the steep mountain slopes along the north side of the route come down from rain forests above, bringing water and mud sluicing down onto the road. What doesn't get washed away gets covered with mud. The lesson here is to make inquiries about taking a shortcut from Fortuna to Tilarán. When the road is good, it is very, very good; and when it is bad, it is horrid.

NUEVO ARENAL The town on the lake is called Nuevo Arenal or, quite often, simply Arenal. This is a surprisingly prosperous-looking place, with neat little houses interspersed with expensive-looking ones. The town sits high on the sloping bank of Lake Arenal, and most homes and businesses are situated with a lake view in mind. Streets are well paved, and more are in the process of being paved in anticipation of a population explosion. Parts of town have an oddly unfinished look, as newly paved streets and vacant lots mix with an occasional house. The center of town has the inevitable soccer field with spectator benches curiously pointed toward the street, away from the field, as if the soccer team is so bad that locals would rather watch the traffic, scarce as it is.

Arenal obviously was a development planned by the government during the dam's construction phase. Many of today's homes here are left over from that era. Unlike the traditional Latin American residential style—built close together and against the sidewalk to allocate space for interior patios—some Arenal homes have real lawns, reminiscent of small-town USA. This adds to Arenal's strange, non–Latin American look.

Because of the area's beauty, the temperate-tropical combination climate, and the low cost of real estate, the Lake Arenal region is undergoing a buying frenzy. Buyers from Canada, the United States, and Europe are furtively looking at property and investing. Germans, Swiss, and Italians appear to be the biggest sharks, biting off chunks of the land as quickly as they can. They try not to appear eager as they snap up bargains, and they do their best to keep this place a secret, lest hordes of other foreigners descend upon paradise and ruin their plans of being the only ones there.

It's not surprising that prices are going up on property around Arenal. It's a very desirable area. Still, it's hard to conceive that inflation could be anything like that along the Pacific beaches. Another favorable circumstance: Since this is lakefront property, it doesn't fall under the complicated and restrictive laws that regulate ownership and construction on beachfront parcels. Here waterfront property is owned outright instead of being leased from the municipality. However, be aware that the water level in the lake fluctuates from dry season to wet season as water is drawn off for irrigation and hydroelectric power. Your waterfront lot could end up with a broad frontage of dry land in the dry season.

ARENAL VOLCANO No trip to Costa Rica can be considered complete until you've visited the Arenal Volcano. Active continuously over several centuries, the volcano's northern slope suddenly exploded about twenty years ago, destroying a village and killing more than sixty people. (A geologist had tried to warn them of an impending eruption, but nobody believed him.) The nearest and best place to observe the activity is in the hot pools of Tabacón, a resort wedged into a steaming-hot river canyon at the volcano's base. You can sit on underwater stools by the bar and sip piña coladas while you listen to the thunderlike explosions accompanied by puffs of smoke and red-hot boulders coughing from the volcano's vent.

The volcano has done marvels for tourism hereabouts. The nearby town of Fortuna has become prosperous, serving the needs of the hordes of sight-seers. New hotels, restaurants, and stores are appearing each season. Fortuna is an exceptionally neat and pleasant community, one that could well make a good place for retirement. With a new road going through San Ramón, San José is only a two-and-a-half-hour drive away.

LA FORTUNA This small town with a friendly atmosphere, spic-and-span streets, and a great climate has my prediction of a place that will some-day have a sizable expat community. Sitting at approximately 400 meters above sea level, Fortuna is too high to be tropical, yet it's low enough to avoid chilly winds. About 16 kilometers from the entrance to Arenal Volcano National Park, La Fortuna serves as an ideal base for tourists visiting the volcano, popular Tabacón Hot Springs, and Lake Arenal. Not far from Caño Negro Reserve and such outdoor activities as windsurfing, fishing, and white-water rafting, it's almost obligatory to stay at or pass through La Fortuna to enjoy these facilities. The tourism potential will do nothing but grow over time, and this will bring more North American residents. The town and vicinity have a growing mumber of hotels, cabinas, restaurants, and travel/tour agencies. As you depart La Fortuna toward Tabacón and Lake Arenal, several new tourist facilities with terrific views of the volcano are under construction.

A small group of foreigners are now settling into the Fortuna area. Of course everybody knows everyone here, but to date they haven't formed any residents' club or formal organization. That will come later, when a critical mass of expatriates forms around La Fortuna. In the meantime, as one resident says, "We come here to enjoy living with our Tico neighbors and being independent."

SAN CARLOS When people talk about "San Carlos," they could be referring to the northern region of Costa Rica, from below Ciudad Quesada on up to the Nicaraguan border at the San Juan River. They could also mean the small city known as San Carlos, a place of about 30,000 residents

located in the more southern portion of the San Carlos region. To add to the confusion, you won't find the city of San Carlos on the map, because officially it is called Ciudad Quesada. However, for some reason unknown to me, Ticos always refer to Ciudad Quesada as San Carlos.

San Carlos is another example of Costa Rica's microclimates. With a lower elevation than the Meseta Central, the region is warmer than the San José area and receives more rain during the dry season. Yet it doesn't have the heavy rainfall of nearby Lake Arenal area. Agriculture is a year-round activity, with citrus, macadamia, and other orchard crops as well as numerous *fincas* (ranches) with horses and cattle tended by expatriates.

These lands were once tropical forests, which during the past decades have been transformed into cattle pastures and fruit plantations. The exceptionally rich farmland here has attracted a number of gringo farmers and would-be agriculturists. San Carlos's agricultural zone devotes almost 70 percent of the land to raising cattle. The area produces first-quality milk, beef cattle, and agricultural products. Expatriates have set up on small to moderately large spreads; some experiment with reforestation. Some people have been planting teak, even though some experts claim that teak needs definite dry seasons alternating with wet periods to force the tree to produce oil and densely grained wood. Time will tell, because it takes many years before teak is ready to harvest.

Ciudad Quesada, or San Carlos, or whatever, is the main center of services and commerce for the Northern Zone. This prosperous-looking city-town was settled in 1840 when the Quesada family moved here from San Ramón and founded a village. As is the custom, the center of town holds a central park and the inevitable Catholic church. Nearby is the customary central market full of colorful stalls selling fruit, vegetables, herbs, and locally made leather products and crafts.

ACOSTA Recently the Ministry of Tourism came up with the idea of promoting "rural tourism" as an economic development project for communities with limited tourist attractions and no hotels or other tourist facilities. The idea is to attract certain types of tourists, those who aren't looking for golf courses, beaches, discos, and the traditional tourist glitz that draws many foreigners to Costa Rica. This special kind of tourist will be curious about the everyday life of the Ticos: who they are, what would it be like living in a "typical" Costa Rican village. Since these isolated communities rarely have hotels suitable for tourists, local residents organize to turn their homes into bed-and-breakfasts and welcome visitors. Since the community goes all out to make visitors welcome, it occurs to me that retirees might be received even more warmly as permanent economic benefits to the area. A few expatriates have already settled there. (A Web site describing the program is found at www.costaricanruraltourism.org.)

Finding this idea intriguing, I decided to investigate by making a trip to one of the designated rural tourism areas, an area known as Acosta, the general name given to a half-dozen villages in the mountains south of San José, about an hour's ride by bus from the center of the city. An excellent road snakes its way upward, winding through small villages and past some very interesting homes. The drive is spectacular, with deep valleys and ravines, lush vegetation, and spectacular views of San José and the Central Valley way down below.

The largest village is San Ignacio de Acosta. It's difficult to know the population, because none of the people I met there could make an estimate that agreed with anybody else's. There's a lovely church and a large, landscaped park. The surprising thing is the high quality of the housing. It was explained to me that at one time the Tico government was making low-interest loans for quality housing, and many people took advantage of this and upgraded their homes. The setting is overwhelmingly beautiful. San Ignacio de Acosta is perched on the top of a rounded mountain, with an astonishing view of other villages so far below that the houses look like toys. San Luis de Acosta is about five minutes away, looking down the other side of the mountain into other valleys. Coffee farms are interspersed with forested land and small farm homesteads. Except for the main roads and some town streets, all roads are graded gravel, some in excellent condition, others not so great. The climate is superb, one of the best in the country, at least for those who like permanent springlike weather. The temperatures are seldom over 75 degrees or below 65 degrees, year-round. Air-conditioning and heating is unknown here.

I was welcomed enthusiastically as a visitor and was given a room in a private home, where I was treated as one of the family. I joined with the family in the local fiesta celebration and was very impressed. In my opinion, a place such as Acosta is a retirement option for certain types of North Americans: those who speak at least some Spanish or those who are willing to learn. Acosta would be appropriate for those who do not require a large circle of English-speaking friends. The local Ticos are exceptionally friendly and open. I feel that before long, a retired couple could easily be involved with the Tico society, with friends and volunteer activities keeping them very busy. ∎

CHAPTER FIVE

THE
CARIBBEAN COAST

The same mountain chain that creates the delightful weather in Costa Rica's highlands further separates the country into eastern and western tropical zones. Because of this separation the Caribbean and the Pacific zones have distinct personalities. Not only are the differences in weather patterns and varieties of animal, plant, and marine life, but marked cultural dissimilarities exist as well. The Caribbean is Jamaican/African; the Pacific is Latin/European.

The word *tropics* implies long stretches of deserted beaches, with thick jungle hovering at the edge of the sand. It means monkeys jostling branches in the strangler fig trees while parrots, macaws, and 1,000 other birds screech, twitter, and sing lyrically in the sunset. Costa Rica's tropics have all of this and much more.

The Caribbean Coast has two distinct regions. Its southern portion, which is lightly populated, reflects Jamaican and African influences, blended with Costa Rican and Spanish personalities. The northern half of the coast is almost uninhabited, visited mostly by fishing fanatics, tourists, and ecology students. (Incidentally, Costa Ricans usually refer to this coast as the "Atlantic" rather than the "Caribbean.")

CARIBBEAN **COAST**

Caribbean
Sea

★ San José

Limón ●

Cahuita ●
Puerto Viejo ●
Sixaola ●

Pacific
Ocean

The northern inland lagoons and waterways are famous for world-class fishing of all kinds. Record-size tarpon and snook are routinely hooked in these scenic jungle rivers and inlets. The best snook angling is usually from the shore, around river mouths, with twenty- to thirty-pounders not uncommon. Fishermen also bring in jacks, mackerel, barracuda, snapper, and other species when fishing the Caribbean Coast. While waiting for exciting action, you are treated to the sight of monkeys frolicking in the trees, an occasional parrot or toucan darting among the branches, and sometimes a crocodile lurking along the shoreline. The Tortuguero area is known as an important nesting place of the endangered green sea turtle.

No roads enter this northern region; the only way to get here is by airplane or motor launch. My belief is that the area is far too isolated and the climate too humid for development other than ecotourism projects.

SOUTHERN **CARIBBEAN COAST**

The southern Caribbean Coast attracts surfers, snorkelers, and reggae enthusiasts, as well as ordinary tourists and ecology buffs who want to savor the unique tropical environment. Weather patterns here are unpredictable, with no sharp distinction between winter and summer. Rain can fall at any time and usually does. Winds often blow down from the north, sometimes causing the Caribbean Coast to duplicate Miami's weather. The plus side of the Caribbean weather is that things stay green and lush year-round, unlike the Pacific Coast, where it seldom rains between December and May. The downside is that this weather is always more humid, and insects tend to grow healthy and robust on this edge of the continent.

LIMÓN The city of Limón, a two-and-a-half-hour drive from San José, is where Columbus sighted the American mainland for the first time, back in 1502. Apparently he thought it was another island and didn't bother going ashore himself. At best, Limón has always been a ramshackle affair—a tropical banana port, too large to have the charm of a small town, yet too small to offer the amenities of a real city.

Having exposed my bias against Limón, I must point out that there are those who disagree with me. A number of North Americans who reside in the community testify to the charm and friendliness of their African/Jamaican neighbors. Racial tensions, resentment, and animosity that are so common in some U.S. cities are virtually unknown here. The social atmosphere here is relaxed, friendly, and neighborly. In fact, Costa Rican race relations and attitudes toward citizens of color are very different from those in many other parts of the world. Because people in Limón speak perfect Spanish as well as English with a British Jamaican accent, those with education are much in demand in the business world. They often find positions as supervisors or managers. They can communicate with London, New York, or Geneva (English being the lingua franca of business today), and they can deal with North Americans and Europeans who speak very little Spanish.

The number of foreigners living in Limón is difficult to ascertain. I asked a friend who lives in Limón to make an estimate. Curt Johnson (from Florida) replied, "I can't put a solid number on the expats here, but we just celebrated Thanksgiving with about twenty-five of them. We had a great dinner with turkey and all the trimmings—a full-blown Turkey Day, including watching football. I've met teachers in the Caribbean School (English-Spanish), Peace Corps people, semiretirees, Evangelical missionaries, and ship's chandlers (people who are commissioned to buy or supply provisions for all the freighters that come into port). We have also run into a few retired people who have been here for many years and still haven't learned any Spanish."

Curt (aka Capt. Curt) and his wife, Cindy, moved to Limón a few years ago. "We lived in an area of Limón called *Zona Americana*," says Cindy. "These were luxury homes built fifty years ago for executives of United Fruit Company. Ours is spacious, yet cozy, with 10-foot ceilings, polished wood paneling, and French doors that open onto the veranda. We have a 180-degree view of the Caribbean and continual breezes. No marinas, no loud high-speed boats going by—nothing but an occasional banana boat or a cruise ship off the coast."

CAHUITA AND PUERTO VIEJO One hundred and fifty years ago, the beaches of Cahuita and Puerto Viejo were uninhabited except for seasonal campsites of Miskito Indians who followed the migration of green and hawksbill turtles. ("Miskitos" are a mixture of native Indians and escaped African slaves who fled Jamaica and Cuba to settle the coasts of

Nicaragua and Panama.) They named their camp *Cahuita*, which means "Point of blood trees" in the Miskito dialect, because of the large number of blood trees growing on the promontory now known as Cahuita Point.

The region remained uninhabited until the late 1800s, when William Smith—an English-speaking Afro-Caribbean who came from Panama every year to fish and hunt turtles—decided to build a permanent home on Cahuita's beach. He was joined by a group of Jamaicans who originally came as construction workers on the railway from Limón to San José. In addition to working on the United Fruit Company's banana plantations, the settlers did subsistence farming, hunting, and fishing and small-scale cultivation of cocoa. The settlers were pretty much self-sufficient, having had little contact with the rest of Costa Rica. (In fact, for many years the central government prevented people from the coast from traveling to the highlands for fear of spreading yellow fever and malaria.) The first road to Cahuita didn't connect with the outside world until 1976. This isolation enabled people here to preserve their African-Jamaican-Caribbean heritage and bring it intact into the twenty-first century.

Because English is the area's first language (sometimes spoken with a delightful Jamaican patois), this area is favored by tourists and visitors who don't want to bother learning another language during their stay. The genuine lack of racial tension here is refreshing for those of us who have been used to the self-imposed social barriers and chasms of hostility that separate black from white in some areas of the United States. I personally feel welcome here and enjoy basking in the warmth of genuine hospitality.

From San José three and a half hours of scenic driving brings you to the village of Cahuita. (It's about four hours by bus.) The village has a picture-book quality in its tropical Afro-Caribbean setting. Many houses stand on stilts to discourage insects; some buildings are painted with bright, contrasting pigments similar to the flamboyant styles of Jamaica. Slender, colorfully dressed women and girls carry bundles on their heads with grace and enviable posture. It's easy to imagine you are in an African seashore village.

The main road follows the shore, past black sand beaches and coral reefs to the north and past more coral and beaches of yellow sand to the south. Along the yellow sand beach is Cahuita National Park, a 13-

kilometer stretch of jungle complete with howler monkeys (which the Costa Ricans call *congos*), feisty parrots, and wildlife of all descriptions. A foot trail parallels the beach through a thick tangle of tropical trees, vines, and orchids. Butterflies, orange and purple land crabs, and iguanas keep you company on the hike.

Many North Americans and Europeans live here year-round, some operating successful businesses. Others regularly arrive in November and head home by May. I had the good fortune to meet a young California couple who invited me to visit their winter quarters in Cahuita. They lived in a picturesque, thatch-roofed cabin perched next to a coral reef and shaded by graceful coconut trees. Their house was very rustic, with minimal furniture, but they enjoyed their winter home immensely. The surf washed at their front door, spilling into a small depression of smooth black rocks where their children played as if in their own private saltwater swimming pool.

Tourism in Cahuita and Puerto Viejo has been negatively affected by publicity about crime in the region. Residents readily admit that petty crime happens—perhaps more than normal—but they blame insufficient police protection as part of the problem and protest that some publicity is unwarranted. Not long ago, after a shocking crime gained national publicity, local residents became outraged. They organized a protest and demanded that the government provide more and well-trained police. After a vigorous campaign, with public demonstrations in San José, the government did indeed install a more modern system of law enforcement.

To ensure the town's reputation as a safe and friendly place to visit, local citizens maintain the Cahuita Security Committee. The goal is to prevent crime rather than deal with a problem after it has happened. The committee establishes a round-the-clock checkpoint between Cahuita and Limón during celebrations that attract throngs of tourists into the area. The committee members work with the police to patrol the beaches. They not only work with law enforcement but also check on the police to make sure they're doing their job. This has had a very positive effect on the tourist business and upon visitors' confidence in their personal safety here. While not exactly crime-free today, Cahuita has become more tranquil.

The southern Caribbean Coast is particularly attractive to younger, more active expatriates. Special emphasis is placed on youthful activities, with reggae music thumping loudly from tropical bars and with surf-boards, snorkel gear, and brief swimsuits the order of the day.

The village of Puerto Viejo is 16 kilometers south of Cahuita by road and somewhat less by the beach trail. To make matters a bit confusing, there are two Costa Rican places called Puerto Viejo. The one here is for-mally called Puerto Viejo de Limón, and the other is a small river town in the northeast, near La Selva Reserve: Puerto Viejo de Sarapiquí. The Puerto Viejo on the southern Caribbean Coast used to be much more sleepy than its sister village of Cahuita. Things have changed, with surfers, Rastafarians, and tourists of all descriptions now thronging through the town.

A problem for those planning on buying property as absentee own-ers: This region is susceptible to organized squatter activities. A friend told of losing about a third of his land when he neglected to watch over it for several years. He thought he was safe because he had hired a guard to watch over it. Only when it was too late did he discover that the guard was one of the squatters. So if you decide to own property here, be sure to keep your eye on it and remove *precaistas* before they establish rights. (See Chapter 10 for preventive measures.)

People who love Cahuita and Puerto Viejo will tell you that the rest of Costa Rica is too tame for them. They prefer this movie-set tropical ambi-ence—romantic, picturesque, and inexpensive. One bar in the very center of Cahuita features on its front porch extraordinarily powerful loudspeak-ers that blare Jamaican rock music day and night. The volume is such that it rattles windows a block away and peels the paint off passing automobiles. I love to visit here, but for long-term living in the tropics, my personal preference would be the Pacific Coast. It's my age I suppose.

WHY THE CARIBBEAN COAST? I've always enjoyed visiting the Cahuita and Puerto Viejo areas, and I've made friends with several resi-dents there over the years. However, it's always been my impression that the gringo population consists mainly of young people who are more interested in surfing and reggae music than in settling down to home life or going into business. That's a gross exaggeration, of course, but the east coast has never been a place where I would consider living on a long-term basis. That's just my personal bias.

Many others have a completely different take of lifestyles on the

Caribbean. To get some insight into the question, I took advantage of my friendship with a couple who make their home in Puerto Viejo by asking how they made their decision. Doug and Rosin Warren, who moved here from Arizona a couple of years ago, said that numerous other people had E-mailed similar questions about living on Costa Rica's east coast. They wanted to know the "whys" of choosing the Caribbean side rather than other, more popular sections of the country.

"We made our decision from the position of someone who wants to live on or very near a beautiful, tropical beach," Doug says. "We realize we're in the minority, since many more people prefer the Pacific beaches. Our viewpoint is sort of a Caribbean versus Pacific comparison, so here it is:

"We honestly believe that the southern Caribbean Coast is the best-kept secret in this entire country. The 20 miles or so from Cahuita down through Puerto Viejo and Manzanillo and to the Panamanian border have some of the most beautiful beaches I've ever seen, with white sand and palm trees, where the jungle comes right down to the shoreline. For the most part the beaches are almost deserted. You can have a whole cove all to yourself if you want.

"The last 5 miles of this section, from Manzanillo to the border, there's not even a road! You walk along an easy trail, right on the beach, and you see nobody. The beaches are spectacular, clean, unspoiled—if you feel like skinny-dipping in crystal-clear, warm water, knock yourself out!

"Weather is another important factor: 70 degrees early in the morning and then about 85 degrees in the afternoon—that's all twelve months of the year! We don't keep blankets on the bed, just a couple of sheets. The downside is that there is no defined dry season. It can rain anytime, but the showers are usually short, and the rain is always warm.

"Another big reason for choosing this area is the price of land. It's much cheaper than just about any place the Pacific side. Our house is 100 meters from the beach, sitting back in the jungle. When we relax on our veranda, we can hear the ocean, but we can't see it. On all four sides of the house trees grow 30 to 60 feet high; it's lush with vegetation—all you can see is green. In the front yard we frequently see three-toed sloths, iguanas, parrots, gorgeous blue morphus butterflies, and more. I'm the first to admit that this is not paradise, but it is damn close to it!

"We had the house built two years ago: two bedrooms, one bath—a little more than 1,300 square feet, with a huge veranda out front, a covered carport, and gorgeous hardwood floors (we sort of splurged on that). The total cost of the land and building was about $45,000. Try doing that over in Tamarindo—with just a minute walk to the beach!

"Another reason we love it here: Small villages are cool places where everyone knows everyone else. When we go into the grocery store, the hardware store, or the bank, they call us by name. That's a touch you just don't find anymore. Yes, I've read about how crime is so bad on this side of the country, but I really have no idea where all that comes from! Sure, petty theft is 'alive and well' over here (as it is everywhere); we've had hiking boots and other items taken from our porch when we were foolish enough to leave them out at night. But neither our house nor our car has ever been broken into. (By the way we do not have bars on any of our doors or windows. I refuse to live in a prison.) We feel perfectly safe strolling through the village at night or walking along the beach at any hour. We do it all the time; we just use common sense.

"Maybe the main reasons we chose this coast are the attitude of the people and the laid-back lifestyle. There's a very strong Jamaican 'yea, Mon' sort of thing here; it's unlike anywhere else in Costa Rica. You almost get the feeling that time stood still on this coast. They say it looks pretty much the way it did forty years ago. On the other hand, you'll find places on the Pacific side where, if you didn't know better, you'd think you were in San Diego or Hawaii. Thank God, the big resorts and commercial developers haven't discovered this place yet.

"I will be the first to agree that this coast is not for everyone: no shopping centers, no movie theaters, no golf courses. But that is *exactly* why we live here! If we had wanted all of that other stuff, we would have stayed in the States! To sum it up in terms of my '60s generation: 'If you were a yuppie, you belong on the Pacific side. If you were a hippie, come on over here!'" ∎

CHAPTER SIX

THE
PACIFIC COAST

This side of the country is characterized by wet summers, dry winters, regular surf from the open ocean, and a much larger population of foreigners. Although most come from North America, a considerable number of Europeans are moving into the area. Many come from Germany, Switzerland, and Italy; other nationalities are well represented as well. Some expatriates operate successful hotels, restaurants, and other tourist-oriented ventures that the business-friendly Costa Rican government makes possible.

The west coast of Costa Rica can be divided into three basic geographic sections: the Nicaragua border to the end of the Nicoya Peninsula area, the beaches from Jacó to Uvita in the center, and the Golfo Dulce–Osa Peninsula area to the south. Each area has its boosters who will assure you that there is no place in all of Central America as nice as their favorite location. I've seen them all, and I can say that making a choice among them would be difficult indeed.

A nice feature of all the tropical beach areas is that they are accessible from the Meseta Central, within a few hours' drive by bus or automobile and almost no time at all by airplane. Some locations require

NICOYA **PENINSULA**

longer driving times than others, but as pavement replaces gravel roads, travel times will decrease.

Certain areas are highly developed, focusing on tourism, with discos, restaurants, and boutiques as well as expensive hotels and homes. Other places are oriented toward permanent and semipermanent residents, especially retirees. Still other locations are almost totally deserted, offering no facilities other than what you carry with you. Bring camping equipment if you care to; camping is permitted on all of Costa Rica's beaches except for parks and residential areas. The law considers the first 50 meters of beachland public property. Costa Ricans take full advantage of camping, and during the traditional summer vacation period (January and February), you'll see a multitude of tents lining the beaches as Tico families enjoy economical vacations. Many foreign tourists and some residents enjoy camping as well. But they stress that you must be careful about leaving valuable belongings in a tent while swimming or visiting a nearby village for supplies. That's probably good advice for beach camping anywhere in the world. (I wouldn't know. My wife and I prefer a comfortable hotel room with cable TV and room service rather than a sleeping bag on the ground.)

Eastward from the ocean's surf, rolling hills of forest and farmland spread inland and up the mountain slopes, becoming steeper and more picturesque with each kilometer. Much of this land is wilderness, traversed by occasional dirt roads that become quagmires in the rainy season. Despite isolation and transportation difficulties, foreigners find these rustic sections exceptionally desirable places to live. As the government gradually paves the roads along the coast and into the interior, more and more settlers are swelling the ranks of North Americans and Europeans who live here and operate businesses. With easy access, property values ought to increase dramatically.

GUANACASTE'S **PACIFIC COAST**

A number of important beach locations on the North Coast attract Costa Ricans and foreigners alike for vacation, retirement, or business opportunities. These beaches are easily reached from San José in three to five hours by car. The main highway is paved and in generally good condition but can be agonizingly slow when you are stacked up behind a string of slow trucks on their way to or from the Pacific docks. Slow as this stretch may be—about 10 miles or so—you will be glad you have to go slow, because there are some shoulder drop-offs that could be dangerous if you drive carelessly. The secret to driving this section of the highway is not to be in a hurry. Relax and go with the flow. Enjoy the spectacular and ever-changing scenery of the Pan-American Highway.

Rainfall is lower here than anywhere else in the country. Unlike most of Costa Rica, here the dry season is truly dry, with almost no rain falling from January to May. Grass turns parched and yellow; some trees lose their leaves, often replacing them with a gorgeous display of colorful blossoms. Around homes or along inhabited beaches, however, you'll see more evergreen, leafy trees because they've been deliberately planted and cared for.

PLAYAS DEL COCO AREA A quickly developing complex of *playas* (beaches) begins at Playa Hermosa and Playa Panama, stretching south through Playas del Coco and ending at Playa Ocotal. A nice beach in this complex and one with development potential is Playa Hermosa. *Hermosa* means "beautiful" in Spanish, and Playa Hermosa lives up to its name. This is a lovely place, with a curving shoreline of clean sand and a peninsula that shields it from the open ocean and dangerous riptides.

Development in Hermosa lags behind that in nearby Playas del Coco, the most commercially developed of these beach communities. Since the pavement ends in the center of El Coco, tourists tend to stay here rather than braving annoying stretches of washboard gravel roads to get to nearby beaches. In contrast with neighboring communities, which are sleepy and tranquil, in Playas del Coco the restaurants, bars, and discos stay open late on weekends, with happy people singing and shouting in exuberance all night long. (At least it seemed that way to me one weekend when I was trying to catch up on my sleep!)

Playas del Coco is a fun place to be, with potential for investment opportunities. Numerous North Americans have settled in Playas del Coco, some operating viable businesses, others enjoying ocean fishing and the beaches. But for retirement or long-term vacations, I might choose one of the quieter, nearby places. A number of foreigners own homes along the fringes of the less populated beaches. I understand that many North American families live in Hermosa Beach and more are in the planning stages of building. Italians and Germans are represented here as well.

One resident, a retired Air Force sergeant, related his reasons for settling here. First, he bought ten acres (by mail) before he retired from the military. Then before he had the chance to visit the property, he received a letter offering to trade the ten acres for one and one-half acres of jojoba bean property. This seemed to be a good deal, so he signed the papers for a trade—again, all by mail. When he finally retired and arrived in Costa Rica to claim his jojoba bean plantation, he discovered that jojoba beans don't grow in this area. Furthermore, the property was not only inaccessible by automobile but had a Nicaraguan family living on it who were not inclined to move simply because the owner wanted them to. While he was looking for a way to visit his jojoba bean farm, he fell in love with a Costa Rican woman and got married. He forgot about his agricultural fiasco and settled down in his wife's village. "Now I have a seven-year-old daughter, a house in a village where I am the only gringo, and I have a good life. My pension is only $855 a month, but I live like a king." He took a part-time job as night watchman at a tourist hotel to supplement his pension. "The only thing I don't like about being a night watchman," he said plaintively, "is weekends, when guests party all night; they make so much noise I can't sleep." He was right; they kept me awake, too.

There can be no question about Coco's potential for business, retirement, or long-term living. Several very successful American-owned enterprises operate here, and more are on the way. But if I don't sound particularly enthusiastic about the place, it's probably because this is where I locked my keys in my rental car and struggled for two hours in the hot sun before figuring out a way to get inside without breaking a window. A good car thief could have done it in less than twenty seconds.

A few kilometers to the south is Playa Ocotal, a place that maintains a village atmosphere despite also having a deluxe tourist resort. The accommodations are tasteful, blending in with the natural surroundings. The village is on the shore of Bahía Pez Vela (Sailfish Bay), and the fishing is said to live up to the name. Each time we visit, we see a noticeable increase in housing, making this another viable retirement option.

FLAMINGO BEACH The next beach complex is just a few kilometers away and is probably the most popular of all on the Pacific Coast. New paved roads have opened the area to increased settlement. This array of beaches starts with Playa Pan de Azucar and continues south to Playa Tamarindo, including the beaches of La Penca, Potrero, Flamingo, Brasilito, Conchal, Playa Grande, Tamarindo, and Langosta.

By far the prettiest beach is Playa Flamingo. A wide, curving stretch of white sand with startling blue waves that turn to white-capped rollers before crashing loudly against the shore creates one of the loveliest scenes imaginable. Hotels here cater to affluent tourists who can afford to fly in from San José and spend $150 a day for rooms. Tourists on ordinary budgets will find few (if any) reasonably priced rooms. Ongoing building activity may change all this.

As you might imagine, foreigners have taken over this beach and have built some very spiffy places. I consider Flamingo the "Cadillac" of Costa Rican beach communities. The hillsides display sumptuous homes, set in tropical landscaping and overlooking a gorgeous beach view. The scene is reminiscent of Acapulco many years ago when it was the playground of the Hollywood and European jet set. Needless to say, Flamingo is not the place to look for inexpensive ocean-view lots!

Some private homes offer rooms for rent and probably do well, for there were absolutely no vacancies in town when I last visited here. Most of the nondeveloped beachfront is also owned by foreigners. However, local authorities have done well in keeping the first 50 meters of beach open, affording the public unlimited access.

The beach adjacent to Flamingo is Brasilito. Instead of having a tourist resort atmosphere, the village of Brasilito is more like a typical Costa Rican pueblo—complete with a soccer field, small bars, and restaurants. This a "bedroom community" for workers employed by affluent residents and businesses in Flamingo. It's also an inexpensive place for Ticos and foreign residents on a budget to find an inexpensive *cabina* or a room and enjoy the beach. The beach isn't bad at all; I'm surprised there isn't more commercial development and foreign settlers. For a beach community, property is reasonably priced.

The next village is at Playa Conchal. The Spanish word *Conchal* refers to the shells on the beach. In fact, the entire beach is composed of tiny, water-worn shells instead of sand. This area has attracted numerous expatriates in the past few years. Although the place is still somewhat quiet and undeveloped, a rumored 5,000-room resort could change all that.

About 2 kilometers north of Flamingo, the village of Potrero has a growing population of foreign residents. They're building along the beach toward Flamingo, eventually to become an integral part of one community. The village itself is much more laid-back and relaxed than Flamingo, with some residents' homes built on the hillside overlooking Potrero's exceptionally gentle beach.

TURTLE **BEACHES**

An excellent example of how tourism and conservation can work hand in hand is found south of the Flamingo Beach complex. Starting at Playa Grande and continuing south to Playa Tamarindo, a broad, sandy beach serves as nesting grounds for endangered leatherback turtles. It used to be that local residents awaited the arrival of these huge, prehistoric survivors, collected the eggs in buckets as they were being deposited, and sold the harvest to bars and restaurants all over the country.

Alarmed by the possibility of the turtles' extinction, the Costa Rican government instituted a model conservation program. Local people are enlisted to help protect the nesting grounds. Guarding the beaches and guiding tourists through the nesting grounds put local people to work. Hotels and restaurants have opened to accommodate the ever-increasing number of tourists. Jobs are created for even more local residents. This boom has only begun; future ecotourism development seems inevitable.

Conservationists have expressed mixed feelings about this program. While they praise the protection of the nesting grounds, they point out that the extra tourist foot traffic causes damage when visitors inadvertently step on the hatchlings. On the other hand, the number of baby turtles killed in this manner is nothing when compared with the unborn ones that used to end up as a tasty *boca* in San José bars.

PLAYA GRANDE Turtles need a wide, sandy beach with ample portions not touched by high tide; Playa Grande fills these requirements admirably. It's long and relatively unpopulated, with few human footprints to disturb the solitude. A few years ago only a handful of homes and one or two tiny motels were to be found near the beach's access roads. Today the development is rapid. As part of the Tamarindo Refuge, the area will always be somewhat restricted in tourist development, even though the region's natural beauty and wildness are bound to attract even more people in the future.

I looked at several developments here, most catering to luxury homes, on beachfront lots as well as away from the ocean. The cost of land in the spiffy developments was surprisingly expensive, particularly right on the beach. However, the vast majority of Playa Grande's land is undeveloped and presumably far less expensive. It has a tremendously long way to go before it could approach being "crowded." Services—such as grocery shopping, hardware stores, and doctors—require a long drive.

One place I looked at was a large, tastefully constructed home with a neatly manicured lawn ending at a beach wall marking the 50-meter boundary. The owner half-apologized for the home's isolation and lack of anything to do, adding, "The hope of this little community is that things won't change. What we offer here is location, nothing else." He indicated the broad expanse of beach visible through a stand of coconut palms and said, "The whole idea here is to fit into the ecology without disturbing things, particularly not the nesting turtles and their life cycle." The

house's window frames were made of wood instead of the more practical aluminum "because metal frames reflect moonlight and confuse the hatchling leatherbacks. We don't allow any lights from our homes to escape at night. For bright lights and nightlife, you have to go to Tamarindo." Since my writing of these lines, several bars and restaurants have opened near Playa Grande, and a couple of housing developments are under way. But Playa Grande is still a very quiet place to live.

A local resident reports some good news about the leatherback turtles. The number of turtles visiting the beaches to lay eggs in 2003 doubled from the previous year, with new turtles joining the flock (or should it be *covey*? *band*? Could it be a *herd* of turtles?). The numbers still remain way below what they were in the 1980s, but locals are hoping this will become a trend.

PLAYA TAMARINDO Playa Tamarindo begins where Playa Grande ends, a picturesque estuary separating the two. Tamarindo is where leatherback-turtle watchers find hotels. Launches begin ferrying passengers across the estuary around midnight. Visitors tiptoe quietly along the beach and pause to observe the huge turtles as they awkwardly pull themselves up on the beach to bury their eggs 6 feet deep in the sand. This is an unforgettable sight; some of these turtles are said to grow to more than 12 feet across and weigh up to 1,500 pounds! The one I watched laying eggs may have been a pygmy; she was barely 8 feet wide. Our guide claimed that during the peak of the season, as many as 350 turtles can be on the beach in a single night.

Because of excellent surfing beaches and nearby Playa Grande turtle beaches, Tamarindo has always been a magnet for tourists of all ages. The coastal region here is easily accessible by pavement rather than gravel and dirt roads, which ensures a steady stream of visitors as well as new residents who often become part of the business community. Another development is the new international airport in nearby Liberia. The airport is now served by Delta (Atlanta), American (Miami), and Continental (Houston). Tamarindo has become a textbook example of foreign development of a Costa Rican beach village with a cosmopolitan mix of nationalities. Almost all businesses—restaurants, hotels, shops, bars, and so forth—appear to be owned by foreigners: Italians, Germans, French, with several other European nations represented. American businesses are in the minority in Tamarindo.

This highly successful development changed the town from the sleepy village of ten years ago into a busy, highly commercial entity. Some residents and longtime visitors lament these changes, while others appreciate the presence of upscale restaurants, quality retail and food shopping options, including a supermarket, and other conveniences that a mere village would lack. While some yearn for the "good old days," Rob Gibson, a Tamarindo homeowner, says: "The surroundings are still spectacular, and the relative success in protecting Playa Grande and the estuary behind it from unbridled development has been key to maintaining its attractions. Even the beach at Tamarnido is large and long enough to take a lot of development without losing its attractiveness. The walk to Langosta still evokes a feeling of Big Sur more than Playas del Coco ambiance." (Playas del Coco is the epitome of tourist beachside development.)

The emphasis in Tamarindo is strictly on foreign tourism and foreign residents. A few years ago, a Tico complained to me: "We keep selling our land and moving farther back into the hills. Now we are working for foreigners on land we once owned. Before long we won't be able to afford to live in our own village!" That prediction has come true; the price of real estate makes property ownership impossible for local families, and hotels are priced out of range for vacationing Tico families. However, Rob

Gibson—who speaks Spanish with local working people—observes no general sense of resentment. "Most Ticos say that tourists and part-time residents are good because they bring money and create jobs in the area. I love the practicality and lack of xenophobia among Costarriqueños, and if we gringos behave decently, perhaps we can keep it that way." Rob also points out that there are definite advantages to living in an expatriates' enclave. "I don't know how much your gringo neighbors would help you in a crisis, but it is nice to have so many of them around."

For those with school-age children, this is the only region outside the Central Valley with an international K-12 college-prep school. Country Day School Guanacaste is a private facility located between Tamarindo and Flamingo. It isn't inexpensive, but as one parent said, "The school is small enough for the teachers to have a one-on-one relationship with their students." There's also a bilingual elementary school, Niños del Mundo, with classes for students in pre-kindergarten to fourth grade.

PLAYA JUNQUILLAL South of Tamarindo the coast seems to be rather unpopulated by foreigners and Ticos alike. This is partially due to the seasonal condition of the dirt roads along the coast. Since most residents believe that a paved road will not be far in the future, this area might have potential for development. A series of long beaches front the Pacific along this coast, some with tiny villages, others almost unpopulated. Among the beaches are Playa Avellana, Playa Negra, Playa Junquillal, and Playa Lagarto. These beaches are graced by large waves rolling in from the open Pacific and are very picturesque. Since I'm not an expert swimmer and know little about ocean currents, undertow, and riptides, I can't vouch for the safety of these beaches. You'll need to consult local authorities on the subject. This is a sensible practice anywhere in the country.

Junquillal is a growing village that sits on one of the longest beaches on the peninsula. The region is known for exceptional surfing waves in the Playa Negra and Junquillal areas. Endangered leatherback and green turtles come ashore to lay their eggs in the sand. Most businesses in the area are owned by Americans, Canadians, Italians, and Germans—who are trying to develop more tourism in the area. Meanwhile, residents are hoping that Junquillal doesn't develop to the same extent as the more popular beach towns. One Canadian expatriate said, "We like progress, but we'd prefer to keep the area as a serene place to come for relaxation and the natural beauty of the area."

One small hotel, right on the beach, is owned by several gringo couples who take turns managing the establishment as their excuse for a working vacation, presumably tax-deductible. One partner said, "It's a very small operation. We consider a month successful when we don't have to dig into our pockets to make the payroll." A few kilometers from the village center, an elaborate residential development is being purchased exclusively by Canadians and Americans. Construction quality is tops, with all amenities. Since Junquillal has such a small population, major shopping and other services are about forty-five minutes away.

BEACHES OF NOSARA About 80 kilometers south of the Tamarindo-Flamingo region is an area with a different developmental emphasis: the Beaches of Nosara. Starting at the Nosara River, three lovely beaches and a wildlife reserve extend south—from Playa Nosara and Playa Pelada to Playa Guiones. Nosara is an experiment in different concepts of foreign development. The emphasis here is on private homes and pristine beaches rather than tourism and commercial enterprise. Residents have formed a militant organization of property owners and have so far successfully kept this part of the coast residential and natural. Along more than 5 miles of beaches, only one small restaurant is located right on the beach. As you stroll the beach, you'll see natural vegetation, trees, and mangrove along the edge of the sand—no discos, fast-food places, miniature golf courses, or any other evidence of higher culture. Just beach and jungle.

Don't misunderstand; you can find services like the above (well, maybe not miniature golf), but not right on the beach. Two hundred meters is as close to the water as they can be located. So when you are strolling the beach, swimming, or sunning, there's nothing to remind you that you are not in pure paradise. The exception to this rule is a small Tico bar and restaurant, Olga's Bar, which has occupied a patch of beachfront for the past thirty years and is therefore grandfathered (or grandmothered) into acceptance. (As many thirsty tourists have remarked, "We need at least one bar on the beach!")

About twenty-five years ago a farsighted American investor purchased a huge tract of beachfront and decided to develop the property in a way that preserved its natural beauty and wildlife resources. He did a marvelous job, developing each lot with its own part of the wilderness. Almost all buyers were from the United States or Canada; they loved the isolation and the idea of preserving beaches, forest, and animals.

Things were going well until a few years later, when the original developer unexpectedly dropped out of the picture. Residents feared that the area could turn into tourist-oriented, treeless commercial zones, as other unregulated coastal areas have done. So the property owners formed an association totally committed to protecting the unique environment. To forestall commercial development, residents dedicated the entire beachfront to the government as a wildlife and nature reserve. The association provides housing and pays the salary for a government ranger to keep an eye on forest and wildlife conservation. It has spent a good deal of money for legal fees, even taking a case to the Supreme Court in an effort to keep large developers from turning Nosara into a new Miami Beach. So far the association has been successful, limiting new business to small, low-impact, family-operated enterprises. However, Nosara isn't unfriendly to tourists. On the contrary, the community welcomes them and is happy to see tourists patronize the many small hotels and restaurants that are located a few hundred meters from the beach. Consequently, Beaches of Nosara draws a different type of tourist: one who appreciates quiet, uncrowded, and natural beaches and who doesn't require discos, T-shirt emporiums, or beachfront pizza parlors to keep him- or herself amused.

"One major problem we have," explained one of the longtime residents, "is that newcomers aren't as ecologically aware as the original owners. Over the years, many of the old-timers have died, grown old, or lost interest. So we try to educate newcomers about the treasures we have here, about the importance of not cutting down the trees or destroying our animals' habitat." The howler monkeys have regular "trails" through the treetops that they use daily to go from one feeding area to another. When the trail is broken by clearing trees, the monkeys never return.

When this book first described Nosara, development was still in its infancy. Services were limited and property prices were very modest, probably one half to one third of more accessible beach locations such as

Tamarindo or Flamingo. Numerous creeks and small rivers had to be forded; for part of the rainy season, the road was impassible. Gradually, culverts and bridges made the route easier, bringing more tourists and visitors who began buying property and building homes. Then, about four years ago, change began accelerating. Nosara was "discovered."

Newcomers are arriving in a steady stream—no flood as yet, but the level is rising. Construction seems to be going on everywhere. Near the beaches a bakery specializing in German and Italian goods has appeared, as well as several grocery store–delicatessens to supplement the two supermarkets already in place. More *cabinas* and small hotels are popping up, and a dozen new homes are under construction at any given time. The airstrip (one of the few cement runways in the country) handles numerous flights daily.

The nearest hospital (in Nicoya) requires an hour and a half drive, making access to sophisticated medical care somewhat difficult. Because of the increased population, not only residents and tourists but the number of Tico workers who work in construction, the government has installed a new medical clinic in the village of Nosara. For life-threatening emergencies, an air-evac flight to a San José hospital takes thirty minutes from the Nosara airstrip.

It's interesting to compare the Nosara area with the resort area of Sámara, just 25 kilometers to the south, or other. There the natural vegetation has been stripped away to make room for commercial projects. Much of what is left is often burned off every dry season to make room for new plant cover during the coming rainy season. Native plants, those specially adapted to this climate, have been crowded out by plants whose natural winter state is to lie dormant or by those whose seeds resist fire. None of this is to say that Sámara isn't a beautiful place—with its gorgeous beach and paved road access, it can't miss.

REGIONAL DEVELOPMENT   The entire west coast of the Nicoya Peninsula is slated for tourism development by the government's tourism ministry (ICT). Of particular interest, with short-term plans in the works, the stretch from Sámara north to Tamarindo is drawing a great deal of attention. Two circumstances account for this recent flurry of building activity. The first item is the newly completed bridge over the Tempisque River, which cuts at least an hour's driving time from the trip from San

José. The second is the inevitable paving of the road from Sámara north to Tourism Institute (ICT). This plan sets out certain areas as high-density tourism centers—suitable for large hotels, intensive usage of beachfront, and full-service tourist facilities. Sámara and Garza are so designated. Other places are planned for residential and low-intensity tourism. Nosara falls into the latter category—much to the delight of local foreign residents. This is precisely what they wanted: protection of the beach and forest, yet development of low-impact tourism to boost prosperity for the natives. The residents of Nosara expect to have a continuing battle over the beaches and forest, and they expect to lose once in a while. But over-all, they feel good about what's been accomplished so far.

SÁMARA AND CARRILLO A welcome development for those traveling to the Pacific Coast from San José and points inland is the "Friendship Bridge" constructed by the Taiwanese government. This bridge replaced the cumbersome ferry across the Tempisque River. In the time the ferry could take forth vehicles across the 2-kilometer-wide crossing, a thousand cars and trucks can zip across the bridge. Travel time has been shortened by about an hour. This new access is having a profound impact on the development of the entire coast, with Sámara and Carrillo being affected the most.

Something that would give the beach areas a real boost: a proposed governmental designation of the town of Nicoya as a duty-free center similar to that in Golfito (described later in this chapter). If this happens, anyone from San José or other parts of the country, resident or tourist, would be able to visit a duty-free warehouse to purchase goods free of customs duties. Since the procedure is to make your purchases one day, and pick them up the following day, the buyers will have time on their hands, a day to kill. It would be natural for visitors to make their pur-chases, go to Sámara or Carrillo to play on the beach (spend money on a room and meals, of course), and return to Nicoya the next day to com-plete the purchase. Several nice hotels and restaurants are already in place for the rush. Although this plan is in the works, it may never become a scenario, but if it does, look for lots of momentum along this section of the Pacific Coast.

Much of this area is already developed, particularly in and around

Sámara. New hotels and condos are going in, and more expats are building homes south of town, extending toward Carrillo. However, this is only the beginning. As we noted earlier, the Tourism Institute has targeted the Sámara-Carrillo area for high-intensity tourist use. We expect to see some large hotels and probably a resort going in before long. Smaller hotels, restaurants, and shops will naturally follow. If Sámara develops as did Tamarindo, we can expect a large percentage of new businesses to be owned by North American entrepreneurs.

The area is quite appropriate for this kind of development. Sámara and Carrillo share opposite ends of the same bay, one of the most beautiful imaginable in a country of beautiful beaches. Several long stretches of beach are flanked by a wide road fringed with coconut palms, making the beaches freely accessible to all. At the northern portion of the bay, Sámara attracts more Tico tourism from the Meseta Central area at the moment (on weekends and holidays they arrive by the busloads). Toward Carrillo, more hotels cater to foreigners and are higher priced. This is where the airstrip is, which makes it handy for visitors.

All along this part of the coast, some low mountains sit back about a kilometer from the shore, and here is where many expats make their homes. The views of the bay are magnificent up there, whereas homes built at sea level have views of nothing but trees or the nearby hotel.

An item of interest about Carrillo: About 1 kilometer south of the airstrip there is a bridge over a small river where two large crocodiles lurk. Local residents regularly feed them by throwing frozen chicken carcasses—tied with nylon line—into the river. They then troll the tasty morsels toward the bridge to lure the monsters from their hiding places. Although the river isn't posted against swimming or wading, I would strongly recommend that you refrain from this activity. The crocodiles strongly disagree with this advice.

CABO BLANCO   On the southern tip of the Nicoya Peninsula, a string of beaches with tremendous potential are undergoing development. The beaches run from Naranjo, on the Gulf of Nicoya side, to Cabo Blanco, at the very tip of the peninsula, and then up along the coast via unpassable roads, toward Carrillo. Most investors agree that the developmental potential between Cabo Velas and Cabo Blanco is among the best in the country. It all depends upon when (and if) the roads will be made passable.

Getting to this area from the northern part of the peninsula has always been a problem. The paved highway ends abruptly at the little town of Carmona, presenting about a 30-kilometer stretch of dirt road to the coast. The road paralleling the Pacific Coast dwindles to a trail from time to time, and you have to ford several good-size streams. Even rugged four-wheel-drives avoid the coastal route. An easier way is to take a ferry from Puntarenas to Playa Naranjo or Paquera, which shortens the drive considerably. It's possible that the road is currently in much better condition. Make inquiries first.

Conditions are changing. For better or worse, progress arrived on the southern peninsula in the form of a huge construction project—a large resort—at Playa Tambor. To encourage the development, the Costa Rican government agreed to install a new ferry terminal to bring tourists from Puntarenas, to pave the road to the hotel, and to provide housing for construction workers who are building the project and who later will be employed by the resort.

I say "for better or worse" because the construction caused a maelstrom of controversy, with ecologists accusing the hotel chain of doing extreme damage to the environment in the construction of the hotel. The resort denied these reports, and went ahead with the blessings of the Costa Rican government.

Oddly enough, the huge Tambor resort doesn't seem to affect the atmosphere of the village of Playa Tambor. It's the same laid-back, friendly place as before—somewhat larger however, and still growing.

The reason that tourism at the expensive resort hasn't affected the town could be the fact that the hotel and grounds are self-contained and guests seldom venture elsewhere. Also, the hotel has a nice white sand beach (that ecologists complain was imported from elsewhere), whereas Playa Tambor has dark volcanic sand that appears dirty but really isn't; it's just black sand. The little surf the beach gets is rather gentle, always peppered with little Tico children splashing and laughing.

Probably because of its unattractive beach, Playa Tambor lags behind in foreign tourism, although the backpack set and Tico vacationers enjoy it, especially the less expensive accommodations and house rentals. A little farther west, the gated community of Tango Mar provides an elegant contrast to funky Playa Tambor. Tango Mar is basically a private (and expensive) resort with deluxe accommodations; it is also a retirement community featuring a small golf course, tennis courts, and a lovely beach.

MONTEZUMA Located about 30 kilometers down the road from Playa Tambor, the village of Montezuma is the entry point to a beautiful string of beaches. Monkeys, parrots, and other wildlife are frequent visitors. Montezuma is a friendly and exceptionally laid-back place with at least as many gringo residents as Ticos. A popular and unique beachside community, it has a widely held reputation among the younger set as a "party town." However, the place is not only a mecca for backpackers and surfers but also a retirement place for more mature counterculture people. (Maybe I fall into the latter category, because I've always felt right at home in Montezuma with kindred spirits my age blending into the scene.)

Residents and businesspeople are very ecology minded and maintain a continual campaign for clean beaches. They also try to discourage some of the scruffy and troublesome visitors, knowing they are bad for business. Residents want to attract all age groups, especially those with money to spend, rather than become focused only on the frat-house and hippie crowd. Gringos who live in Montezuma enjoy a lively and active social life; those who covet peace and quiet might want to look elsewhere. The last 7 kilometers of road to Montezuma used to be rather bad during the rainy season; hopefully it's better now.

MALPAÍS Spanish for "badlands," Malpaís lives up to its name at the tip of the peninsula, where some spectacular rock formations break up the

MID-PACIFIC **COAST**

Herradura

Jacó

Parita

Quepos

Manuel
Antonio

San Isidro del
General

Dominical

Uvita

Cinco Ventanas

Palmar Norte

*Pacific
Ocean*

Paso
Canoas

Golfito

Zancudo

Pavones

Osa Peninsula

surf as waves from the open ocean crash into foam. This is as far as you can go; the road up the other side of the peninsula is just about nonexistent. I have heard people claim they've driven four-wheel-drives up the western edge, but it seems reckless to me.

This area is sparsely settled, with not much in the way of a village commercial center. Rather it's a long collection of houses, restaurants, and small hotels scattered along 3 kilometers of gravel road parallel to the ocean. Cabo Blanco Nature Preserve is to the south. Despite the small population, a surprising number of expats live here. They live in houses dotting the beaches, some more cliff than beach. The area seems to be peaceful and quiet, probably as quiet as Montezuma is noisy. The last time we visited, there were a number of building sites being laid out in anticipation of new expatriate settlers.

Along with most of the Nicoya Peninsula's tourist areas, the Malpaís area is continually growing and attracting more retirees and businesses. I can see a promising future for the region. The government is eager to develop places such as this and will surely devote whatever resources available for roads and infrastructure.

MID-PACIFIC **COAST**

If there is any place in Costa Rica that's bound to bloom with foreign investors and retirees, it would have to be that stretch of beachfront from Jacó to Dominical and, with the newly paved road, south toward Palmar Norte.

Although pretty beaches line both sides of Costa Rica, these are particularly accessible for residents of the populous Meseta Central. A short drive or bus ride makes this coast practical for overnight sojourns. A weekend home here is convenient and usable by family and friends, whereas one that requires a five-hour drive over horrible roads might sit vacant most of the year. When the main route has been paved and time-saving shortcuts completed, a drive from Escazú or other suburbs will take as little as an hour to Jacó or two hours to Dominical.

PLAYA JACÓ For the million-plus people who live on the Meseta Central in and around San José, the Playa Jacó region offers the closest opportunity to enjoy Pacific Ocean beaches (as opposed to those facing the Golfo de Nicoya). From the residential resort at Punta Leona to Playa Hermosa south of Jacó, a string of beaches bring thousands of weekenders for surfing, swimming, and partying. Since it's only about a two-hour drive from San José, it's entirely possible to drive here in the morning, enjoy the surf, and be home in time for supper. Not surprisingly many Meseta Central residents have weekend homes here, and a large number of expatriates live here full-time. Several hundred North Americans and many Europeans make their permanent homes here.

Jacó is the largest and most developed town along the entire coast (about 4,000 inhabitants), and it has everything you need, from good medical care to discos and casinos. The main street is sprinkled with open-air restaurants where members of the foreign community can be seen socializing, day or evening. Since Jacó is one place where beach property can be owned rather than leased, it's possible to find a home right on the ocean, with beach and surf for your front yard.

Many if not most tourist businesses here are owned by gringos and Europeans. Some do quite well because the area's many tourist attractions bring streams of visitors in search of adventure. Every surf and nature sport, from surfing to crocodile safaris, ensures plenty of tourist business. Two eighteen-hole golf courses are open to public play here, one at Marriott's Los Sueños resort, 5 kilometers north of Jacó, and another about 15 kilometers south at Quebrada, Amarilla, the Tulin Resort.

When I asked Mike Gernazian (better known as "Gringo Mike") why so many Americans choose to live in Jacó, he replied, "We want to be close to the big city but still have the pleasure of the clean air and the beach. There are several hundred of us in the area, yet Jacó is small enough that we all know and help one another. If you need to borrow a tool, there is always someone to help. The only spat I have ever seen is over the one copy of *USA Today*'s crossword puzzle at Zarpe's Bar (a gringo hangout). We all want to work it." Mike rents cabins near the beach and says business is booming.

PLAYA HERRADURA Playa Herradura is smaller than Jacó, enjoys gentler surf, and has more shade trees. At the moment Herradura offers economical tourist hotels and weekend homes for highland residents, both Ticos and gringos. But the town extends a promise of better things to come. For a beachfront community Playa Herradura boasts property that is reasonable—at least compared with prices at Jacó or Manuel Antonio. Many building lots can be found within walking distance of the beach, and construction is booming. An upscale development known as Los Sueños is under way at Playa Herradura. With its large-scale marina, luxury homes, and condos, Los Sueños will raise the general tone of Herradura and bring in more development. At the time of my last visit, spring 2000, the golf course was almost complete.

About 10 kilometers north of Herradura (about 30 kilometers north of Jacó), Punta Leona has an attractive private club (with day admission for nonmembers) with a complex of condos and cottages owned by retirees and weekenders from the Meseta Central. Like Los Sueños in Herradura, there is a very safe feeling about these gated communities, but prices reflect the additional costs of privacy and luxury.

MANUEL ANTONIO It was the middle of February, and we were sitting with a group of friends in a restaurant overlooking the Pacific. A long, palm-fringed beach stretched out into the distance as far as we could see. Behind us loomed mountains covered with rain forest, sweeping down to accent the beach, with its azure-blue water and sparkling surf. The sun was at its zenith, beating directly down with dazzling strength. Two members of our group were complaining about the heat. We consulted a thermometer and found that the temperature was 85 degrees. Suddenly they broke into laughter as they realized that Baltimore, their hometown, was dealing with 4 inches of sleet and snow. Two weeks of Costa Rica's idyllic weather had turned them into indignant complainers over an ordinary 85-degree day at the beach! We all ordered a cold beer served over ice cubes (a Costa Rica tradition) and looked out over the panorama with renewed appreciation for where we were: Costa Rica's famous Playa Manuel Antonio.

What kind of name is that for a beach? According to legend, a husband, worried about his pregnant wife, placed her in a dugout canoe and headed north for Puntarenas, hoping to find a doctor to deliver the baby. But before they could go very far, the wife went into labor and they paddled ashore to camp in the shelter of a gentle beach cove. His wife gave birth to a healthy child, whom they named Manuel Antonio; the beach has been called that ever since. Travelers who have visited beaches all over the world swear that Manuel Antonio is the most beautiful of all.

The coastline north of Manuel Antonio is a long shore of golden sand that catches the full force of the Pacific's waves as they roll in from China. Then, at Manuel Antonio Park, a narrow peninsula juts out into the ocean, curving about to form two protected coves on either side of the land. Here the waves suddenly become gentle, a place where you can float on your back for an hour without worrying about getting surf in your face. You'll often find a sailboat or two anchored here, gently swaying, resting on the way to the Panama Canal or the big voyage north to Acapulco.

Originally United Fruit Company banana property, the area was made into a national park in 1972 with almost 700 hectares of land, partially expropriated, partially donated. The park contains three beaches, each with its own character. The first is Playa Espadilla Norte, which sees occasional riptides—although many people swim here anyway. Next is Playa Espadilla Sur and then Playa Manuel Antonio, both quite safe for swimming and snorkeling. From the beginning the emphasis has been on preserving the natural beauty and protecting wildlife. Whiteface capuchin monkeys frolic in the trees, competing with arboreal iguanas for food. A tropical storm in 1993 ripped up some of the trees, causing the sloth population to go elsewhere, but other than that the damage was minimal.

One of the earlier tourist developments, Manuel Antonio soon became a popular place for retirement and vacation homes, hotels, and restaurants. To protect the area from total development, the government demands that new construction be connected with tourism in some manner. Buildings cannot be more than three stories high and must provide a minimum of three times the square footage of green space for each foot of building. To satisfy the requirement that development be tourist-related, several North Americans have built homes with rooms or apartments that can be rented out to tourists; they keep part of the house as living quarters.

Since Manuel Antonio's fame makes it an almost obligatory part of a tourist's itinerary, a bed-and-breakfast or room rentals can be a very viable business. Rooms are likely to be rented solidly through the summer (December, January, and February) and to have low vacancy rates during the rest of the year. During a recent trip we rented an apartment from a woman who came from Florida several years ago to build a small house for herself. She added a couple of rooms for extra income during the tourist season. As the volume of tourism during the off-season increased, she added more rooms, until she now has a pleasant ten-room hotel plus two apartments across the road—all with a splendid view of the ocean. "I hadn't considered becoming a hotel owner when I came here," she explained. "It just happened to work out that way."

Over the thirty years that I've been visiting Manuel Antonio, I've seen the most profound changes of anywhere in the country. It has changed from a very rustic, low-density tourist destination to a full-tilt, full-service community. The road from Quepos to Manuel Antonio Park is jam-packed with hotels, restaurants, and other tourist accommodations. Scarcely a square meter of land remains undeveloped. Oddly enough, this doesn't seem to detract one iota of the region's beauty and charm.

DOMINICAL   South of Quepos and Manuel Antonio, along the 45-kilometer stretch of gravel road to Dominical, you'll find occasional roads leading to the beach. We've found a few small hotels along this part of the coast, but for the most part this country is either palm-oil plantations or flat farming land. Yet starting with the village of Dominical and head-ing south, this part of the coast is turning out to be another of those "undiscovered" places with potential for retirement and/or investment.

Before long the Pacific Coast Highway will be paved all the way to Panama, joining the Pan-American Highway at Palmar Norte. This route will take considerable pressure off the present Pan-American Highway as well as open the region to tourism and development. Although a stretch of road south of Quepos is still gravel, it's not a bad drive in a rental car; they keep it graded (however, during the rain of the 2003–2004 wet sea-son, parts of the road were in bad shape).

As paved roads replace the almost impassable stretches of rock-and-mud obstacle courses, ever-increasing traffic streams along the coast—tourists looking for rooms and retirees buying property. The village of Dominical and its surrounding communities can't help but flourish. As you might guess, many foreign residents prefer things the way they are; they dread the thought of developments and tourists destroying the peace and tranquillity that has been theirs for so long. But road crews are within reach of completing the task; it is too late for anything but anguish. As one man said, "It is funny to think that in a few years we'll be looking back fondly to the time when there were no traffic lights here."

If you want to drive on pavement all the way to Dominical, travel south on the Pan-American Highway and turn toward the Pacific at San Isidro del General, then just follow the signs through town. Because of

San Isidro's system of one-way streets, you may have to ask directions by pointing in whichever direction you are going and asking "Dominical?" Someone will steer you right.

In its own way, this road is one of the more scenic in all of Costa Rica. The narrow pavement traverses rich farming country, up somewhat steep grades, running along ridges with breathtaking views on both sides of the road, looking into deep valleys where the farmhouses are so distant that they seem like toys. Even during the dry season, the countryside is lushly green, plants heavy with foliage and banana trees shading the roadside. Although the drive is less than 25 miles, it takes about forty-five minutes. That's the way it should be, because the scenery is so spectacular that you might miss something if you could whiz along at 100 kilometers per hour. Also, the pavement has a way of disappearing from time to time, turning into stretches of gravel road where construction crews are still at work. The problem is not serious; just slow down and relax.

The paved highway ends at the newly paved coastal road at the Barú River, a picturesque mountain stream that empties into a lagoon at this point. A turn to the left, over the river's new cement bridge, and you find Dominical. Take the first right turn past the bridge. This is another place I've watched develop over the years, from a sleepy village to an awakening, cosmopolitan community. It is my impression that this region is one of the fastest-growing along the coast—at least as far as residential development is concerned. Excellent restaurants and other retail businesses seem to be popping up in response to the growing number of expatriates in the Dominical area.

Dominical's main street (there are only a few streets here) follows the river past several rental cabins and businesses. It ends at the beach, where another road follows the shore down to Punta Banda, also known as Roque Azul. Camping beneath a grove of shade trees is free on the edge of the broad, sandy beach of Playa Dominical. Rest rooms and showers are strategically spaced along the beach. For the most part, campers are Tico families and backpackers, but all are welcome. As anywhere in Costa Rica, be careful of leaving valuables in a tent while you are surfing or dining in a restaurant

The surf is spectacular, booming in on the sand and making swimming occasionally hazardous, with riptides to harass those not used to handling them. "You usually don't realize what is happening," said a

longtime resident here and the owner of some *cabinas* on the river where we were staying. "It seems as though you are staying still in the water, but the beach is moving away from you. We lose a couple of tourists every year to these tides, and it isn't necessary. Instead of trying to swim against the current, the best thing to do is relax and leisurely swim parallel to the beach, until the shore stops moving away. The current is only a few feet wide. Then work your way back to shore, pausing to float on your back and rest. The water is so warm and salty that you can float all day long and never get tired. There is no reason for anyone to drown in a riptide."

Serenity and calm at Playa Dominical and Playa Barú make this a great place to spend the winter, away from the ice and snow of northern climes. Many people do just that. Prices are particularly affordable if one doesn't need an ocean view. A visitor from the Yukon, a man who has been coming here for several years, was very excited as he described the house he was buying in a nearby village. It was a brand-new, two-bedroom place on three hectares of land. "To make sure everything is all right, I agreed to rent it for two months," he said. "At the end of that time, if the house is satisfactory, I'll go ahead and buy it."

Dominical and surrounding villages sit right on the water's edge, and rainfall is about the same as in other coastal towns to the north or the south. Logically, Dominical's climate should also be similar: hot days and warm evenings. But this is not exactly the case. Mornings and evenings are much cooler, and even during the middle of the day, pleasant breezes come in from across the ocean. At night temperatures drop into a delightful range, making it possible to sleep without an air conditioner.

Don't misunderstand, the climate here isn't like that of the Meseta Central, but it is noticeably cooler here than in many other parts of the coast. This is due to an odd juxtaposition of geographic features. Not far from the beach, mountain slopes start climbing sharply from the flat shelf of land that borders the ocean. They swoop higher and higher until they reach Costa Rica's highest point: Chirripó Peak. During daylight hours the sun beats down on that narrow strip of land between the ocean and the mountain slopes, heating the air and causing it to rise. As the warm air flows upward along the mountain's face, cooler air is continuously pulled in from the ocean. Then in the evening, when the sun's heating action stops, cool air from the high peaks descends (cool being heavier than warm), reversing the direction of the breeze and pushing the humid, muggy air out to sea.

UVITA South of Dominical, as far as the village of Uvita (18 kilometers distant), numerous beaches face the ocean, some with houses or tiny farms, places that will someday become villages. One of the prettiest on this part of the coast is called Punta Dominical. A high point juts out into the ocean, with cliffs and surf reminiscent of California's Big Sur or Spain's Costa Brava. Below a small hotel cliffs and rocks catch the full force of the ocean's strength as waves crash and send cascades of white foam flying high in the air.

Most desirable property along this coast seems to be owned exclusively by foreigners, many of whom don't appear to be particularly eager to sell and, when they do, not at bargain prices. Occasionally a beach-front property can be found at highly inflated prices. Affordable property is found away from the beach, where Ticos have land for sale. I looked at one parcel in Uvita, about 1 kilometer from the beach, five hectares (twelve acres) of land with a comfortable house for half of what it would cost near Dominical. There were many fruit trees and enough pasture for keeping a horse or two.

A longtime resident named Lillian said, "We looked all over Costa Rica before settling on Uvita. We found a ten-hectare plot up on the mountainside. Not only do we have a gorgeous view but there are also six beautiful waterfalls on the property. For me it's like having my own national park." She added, "We are holding it in trust for our two granddaughters, as a future for them."

A difficulty with small communities such as Uvita is a lack of enough residents to form an effective community organization. Local residents hold informal meetings, but not enough attend to get much done. (Most unimproved properties belong to absentee owners.) This is due to change, however, since the pavement now connects with the Pan-American Highway at Palmar, just a few miles south. Rapid development is under way as some prime land is now available for development.

A problem with lightly populated areas like Dominical or Uvita is the lack of sophisticated medical care. Often a resident doctor in the village can handle emergencies, but for serious problems the nearest emergency clinic in this region is in Platanillo, about 13 kilometers from Dominical, or the hospital in San Isidro, some 45 kilometers distant. Uvita's medical needs are taken care of in Palmar Norte.

This problem of medical care was brought home to me on a recent trip. As I was driving from Dominical to San Isidro, a *campesino* ran out into the road and flagged me down. His hand was bleeding from an accident, and he needed to get to the hospital. I had to act as an ambulance driver, not knowing whether to go top speed and risk killing us both or to slow down while my patient bled to death. He was the calm one, as he insisted on trying to show me his wound and describing in minute detail what had happened. Fortunately, we both survived.

CINCO VENTANAS The road from Dominical south to Palmar Norte (where it joins the highway going to the Panamanian border) is brand new and a marvel compared with the old rock-and-mud nightmare trail of a few years ago. Today it is a matter of ten or fifteen minutes from Dominical instead of the hour and a half it took me the first time I made the trip. The road zips on down the coast past areas that before were seen only by four-wheel-drive daredevils.

One very interesting place we encountered last year is called Cinco Ventanas. Even though development here is rather new, there are already 1,400 properties owned by foreigners (not all live there full-time) and a fourteen-unit shopping center including a small supermarket, gasoline station, and restaurant. The majority of the foreign property owners are

French-Canadian, but other North Americans are discovering the area and will be moving in as well.

The developer explained why there are so many French-speaking residents: When she and her husband started their project here, they advertised heavily in the Quebec area as an experiment. They sold building lots by mail, with the buyers being assured that if they didn't like the property when they arrived, they could either have their money back or choose another lot. Before long, most of the lots they had were gone, bought by French-speakers. "They just love it here," she said, "and since French is similar to Spanish, they have no problems with language."

Just east of Cinco Ventanas, the mountains quickly rise to more than 3,000 feet, providing the same kind of "air-conditioning" as in Dominical, with breezes coming inland in the hot part of the day, and cool breezes flowing down the mountains at night. By the way, the name *Cinco Ventanas* (Five Windows) refers to some natural caverns in the cliffs by the water's edge. Residents in this area have exclusive rights to cross the private land between the highway to Playa Ventanas, a small bay with a wide beach and bordered on both sides by rocky cliffs ranging in height from 60 to 200 feet, making this one of the few "private" beaches in the country.

GOLFITO AREA For years I had heard people speak of Golfito and the Osa Peninsula. The area sounded like a place of adventure—panning for gold in forest streams, fishing for trophy sailfish, or hiking rain-forest trails. In order to complete research for this book, I resolved to spend some time around Golfito to collect information. But when I asked folks around San José who either owned property or regularly visited here, I found their answers short and vague, always skirting the subject as if trying to draw my attention elsewhere. When I spoke with a man who owned property on Zancudo Beach, his face burned angrily as he said, "Zancudo is my special place, and I don't want any damned travel writers drawing attention to it! It would destroy things for all of us!"

Obviously, our interview was over, but now I knew I had to go! I jumped in a car and was soon on my way to Golfito, the jumping-off place for the Pavones–Zancudo Beach areas. The drive south on the Pan-American Highway is gorgeous. One unbelievable view after another invites a pause wherever the car can be parked safely off the pavement.

Ordinarily the trip takes six hours, but by the time I stopped several times to sample pork *chicharones,* marvel over the views, and take a nap in the shade of a banana tree, the trip stretched into an eight-hour day. When truck traffic is diverted along a completed new coastal highway, you'll be able to make the trip in five hours from San José.

Golfito is an often neglected part of Costa Rica, with scanty information provided by most tourist guides. The town began its existence as a banana port for United Fruit Company but was abandoned when the company decided that the operation had become unprofitable. When it was a banana port, there was no incentive to develop it as a tourist attraction, although today the area is trying hard to do so.

Sitting on a bay of Golfo Dulce, Golfito's waterscape is absolutely gorgeous, reminiscent of the San Juan Islands in Puget Sound (that is, as long as you are facing *away* from the town!). The coastline and islands jut steeply from the water, green and matted with trees, vines, and thick brush. The water is so calm at times that it is hard to realize that this is not a lake but a protected little bay of the Pacific Ocean. From the slope a rain forest watches over the town as fishing boats ply the calm waters of the Golfo Dulce. During the town's banana-shipping days, the company wisely kept these mountain slopes as a wildlife preserve and watershed, ensuring Golfito a relatively pure water supply.

The town itself can hardly be described as anything but picturesque. It looks like a cliché movie set of a banana-shipping port. Just a few blocks wide, the town follows the water's edge, with some houses actually standing over the water on stilts and others clinging to the cliffs and hanging out into empty space. A couple of excellent hotels accommodate the growing number of curious tourists, but most lodgings are rather rustic.

A surprising number of North Americans live in or around Golfito. One place to meet them is at Louis Brenis Restaurant, which sits across from *la bomba* (the gasoline station). The Costa Rica Surf Bar is another local gringo hangout. The main commercial street, looking ramshackle, climbs a hill paralleling the highway and waterfront. Foreign residents patronize a couple of open-air restaurants here, as well as hardware stores, shops selling tackle and boating supplies, and several red-light bars.

Because of special circumstances, some of Costa Rica's better property bargains can be found around Golfito. A local resident explained,

"When the United Fruit Company pulled out, it left us without our biggest employer." Workers started moving away, selling property for what they could. Next a disease called the "Panamanian Blight" hit the cacao crop, which was the second line of defense for farmers here.

Property became difficult to dispose of. Sellers were plentiful, but buyers scarce. This buyer's-market situation is still in effect to some extent, but demand by foreign purchasers continually pushes beach property prices upward.

The government is working hard to find a solution, trying to attract new businesses to fill the void that United Fruit left when it abandoned the economy. Starting new types of agriculture is not a good option, because the chemicals and pesticides used to grow bananas have made it difficult to grow anything else afterward. One project that helps local commerce is a Free Trade Zone, a special place for manufacturing and exporting by Costa Rican and foreign businesses. Those operating within the zone's coverage are exempt from some taxes and customs on importation of raw materials, components, and parts. This should attract investors who would like to take advantage of the tax breaks and the availability of good local workers.

Another government program that brings hoards of residents into Golfito is the duty-free warehouses. Anybody, resident or tourist with a passport, can obtain a permit to enter these warehouses and purchase a wide variety of goods, duty-free. To make sure that Golfito tourist facilities gain from this, buyers must register the day before—thus ensuring that they will spend money on meals and accommodations. You are allowed $500 per person tax-free every six months.

Buses from San José take seven hours to reach Golfito, leaving San José from Calle 4 at Avenida 18. Spectacular scenery makes the trip enjoyable. For the impatient, daily flights on either SANSA or Nature Air will take you there, but expect to pay a lot more than for a bus.

ZANCUDO BEACH Although Golfito is the central focus of the area, many North Americans prefer to live nearby, rather than in the town. Their homes and business interests are in nearby villages or on isolated bays around the Golfo Dulce. Playa Zancudo is one of the secluded communities that attracts expatriates. It's a relatively small village stretching along one sandy street with a handful of restaurants, cabin rentals, and a small hotel or two. The black-sand beach is backed by homes not far from the water's edge but concealed from the view of swimmers and surfers by the usual coconut and strangler fig trees. Zancudo is a popular place for local Ticos to come to swim on weekends. Unlike Pavones, the famous surfing beach to the south, Zancudo's beach is very swimmable, with gentle surf.

Several bars and restaurants serve as social centers, with occasional weekend dances. A stop at any of the local open-air restaurants will usually find a table or two of North Americans or Europeans discussing local news and making plans for the development of their properties. Paving the road is a common topic. Those who own homes along the beach shudder in horror at the image of the throngs of tourists, property buyers, and developers a paved highway will surely bring. They feel that since they have discovered this part of Costa Rica, it is rightly theirs, and it would be downright rude for others to crowd in. On the other hand, those who have businesses, who depend on tourists and new residents to make their enterprises grow, eagerly look forward to the road and the increased prosperity it will bring.

I spoke with several folks who routinely come here for three months or longer every year. A house or a cabin with a small kitchen, right on the beach, can usually be found at reasonable rents during the off-season. By all means, stay for a couple of months before deciding to invest or build, get to know the other expatriates, and know whether you will find enough compatible friends. This will also give you the opportunity to talk with local residents and get the latest on land values and who has properties for sale.

A local resident remarked, "Everyone wants to come here in the winter months [referring to winter and summer in the North American sense]. People seem to think that summer is a total monsoon. But the weather is wonderful then. It's actually a little cooler during June, July, and August. Every morning is sunny, and at least part of the afternoon is usually rain-free. Often it doesn't rain at all." The hottest month of the year is March, according to local residents. This is just before the rainy season gets started.

Buses and stake-bed trucks bring families from nearby towns on weekends, loaded with children eager to enjoy the beach. The waves are gentle, the water warm, and kids in no danger of anything worse than sunburn. An easier way to get here is by water taxi from Golfito. Schedules vary with the tides.

The shortest way to the beach is a two-hour drive over a gravel and sometimes rocky trail. This same road splits off and goes to Zancudo's sister beach to the south, Pavones. During the rainy season this route requires a four-wheel-drive vehicle, and it's not all that great in the summer. Maps don't help much in finding either Zancudo or Pavones. I have three different maps; for all practical purposes they might as well have been of three different countries, because each has a different version of the road system, none approaching reality. It's best to stop often and make inquiries.

MAPS AND DIRECTIONS One of my favorite Costa Rica map incidents occurred while I was trying to find my way from Zancudo back to the highway. I had been there several times before, but I was forever getting lost. This time it seemed hopeless; I knew I was about two hours away from the pavement up north. I saw a truck approaching and flagged it down. With my three maps, I approached the driver and asked him to give me a clue how to find the sandy trail that headed north.

He puzzled over the maps, shaking his head in despair. "This map is wrong, Señor," he said. "This town is not here, it is way over here, and this road has not been used for years." He took a pencil and began tracing what he thought might be the road I wanted. Finally, with a flourish, he marked the last portion of the horrible road that connected with the pavement near Golfito. He explained once again how to find the correct turning points and, as an afterthought, said, "But Señor, I don't understand why you don't return to San José on the paved road instead of such a bad road."

"Paved road?" I interjected. "These maps don't show a paved road!"

"Of course not. This is a new road and not on the maps yet. Just go 2 kilometers in the opposite direction and you'll reach the pavement!"

PAVONES Pavones is located in the southernmost region of Costa Rica, near the mouth of the Golfo Dulce. This area is the last bit of Costa Rica before the coast becomes Panama. Pavones at one time attracted attention as a possible place for investment and/or residency. Reputed to have the longest surfing beach in the world, Pavones is well known among surfboard enthusiasts, who pilgrimage here from all corners of the world. Some of the land is in what appears to be primary forest, loaded with wildlife and rare plants.

A road parallels the beach for several miles just north of Pavones, with only an occasional ranch house or cabin observable from the road or the beach. Farm clearings alternate with tracts of virgin forest, lovely stands of native trees, tangles of vines, and a profusion of birds and animals.

The Pavones Coast is a wonderful place to visit, a great place to surf, and famous for its tropical scenery. But at this time it is a very poor choice as a place to buy property. Some land here has been in bitter legal dispute since 1985, and previous editions of this book warned against buying here. Investing in land that has even a shadow of legality hanging over it is a violation of our basic guidelines for Costa Rica real estate transactions.

Squabbling over property rights escalated into armed conflict between landowners and squatters. Both sides began carrying firearms. Two separate Wild West–type showdowns occurred between gringos and local Ticos. In one incident a Tico was killed by a guard protecting an American's property; later an American and a Tico were killed in a shootout. The situation has cooled off, although for a while, a somewhat tense atmosphere existed in Pavones between foreigners who believe they own the disputed properties and Ticos who maintain that the foreigners do not have rights to the land.

Local Ticos insist that this does not represent anti-gringo sentiment. They claim that hostility is focused on only those foreigners who occupy the disputed lands. They stress that others are welcome. Unfortunately, the situation has discouraged tourism in the Pavones area, much to the distress of the vast majority of Tico residents who have no stake in the dispute. Tourists who regularly spend their surfing vacations in Pavones report that Ticos here are just as gracious and friendly as anywhere else in the country. However, if you choose to invest here, make very sure that you know what you are buying. ∎

CHAPTER SEVEN

WHY CHOOSE
COSTA RICA?

North Americans choose Costa Rica for a new beginning for many of the same reasons that tourists decide to spend their vacations here. They've heard all about this small Central American democracy, and they come to enjoy the rain forests, lofty mountains, marvelous wildlife, and gorgeous beaches. They long to have the choice between year-round spring in the mountains or year-round summer at the ocean. Costa Rica's cleanliness and truly welcoming citizens make tourists feel at home and inspire many of them with an idea of moving here to start a business, work, or retire. Those who relocate here are, in a sense, going on a permanent vacation. They get to enjoy all the attractions that bring foreign tourists to Costa Rica's shore—without leaving home.

A cruise ship's one-day shore excursion at a Costa Rican port was enough to convince Tony Waddell that he should take early retirement from a major corporation in California and retire to Costa Rica. "I remember the chaos and aggressiveness of the souvenir vendors at every port of call on that cruise, except for Costa Rica," he says. "When we docked at all the other places, we were overwhelmed by beggars and hustlers selling everything from T-shirts to painted shot glasses.

Not so in Costa Rica. We were greeted by a group of students dressed in typical clothing, their school band proudly playing the Costa Rican national anthem. I decided then and there that Costa Rica was the place I'd like to retire." (By the way, the national anthem, "La Guaria Morada," praises the national flower, a purple orchid, instead of a militaristic glorification of war.) Tony not only retired here, but his enthusiasm for his new home convinced his sister to visit; before long she purchased a business and moved here, too.

Some point out that Costa Rica's relative affluence and absence of obvious poverty make them feel more comfortable while experiencing the stimulation of foreign retirement. The fact that Americans genuinely feel wanted makes it easy for us retirees to settle anywhere we choose and not feel confined to expatriate enclaves.

Costa Rica's unique selection of climates is a definite drawing card, with fugitives from bitter-cold winters or suffocating summer heat finding welcome relief from weather extremes. "I grew up in Kansas," one retiree explained, "and we had blizzards and frozen ground in the winter, then 110-degree days trapping us indoors in the summer. Where we live now (on the hillside above Escazú) we only need one set of clothing—springtime."

Many who fall in love with Costa Rica and resolve to live here are much too young to retire. So they come here with the goal of combining a business enterprise with enjoyment of all Costa Rica has to offer. Casey Halloran, who started an Internet company in Costa Rica, says, "While in university I studied a year in Spain and got hooked on travel and speaking Spanish. After one year in the U.S. workforce as a marketing manager for a software firm, I decided to try to start my own company. After reading books on living and retiring in Latin-American countries and researching the Internet to see if anyone was already doing what I had planned, I chose Costa Rica. After three years here I've had a great experience and do not intend to leave soon."

Some relocate to Costa Rica for the sheer exhilaration of living in a foreign country. When asked how she and her husband made the decision to move to Costa Rica, Hilary Aeschliman said, "We probably did things differently than most sane people do. We decided to move here without even visiting. We had traveled in Mexico, and everyone we spoke with compared it favorably. In fact, most liked Costa Rica better than

Mexico, so we decided we could handle it without testing the waters first. Our initial plan was to spend three years here, rent furnished homes, learn the language, and take back our experiences. However, our children are enjoying school here, so after one year into it, neither of us feel an inclination to hurry back to the States. I suspect we'll stay longer than three years; after that we'll be part-time Ticos for a long time to come."

LOW COST OF LIVING? One of the side benefits of living in Central America is a significantly lower cost of living than can be found in the United States or Canada. But those who come to Costa Rica solely because they need a cheap place to live usually suffer frustration and disappointment. They end up not seeing the beauty of the country because they are comparing prices of everything.

It's always amusing to hear some tourists—and even an occasional resident—complain about high prices in Costa Rica. For some reason these people assume that property, goods, and services ought to be dirt cheap in a developing Central American country like Costa Rica. They feel cheated to discover that some things cost as much here as they do back home—imported goods even more.

Those who are disappointed that the cost of living is not next to free, the longer they live in Costa Rica, the more critical they become. They tend to forget what prices were where they came from, and they think in terms of colones rather than dollars. When they see the price of an item rise from 500 colones to 1,000 colones over time, they complain that the cost has doubled. They overlook two important facts. First of all, a 1,000 colón bill is worth a little less than $4.00, whereas back then, a 500 colón bill was also worth a little less than $4.00. Secondly, the same article purchased in Ohio might cost $8.00.

My favorite example of this was once when we were having dinner in a local restaurant while an expatriate couple at the next table complained bitterly about high Costa Rican prices. They had moved to Costa Rica three years earlier. After a long tirade I interrupted to point out, "You are drinking a bottle of beer that costs $1.00, and you ordered a large meal that costs a little more than $3.00. What would you pay where you come from?"

"Well, those are exceptions," the woman admitted, "but, everything else is sky-high." I challenged the lady and her husband to name some items that aren't imported yet are priced outrageously. After some thought the woman replied, "Cat food and kitty litter." Her husband triumphantly added, "Shaving cream and deodorant." Of course, these items are imported, but that didn't occur to this couple. They ignored the price of food, domestic wages, transportation, housing, and other essentials that are priced from one-third to one-half the cost in the U.S. For some people, no matter how low the price, it's still too much.

When it comes to real estate, these same people are sorely disappointed when property isn't next to free. Not long ago I was showing guests from Michigan a gorgeous beach-view lot we were considering buying. Our guests were shocked when I quoted the price. "Why, back home, we could buy a larger lot for *half* that amount!" they exclaimed. I wanted to ask whether the Michigan property had a good view of the Pacific. For sure, a California lot with a similar ocean view would command several million dollars instead of the $38,000 price in Costa Rica.

Although I have a hard time imagining a quality place in the United States or Canada that makes Costa Rica look expensive, my routine reply to bargain hunters is: "If rock-bottom prices are your priority, look elsewhere." Many places in the world offer cheaper living than Costa Rica. But is the quality of life the same? Is the weather as nice? Are the people as friendly?

You're in for a disappointment if you expect to pay $3.00-a-day wages for your gardener or maid, buy gasoline at 68 cents a gallon, or purchase ocean-view property at Texas Panhandle prices. If you anticipate luxurious $10.00-a-day hotel rooms and lobster dinners for $5.00 when traveling about the country, this might be the time to return this book to your public library.

In general, I estimate that most Costa Rican prices are about one-half to two-thirds of those in most North American communities. Of course, imported goods can be twice as much, even more. The rooms in hotels that Costa Rican residents patronize usually range from $25 to $45 a night for a couple, including breakfast. These aren't luxury establishments by any definition, but they clearly offer far more than budget hotels in the United States or Canada for the same price. Backpackers are delighted to find rooms for $5.00 to $10.00, since they don't mind sharing a bath. Yes, some luxury Costa Rican hotels charge $80 to $120, but similar hotels in many parts of the United States or Canada will easily eclipse that. Restaurant meals? Go to just about any good restaurant in Costa Rica and

check the menu. Few entrees are priced over $9.00. A juicy steak goes for about $6.00, and if the item exceeds $13.00, you're probably ordering lobster or jumbo shrimp. (For some reason shrimp is expensive in Costa Rica.) If you're into *tipico* Costa Rican food, you can order a *casado* for about $2.75: a huge plate of beans, rice, fried banana or yucca, salad, and your choice of chicken, fish, or a pork chop. All for less than a hamburger back home, and delicious.

Let's forget about hotel prices and restaurant costs; they don't figure heavily in most long-term residents' budgets. More important is comparing the cost of everyday living here with the lifestyle the same amount of money provides elsewhere. You would be hard-pressed to find another place with so much to offer for such a reasonable outlay. Let's start with housing prices.

In many foreign countries North American residents feel they must live in certain "safe" areas, for which they pay premium prices. Because Costa Rica is not a highly stratified society, North Americans feel comfortable living in just about any neighborhood. This translates into a wide selection of rents and housing prices. While you can pay $1,200 a month for rent in a luxury section of Escazú, you also can often find a nice place for $600 a month in the same neighborhood. For $300 you can find accommodations in a very livable area like Alajuela or San Pedro. All three locations are just a few minutes away from shopping and conveniences, and all offer quality living with superb climates. If you're content with less sumptuous digs, your rental costs can be even less. I have a friend who lives in a small house near San José that he rents for $170 a month.

Utilities, a significant part of most budgets, seem almost free in Costa Rica when compared with the United States or Canada. Our telephone bills usually total around $7.00, which includes many local calls and calls to various places around the country. Internet charges are extra. Homes on the Meseta Central have neither furnaces nor air conditioners to drain money from budgets. Electric bills for our condominium in Rohrmoser averaged $13 a month, a fifth of what we pay back in California. However, electric, water, and garbage rates vary from community to community. At our Costa Rican Pacific Coast home, electric bills are considerably more (why I don't know), and water bills are very high (because local bills include road maintenance and other services). No matter, we have friends in Missouri and Ohio who spend more to heat or cool their homes every month than most Costa Ricans earn in a month! Compare the cost of living here with that in your own hometown and then tell me Costa Rica is expensive.

Food is affordable, too, with tropical fruits and veggies not only at giveaway prices but deliciously fresh. Costa Rica produces tasty grass-fed beef; a filet mignon in a San José supermarket costs about the same as round steak in a Baltimore supermarket. Some new residents here report spending a third less on their food budget than they did at home. The key is to buy local foods and avoid imported goods, which carry heavy import duties.

Property taxes are almost nothing, at least for North Americans accustomed to forking over big money for taxes. According to people I interviewed for this book, an average middle-class home—with three bedrooms and two baths—is taxed at the rate of $40 to $200 a year. Most U.S. communities collect more taxes than that every month. Tax reform laws passed in 1996 boosted some property taxes but were basically aimed at collecting from those who previously had evaded taxes altogether. However, tax reform laws passed in 1997 dropped property taxes! (I'm almost embarrassed to report that the assessment on our two-bedroom home—a basic, nonluxurious place—dropped from more than $100 in 1997 to only $46 in 2004.)

Besides affordable housing, utilities, taxes, and food costs, what other bargains does Costa Rica offer? Oh yes—servants. A housekeeper will clean your house and wash and iron clothes for about $250 a month. That includes benefits such as Social Security, paid vacation, and a Christmas bonus. (See Chapter 12 for further details.) We pay our gardener-handyman $2.00 an hour for part-time work, and that's well above minimum wage. We have a delightful cleaning lady who comes in one half-day each week. She washes clothes, changes bed linens, mops and disinfects floors, and waxes the veranda deck—also for $2.00 an hour. (By the way, what do you pay servants in *your* hometown?)

Is everything inexpensive in Costa Rica? Of course not. Clothing prices here will probably be the same as where you came from. Gasoline is much more expensive, depending on the current world price of crude oil and whether the government needs more tax revenue.

Since the bulk of Costa Rica's governmental income comes from customs duties, obviously anything imported will be pricey. Cameras, TVs, electrical goods, and other imported items will cost much more because of high tariffs. Tropical countries aren't suited to wine production, so drinkable wines are imported from Chile, Europe, or California. (Chilean wines are very popular and inexpensive.) Almost anything from Europe or North America is expensive; local consumers solve this problem simply by making do with goods made in Costa Rica or other Central American countries.

High import taxes are a way of life in almost all Latin countries. This makes automobiles *very* expensive. You'll need to brace yourself before asking the price. Until a couple of years ago, customs and taxes cost more than 100 percent of appraised value! It's a little better today, running from 40 to 77 percent of the vehicle's value. Undoubtedly these tax-rates will change from time to time, but you can be sure that Costa Rican cars will always be expensive. Calculations are made from something called the "Black Book," listing new and used car wholesale auction prices (a bible for U.S. car dealers, loan officers, and Costa Rican customs agents).

Fortunately, public transportation is excellent and inexpensive. Depending on where you live, a family car may not be the absolute necessity that it is back home. Buses travel all over the Meseta Central, at frequent intervals, for as little as 65 colones (15 cents), more for longer distances. Taxis are plentiful and inexpensive. Even in the country, far from city conveniences, buses and taxis are abundant. Where public transportation is all but nonexistent, the custom is for automobiles and trucks to pick up pedestrians. I've made several acquaintances that way.

SOCIAL **LIFE**

I've never promoted the idea of retirement in Costa Rica on the basis of cheap living. The attraction here is *quality* living: an adventurous, interesting life in a superb climate, with exotic tropical surroundings. The icing on the cake is affordable costs. When asked why they decided to live in Costa Rica, most people begin by describing the gorgeous weather and magical tropical surroundings. They'll rave on about favorite beaches, mountain retreats, and cloud forests, and eventually they'll mention the affordable cost of living. But oddly enough, when you ask them to pinpoint the most important factor in making the decision to relocate to Costa Rica, most people will agree that lovely surroundings are only part of it. There must be something else involved; after a while any pretty, exotic scenery becomes like new wallpaper: You get used to it. When you pin most people down, they'll admit, "We like the many friends we've made and our social life here."

It turns out that North Americans who live in a foreign country tend to cling together, to form close social groups, to reach out to draw newly arrived English-speakers into their midst. This is partly because they feel isolated from non-English-speaking neighbors and crave all the friends they can possibly attract. Since the pool of English-speakers is limited, each addition to their circle of friends is valuable. People with almost nothing in common—who wouldn't even nod at each other back home as they passed on the street—become great pals in a foreign setting.

I've found this to be true no matter which non-English-speaking foreign country I've researched. Expatriates in Mexico, Spain, Argentina, and Portugal affirm this close camaraderie among fellow English-speakers. Whenever I ask, people usually respond by saying, "Everyone is so friendly here! I have more friends and companions than I ever had in my hometown. There I barely knew my neighbors. My friends were mostly people I worked with." Only as an afterthought do they mention the exotic surroundings or afford-able costs. Friendship and social activities almost always head the list of advantages of living in Costa Rica.

Think about it: Let's say you're moving from Syracuse to Scottsdale. You'll enter the neighborhood as total strangers. If you want friends, you must start over. That's not easy; it takes a certain personality type to quickly cultivate a compatible circle of friends from a field of aloof strangers, and it takes a certain amount of exposure (parties, social events, and so forth). In Costa Rica you'll be sought after.

This doesn't mean that you don't have to work at making friends in Costa Rica. You must go halfway. If you wait for expatriates to knock down your door and drag you out to dinner, you may give the impression of wanting to be a hermit.

MIXING WITH TICO NEIGHBORS The usual strategy for newcomers is to seek out a place where most neighbors are fellow countrymen, who speak English, and who are available to help them through the trauma of fitting into their new surroundings. But before Laura and David Streek of Cambridge left England with their two young daughters, they decided that they wanted their Costa Rica adventure to be more than the usual thing. Laura said, "We wanted to be able to integrate into the community and society of a new country where we could lead a simpler, warmer life spent mostly outdoors. We wanted our children to experience a new culture and learn a new language."

They discovered a village they liked on the Pacific Coast and decided to try living there. Instead of joining the foreign community in their tasteful and comfortable homes with lovely views of the ocean, the Streek family rented an older Tico-style house, right in the center of the village. Little stores flank both sides of the house, and goalposts of the village soccer field were across the street. The grade school sits on the sidelines of the soccer field.

Their neighbors are mostly Ticos, with a scattering of North American and Europeans émigrées from Switzerland, Holland, and Scotland—most of whom operate small businesses in the village. They immediately set about making friends and found it rather easy. Soon the family felt comfortable with their surroundings and knew enough of their neighbors to have a party.

Laura said, "We decided to have an open house that weekend, which begged the question: Where else in the world could you have moved to, not knowing a single soul, and within two weeks have met enough likable people to have a house party? We spent a happy afternoon of flower arranging, stringing fairy lights, and setting up the music system in readiness for the night's festivities.

"Soon after sundown, with the house sparkling in the twilight and music drifting out into the balmy air, people began to arrive. Before long the party was in full swing, with guests bringing pots of chili, dips, tortillas, crates of beer, and gifts. The porch was filled with young Ticos and gringos alike drinking beers; the salon held the food, and the children danced the salsa with the more-than-willing grown-ups. The kitchen and back rooms bustled with the usual party activities. The garden was the only place one could find to sit under the stars and enjoy a conversation with new friends."

In many countries, something like this could never happen, but Ticos have a strong sense of equality and think nothing of joining in a multicultural celebration like this one. Instead of meeting foreigners with an awestruck bowing of the head—as is the custom in many Latin American countries—Ticos look strangers in the eye, shake hands, and maybe even invite the strangers to visit their homes. That would seldom happen in other foreign countries—probably not in your hometown either.

Even if your Spanish is far from fluent, communication flows. Most Ticos have learned about as much English as you've learned Spanish. (They probably have also forgotten as much English as you've forgotten Spanish!) So all sides have lots of fun talking, learning new phrases in the other's language, and becoming friends. Making friends among the Tico community is rewarding; however, you should resist the temptation of moving to a totally "non-gringo" community, away from other English-speaking neighbors. Most gringos need a circle of English-speakers to round out their lives. They find that even though communication with Ticos is good, many common elements of understanding are lacking. After a while there's a craving to talk politics, to discuss movies, or to reminisce over the "good old days." You'll receive blank stares from your Tico friends when you start speculating about the Chicago Cubs' chances for the pennant or whether Senator Phoghorn can be reelected. In short, the average newcomer to Costa Rica needs both gringo and Tico friends. Happily, this is possible! Newcomers are attacked with aggressive friendliness.

CLUBS AND **ACTIVITIES**

There's no excuse for being lonely in Costa Rica—too much to do, too many people to meet, too many places to go. Take some Spanish classes, attend a meeting of Republicans Abroad or Democrats Abroad, do some volunteer work, learn to play tennis or bridge. You'll meet more friends than you've dreamed of, and you'll live the rich life you moved to Costa Rica to find.

The biggest mistake some make is not keeping active. Some newcomers will take a drink or two when things get too quiet for them; next thing they know, they're drinking too much. If you haven't already acquired interests to keep you busy in your new location, open the *Tico Times* to the "Club Directory" section and look at the broad range of invitations. (If you can't find a group of friends who are involved in your favorite activity, chances are, your favorite activity is illegal, immoral, or boring!) Volunteer work is another satisfying way to make friends and become involved in fun activities; this can be much more satisfying than sitting around a bar until closing time.

An excellent example of a volunteer project, one in which my wife and I are currently involved, is the establishment of a library in a village in Guanacaste. Local expatriates contributed funds to purchase several shelves of reference material as well as books that are fun to read for adults and that will enhance the local children's interest in education. When enough money was donated, we expanded the library by renting a building separate from the school and opened the facility to adults as

well as children. We now have art programs for children, four computers for teaching marketable skills to teenagers and adults, and fiction and nonfiction shelves in both Spanish and English for gringos and Ticos. Just a slight exposure to worthwhile projects like this increases one's social circle immensely. See www.discoverypress.com/library.

LATIN LOVERS Single women visitors find that Costa Rican men tend to fancy themselves as prototypes of the "Latin lover." It's as a Brazilian friend once explained: "When I was young, my father one day took me aside to tell me the facts of life. He said, 'My son, in this world you must understand one thing. You cannot expect to go to bed with every woman you meet. But, of course, you must at least *try!*'"

That's the essence of a "Latin lover." The stereotype is a playboy supporting one or more mistresses and continually trolling for more conquests. To a small extent this could be true among the more affluent Costa Rican business types (same as anywhere else in the world), but the average eligible Tico bachelor, the type most single women will meet, doesn't earn enough to even *dream* of supporting a mistress! He has a tough time scraping together enough money to keep gasoline in his car's gas tank.

Curiously, according to foreign women I've talked to, every one of the men who try to date them seem to be either "single" or "divorced." Convenient, no? Of course while divorce in Costa Rica is not common, a married man pretending to be single or divorced is quite common. But is this any different from San Francisco or Baltimore?

It's much more common for serious relationships to develop between gringo men and Tica women than the other way around. There are some specific reasons for this, as we'll see later on. Yet I've seen several successful romances bloom in the other direction, when a foreign woman and a Costa Rican man find their niche together. I don't know the statistics, but I'd wager that the divorce rate in these cases is lower than the average in the lady's home country.

This brings us to the question of Costa Rican males being "macho" and their women being obsequious and subservient—the picture most of us have of Latino culture. In my personal experience, and in my firm opinion, this picture is highly exaggerated and confined mostly to those living at poverty level—pretty much the same as in the United States. Yes, I realize that some Ticos beat their wives (that happens in Omaha and Orange County as well), and I recognize that some Costa Rican husbands cheat on their spouses (and vice versa). But from my observations over many years, I staunchly maintain that "machismo" isn't part of the average Tico personality here.

A bit of advice for foreign women who do find that rare, single, marriageable male: Before you consider marriage, check out your intended rather closely. Consider whether you could end up living on an economic level you're not accustomed to—and make it crystal-clear that you do not expect to have a Latin lover for a marriage partner.

WHAT ABOUT SINGLE MEN? "After the divorce, the first thing I thought about was coming here to get away for a while. There's something romantic about the name 'Costa Rica,' and I needed something to cheer me up after all my problems. I just knew this would be a great adventure." This was a typical reply when I would ask a single man why he was visiting here. A common follow-up statement was, "Actually, I planned to stay for only one month, but before I knew it, I met this pretty young lady, and now I'm married again!"

I've known a dozen or more fellow countrymen who married Costa Rican women, but just a few American women who married Costa Rican men. Why? I asked an ex–New Jerseyite who married a Tica woman some time ago. "Why?" he responded. "Because Costa Rican women are different in many ways. It's not just that they are pretty and young—that's not what it's all about. We come here looking for something we think we lost somewhere back along the years. What we find is a pretty young thing who treats us as though we are special and are twenty years younger. They don't nag or complain if we're not perfect. In my case, I found a nice-looking woman who does whatever she can to make me feel at home and wanted."

What's the downside of this kind of relationship? The new groom is often expected to provide not only for his new wife and, often, her children from her first marriage but for his wife's family as well. When Mami needs a new refrigerator or when Papi wants new false teeth, the husband is expected to pay.

Single North Americans tend to congregate in an area of downtown San José that I call Gringo Gulch, around the odd-numbered *avenidas* and odd-numbered *calles*. A concentration of inexpensive hotels and gringo bars here attract a large number of single or divorced fugitives from northern climes. They hang out in these bars of more or less ill-repute, where they drink Pilsen beer and exchange lies about their romantic conquests, financial successes, and the injustice of their divorce settlements. The majority of the habitués of Gringo Gulch are of Social Security age, looking for that one last go-round. Surprisingly enough, some actually find it. Many women who visit the gringo bars really aren't prostitutes. (Prostitution, however, is legal in Costa Rica, with women undergoing mandatory testing on a regular basis.) Often these are simply working women hoping to meet a wealthy foreigner to marry, someone who will "take them away from all this." An older gringo with a $1,000-a-month Social Security check will do just fine. With that kind of income, the woman can quit her job and support her children in style.

One word of caution to would-be Don Juans: Be careful after dark, and especially avoid the *zona roja* (red-light zone) in the opposite corner of downtown as it gets later in the evening. Some street girls here are fairly good thieves. Your wallet can disappear quickly while you are basking in sweet talk from a pretty young thing. Their scam is pretending to be overwhelmed by a man's sex appeal. While several enthusiastic girls hug and caress the delighted gentleman, others are helping themselves to the contents of his pockets. It's usually a nonviolent robbery, and the victim doesn't realize he's been had until he tries to pay for his next drink. Most habitués of Gringo Gulch are transient and ephemeral. Within a few weeks they either move on to discover the real Costa Rica or return home with exaggerated tales of their sex lives in Central America.

Although an occasional visit to the downtown San José gringo bars can be entertaining, it's all too easy to make hanging out here your social life to the exclusion of all else.

If you're single and are looking for someplace to go and people to meet, simply open the *Tico Times* to the "Calendar" section. You'll find a page and a half of listings: classes, art exhibits, concerts, lectures, dances, theaters, political clubs, sports, and every possible activity you can imagine—great places to meet people and make quality friends. There's no excuse for being bored in Costa Rica.

GAYS IN COSTA RICA Several gay couples have written to me, describing their relationships with Tico neighbors. They have all been positive. None of the hostility that is sometimes demonstrated in other parts of the world seems to be encountered in Costa Rica. Costa Rica seems to accept both male and female homosexuality as an ordinary fact of life. ∎

CHAPTER EIGHT

LIVING IN
COSTA RICA

A longtime resident once said, "I don't consider Costa Rica a Third World nation. I'd call it a 'Second World' nation—if there were such a thing. After all, it's a place where you can drink the water and eat the food, where your conscience isn't continually assaulted by beggars and abject poverty. Furthermore, it's a place where the government isn't run by a bunch of military thugs." For these reasons North Americans find adjusting to Costa Rican everyday living conditions rather easy. Of course there are differences in lifestyles, but instead of being traumatic, in most instances the variations are charming.

Whether you thoroughly enjoy living in Costa Rica, however, depends on your approach to life. If you expect people to conform to your ideals, if you want conditions to be exactly as they are in your hometown—you are bound to be disappointed. Costa Rica is, after all, a foreign country, and that's exactly why most of us choose to live here. In this chapter we'll look at some everyday living conditions that make Costa Rica different.

LATIN **AMERICAN TIME**

A difficult notion to understand is the way Latin Americans view time. When one is invited to a social event in the United States or Canada, it's considered ill-mannered to arrive late. Not so in most parts of Latin America. Should you receive an invitation for dinner, say, at 7:00 P.M. and actually arrive at that time, you are likely to embarrass the hosts. She is probably in the shower, and he still at the office. Guests are expected to arrive late. It doesn't matter, because the 7:00 P.M. dinner isn't served until 8:00 or 9:00 P.M. anyway. When keeping appointments with businesspeople, you can arrive at the office a few minutes late without worrying about it. You'll have time to catch up with the latest goings-on in the world by reading *Newsweek* and *La Nación* while waiting for your appointment. Still, even after several decades of exposure to Latin American time, I've never understood it, nor will I ever. When invited for a social gathering at 8:00 P.M., I always ask, "Is that eight o'clock Tico time or eight o'clock gringo time?" The reply is usually a grin and, "Better make that nine o'clock." Most Costa Ricans share this cavalier view of time—not, however, to the extremes found in Mexico or Argentina.

On the other hand, my personal experience with my Costa Rican employees is that they're usually on time. I'm always surprised to see them arrive at my house early, start to work on time, and—after a morning and an afternoon break—go home on time. Maybe this is because I pay more than the going wage scales, but I suspect that the Costa Rican work ethic is unusually positive, at least for Latin America.

COURTESY **AND CUSTOM**

Costa Rican social behavior is a curious mixture of Old World, European formality and a special Tico style of relaxed interaction. You shake hands politely when being introduced or when meeting an acquaintance on the street, women as well as men. Women may also greet other women friends with a kiss on the cheek; with close friends a woman may do the same with a man, but only if they know each other well. Exaggerated hugging and kissing—common in the United States—is not approved of here. Men, when greeting truly close friends, will give an *abrazo*—a quick hug and pat on the back—or perhaps lightly clasp the friend's wrist or forearm instead of shaking hands.

"Getting down to business," as we North Americans are apt to do, without any preliminary greeting and small talk is considered somewhat rude in Costa Rica, but not terribly so. Costa Ricans know how we North Americans are, so they never make a big deal out of it; they realize that "business" is the custom in our countries. To be polite, you might spend a few moments inquiring about someone's children or spouse, or perhaps give a compliment about the person's clothing, the weather, or anything else you might think to say before talking business. Doing so gets things off to a smoother start.

Costa Ricans have a delightful habit of issuing off-the-cuff invitations to visit them at their homes, for dinner or for cocktails, but you should always wait for the invitation and not just drop in. An exception to this is when someone moves into the neighborhood or when you move into a new home. Then it's considered polite to knock on the door and introduce yourself.

A crucial point to remember: In social or business transactions, Ticos just cannot handle confrontation. Unlike the people of some countries—where arguing, shouting, and mock displays of anger or emotion are the accepted norm—Costa Ricans are appalled at such behavior. It's considered not only rude but also degrading. Confrontation is foreign to the culture.

I know a New Yorker who lost an excellent gardener when his gringo temper flared momentarily. Chuck's employee had planted some flowers in the wrong place. As usual when making a point, Chuck raised his voice and waved his hands in the air to signify his displeasure: "No, no! Not here! I wanted them over there!" The astonished gardener loaded his tools in his wheelbarrow and left the property, never to return, despite pleas from the homeowner's wife, who tried to explain, "That's just Chuck's way—he doesn't mean anything by shouting."

THE POST **OFFICE**

Although Costa Rican mail service is pretty good when compared with that in some other Latin American countries, it's hardly up to the standards we expect at home (such as they are). In a country where streets rarely have names and houses lack street numbers, home mail delivery can hardly be expected to be reliable. I waited six months in vain for my

first bank checking account statements. Then one day, out of the blue, they all appeared at the same time. Instead of complaining, I was astonished that the mail carrier actually found our house. The address on the envelopes read, "300 meters north from Amistad Park, 100 meters to the east, and 25 meters to the south." (But which house?) The poor guy probably carried these bank statements with him every day for months, just in case he deciphered those directions and figured out which house I lived in. Unfortunately, the statements arrived after we'd sold the house and closed our checking account—having decided that having a checking account wasn't all that convenient.

That's why most folks rely on post office boxes, known as *apartados*. This means a trip to the post office every couple of days, but at least you are fairly certain your mail will be waiting for you. My post office box in the village near our Guanacaste home costs $8.00 a year. I understand the cost is considerably higher at other post offices, and boxes can be in very short supply.

For a while there was a problem with mail being stolen by employees within the postal system. The general impression was that most thefts occurred in the main post office in San José rather than in the smaller substations around the country. It's been some time since newspapers have reported thefts, so presumably a campaign by the government was successful in rooting out the culprits. Not too long ago, the postal system supposedly was privatized, but as far I can tell it hasn't made a lot of difference. The same employees are working in the offices, and things look normal. I still would prefer using one of the courier services or certified mail if anything important or urgent needed to be sent.

Airmail between Costa Rica and the United States or Canada involves ten days each way. That means at best a twenty-day turnaround between the time you send a letter and the time you receive the reply. A practical way to avoid this delay is by using a fax machine. Seems like everybody's got 'em here. A fax to or from the United States or Canada costs about $1.50, but the turnaround for an important letter or document is a matter of minutes instead of weeks. Even better than a fax is electronic communication via the Internet. Now that Internet access is available almost everywhere in the country (there are Internet cafes everywhere you look), the most practical communication method is E-mail. Full information is presented later in this chapter.

Another way to beat the system is with one of several Miami–San José post office box services that offer same-day delivery by air courier to and from Costa Rica. Mail going either way gets there almost as fast as if it were mailed in the States. This is the only practical way to subscribe to magazines or newspapers at domestic rates and receive them in the same season as publication. If you live in the boonies, your mail service company can often forward your mail by bus for pickup at the end terminal.

Among the most popular services: Aerocasillas (P.O. Box 4567–1000, San José, CR; 506–255–4567; fax 506–257–1187); Star Box (5177 Northwest Seventy-fourth Avenue, Miami, FL 33166; 305–257–3443; fax 305–233–5624); and Trans-Express "Interlink" (4437 Hollywood Boulevard, #B, Hollywood, FL 33021; 954–296–3973; fax 954–232–3979).

TELEPHONE **SERVICE**

Telephone service is usually ghastly in Third World countries, with some Latin American countries really rudimentary. A number of factors contribute to this, mostly having to do with the enormous investment required for telephone infrastructure in order to make lines available to all parts of the country. When you have dirt roads or trails leading to isolated backcountry regions, the cost of installing telephone poles and stringing lines becomes prohibitive. Even if lines are installed, village residents and farmers can't afford to pay more than a bare minimum, so there's no profit for the investors. Many *campesinos* aren't interested anyway, because they aren't used to telephones and don't feel that they're worth the bother.

Because private enterprise is seldom willing to invest the fortune required for so little return, the job of installing the communications network necessarily rides on the shoulders of the government. Progress is slow because money is always in short supply.

Costa Rica is different from most other Third World countries in this respect. As much as people like to criticize Costa Rica's telephone and electric company (ICE)—and I am among them—we need to admit that ICE has done a pretty good job overall. No, you still can't expect to have a phone installed the same afternoon you order it. And in some parts of the country you'll still have to wait until they get around to planting poles and stringing lines. But the situation gets better every year. Installation of lines and junction boxes to out-of-the-way places is accelerating. The best part is that you can dial any place in the world from your home and connect just as though you were calling across the street. Try that in Honduras or Guatemala! Charges for local and in-country calls are so low they seem almost free.

Phone service is naturally better in the cities; the per-person installation costs are much lower, making it more financially feasible to provide service. So if you want to live in the provinces, make sure phones are available before you settle in unless you can be satisfied with a cell phone—and your area has cell service. We waited several years for phone service where we lived in Guanacaste because the lines had to stretch 40 kilometers to our community for just 350 telephones. But once the lines are in place, there's no problem having a phone installed in your home with only a few days' wait.

One of the phone company's modernization projects has been to convert some pay phones to accept phone cards instead of coins. The problem with that is when you have to make a call on a public phone, if you don't have a phone card, you have to go somewhere to buy one, because the phones won't accept coins. This is complicated by the fact that not all phones will accept the ICE phone card that has a digital chip embedded. In this case you need a card that allows you to dial an access number, and then dial the number you want. These are the best kind because they work on any phone, regardless of the type, and you can use them when calling from a private phone and not bill your host for the call.

One problem newcomers can encounter is an occasional and unexpected cancellation of their phone service. We're accustomed to waiting for bills to come in the mail, then writing checks and mailing them out. In Costa Rica, it doesn't exactly work that way. Unless you live in the city, you must go to the place where phone bills are presented each month. This could be a grocery store, a stationery shop, or some other local business. The phone bill is rarely at the same place where you go to pick up your electric bill—or pay your garbage collection or your house insurance—that would be much too easy.

I have a friend who owns a small variety store and collects all the phone bills for the area. She speaks almost no English but manages to do okay with gringo customers. However, a couple of times I've had wild-eyed gringos come to me crying, "Please help me, John! I just paid my bill, but that woman canceled my account anyway! She said *está cancelada!*" I calmed them down by explaining that the word *cancelada* does indeed mean "canceled" but it was the *bill* that was canceled, not the service!

When we lived in the city, a telephone employee used to come around to our condominium and leave the bills with the watchman. We had to remember to go to his guardhouse at the proper time to pick up the bill, or there went the telephone again! Then we would take the bill to a nearby supermarket to cancel the bill before they canceled the service. This is why some people hire *tramitadores*—people who remember to do all these chores and who earn money by standing in line. Understand, telephone service improves as time goes by; conditions could be different by the time you read these words.

DIALING IN COSTA RICA To reach an AT&T international operator, you dial 0–800–0114–114, no coin needed. MCI is 0–800–012–2222; Sprint is 0–800–013–0123; Canada Bell is 0–800–015–1162; information is 113. An English-speaking operator will accept your credit or calling card number or place the call collect. Compared with phone service in other countries, where it takes hours of waiting around a telephone office to get a call through, this is a miracle. If you have a phone in your home, direct dialing is not only easy but also the most inexpensive way to place an international call. The telephone directory lists codes for each country. You dial the country code, wait for the connection, and then dial the number you wish to reach. For example, to dial the United States from Costa Rica, first dial 001. To call Costa Rica from the United States, the prefix is 011.

Emergency calls can be made by dialing 911—just as you do back home. The fire department is 118; highway police, 117; the Guardia Civil, 127; and an ambulance (Cruz Roja), 128. To report a problem with your telephone, dial 119. For electrical problems dial 126; for water problems, 223–5555. To receive or send Western Union money orders, go to the office at Calle 9, between Avenida 2 and 4 (283–6336).

THE INTERNET The computer age hasn't skipped over Costa Rica. You'll find stores selling the latest hardware and all the software you could possibly want, at prices very similar to what you would pay back home. Wisely, the government keeps customs duties low on items such as computers and accessories, the idea being to encourage the cybernization of the nation. The government is eager for the country to get on the E-mail and Internet research bandwagon and is offering free computer access (for Ticos and residents) at larger post offices. E-mail convenience in Costa Rica is nothing short of miraculous. Previously we had to depend on expensive telephone calls to keep in touch with the States, or we wrote letters that took a month for a reply. Now, with E-mail, you can touch base daily with family and friends or do business with a click of the mouse.

The only legal Internet provider is the government-owned Radiográfica Costarricense S.A. (RACSA). RACSA offers a $15-a-month, unlimited Internet connection to families and noncommercial users. This service can only be used from the specified home connection. You pay for the phone connection time, but the cost is minimal. Regular commercial connections start at $30 per month.

It's very easy to open an account; you don't even have to go to a RACSA office. Just about any computer store has the applications and can set you up with an account and a password while you wait. But first you have to deposit your $15 into any one of several banks and show the receipt to the computer store clerk. Keep in mind that this account can be accessed only from your home phone number.

If you bring a laptop with you, a RACSA Internet card is very convenient, allowing you to connect anywhere you have a phone connection.
This is handy when using a friend's dial-up connection, when there is an
hourly charge, so you don't run up your friend's phone bill. The cost of
the card is $10 for a ten-hour card, or $20 for a twenty-hour Internet card.
You simply dial 134 and when you connect, enter the password on the
back of the card. These cards can be purchased from RACSA or some
computer stores.

As pointed out earlier, the government has a monopoly over all radio
and telephone communications and is jealously holding on to the very
lucrative Internet business. The service is sometimes erratic and sometimes frustrating, but it is the only game in town. Actually, service is
improving, step by step. The biggest problem is a shortage of high-speed
Internet connections, which many need in order to conduct business back
home while they live in Costa Rica. At the moment, cable connections are
available through AMNET (www.amnet.co.cr) and Tica Cable (www.cable
tica.com), in a cooperative effort with RACSA. Currently the cost is about
$80 a month (for up to two computers), but the speed isn't comparable to
DSL or most U.S. cable services. It's only 246/128k BPS, but still quite an
improvement over ordinary 56k (and less) phone lines.

If you need high-speed connections, check for up-to-date Internet
information when you look for a place to settle down. I will try to keep
the latest developments posted on my book update Web page
(www.discoverypress.com/update).

COSTA RICAN **DELICACIES**

A delightful custom in Costa Rica is the serving of *bocas*, or free appetiz-
ers, with drinks in bars—they may be fried shrimp, a chicken dish, barbecue, or some more exotic specialty. They aren't served as frequently as
they used to be, especially in bars mostly patronized by gringos, since we
don't expect them. But Tico bars usually sustain this custom, so when you
see someone else being served a treat, don't hesitate to ask. You may
have the chance to sample a raw turtle egg—bars are just about the only
place where you can legally find them.

Other treats are small dishes of chicken and rice, or perhaps a
chicken drumstick or wing, a piece of fried fish, or some *chicarones* with

yucca. You are sometimes given a choice of *bocas,* other times it is whatever the cook happens to be doing. Bocas aren't just for serving in bars. We are often invited to expatriates' homes for a "boca cocktail party." On the Pacific Coast, it's a traditional way often to celebrate a gorgeous sunset. Guests are expected to bring their favorite boca to share with other guests. When you have no way to make bocas (if you are a tourist, staying in a hotel, for example), a bottle of Centenario rum, or a bottle of good wine is a good substitute, or if you prefer, a take-out pizza cut into small pieces. Friends compete for new and unusual recipes for tasty bocas.

DINING **OUT**

It's difficult to look at any particular restaurant menu and point out many dishes that could be described as typically Costa Rican. Curiously, in a country with so many unusual ingredients available, restaurant cuisine tends to be rather ordinary. Steaks, fried chicken, and shrimp seem to be almost obligatory on every menu; they taste fine, but after a while one gets very tired of fried chicken or steak. One of the most common complaints tourists have about Costa Rica is the large number of boring restaurants.

On one research trip I stumbled across a new restaurant that advertised "good old-fashioned American cooking." Since it was operated by an American from Los Angeles, I anticipated tasty "California cuisine." I ordered the featured dish of the evening: a specially prepared beef tenderloin. The owner assured me this was not at all like the normal Costa Rican fare. It wasn't. It turned out to be an overcooked slab of dry sirloin, topped with a slice of Velveeta cheese and doused with canned mushroom sauce. The veggies were canned string beans and carrots. So much for good old-fashioned American cooking. The last time I was in that neighborhood, I noticed the restaurant was closed, presumably due to lawsuits by outraged gourmets who object to Velveeta on their steaks.

Not that there aren't some wonderful dining establishments around; it's just that you'll encounter more of the ordinary variety. Around the San José area, you can find interesting dining places, ranging from elegant French restaurants to superb pizzerias. Some excellent Chinese restaurants will surprise you with dishes that are quite different from the Oriental cuisine you

are used to back home. Their style of cooking is a cross between traditional Oriental and tropical American. Some terribly mediocre Chinese restaurants are also to be found (ask friends for recommendations).

One very common Costa Rican food—served everywhere, sometimes for every meal—is *gallo pinto,* which inexplicably translates as "spotted rooster." This is a mixture of cooked rice and black beans—sometimes mixed with cilantro and chopped onions—fried together until the rice turns a purple color. Mixed with eggs and topped with salsa Inglesa or salsa Lizano, it makes a filling breakfast—nutritious but boring when served at every meal.

In small restaurants away from the city, a typical menu item is a *casado*—a large plate with beans, rice, fried *plátano* (a green cooking banana), and some sort of meat, chicken, or egg. (*Casado* means "married man"; why the meal is called this is a mystery.) *Olla de carne* is a tasty meat stew with vegetables such as *chayote,* squash, yucca, and *plátano.* *Arroz con pollo,* chicken with rice, is one of my favorites when properly prepared and not too dry. *Sopa negra* is a soup made of pureed black beans with an egg poached in it, topped with green onions and crumbled cheese or sour cream. Another favorite is empanadas: fried dumplings filled with meat or cheese, often sold by children who carry them around in galvanized buckets. A tortilla in Costa Rica is occasionally defined as an omelet made with chopped potatoes or yucca root. Mexican-style corn tortillas are popular in the countryside and are also called tortillas; these are far more common than the egg-and-yucca variety.

GRATUITIES Restaurants are supposed to add a 10 percent service charge to the bill, then it's up to customers if they care to leave something extra. Some restaurants cheat and don't give tip money to employees, so leaving an extra 5 percent tip ensures that your waitress at least gets something—and guarantees special service next time. Away from the city, many restaurants don't add tips to the bill; it's customary to tip 10 or 15 percent in these cases. Barber shop and beauty salon personnel expect a 10 to 15 percent tip. My last haircut cost 1200 colones ($2.65) and I tipped 300 colones (65 cents).

At Christmastime it's customary to give something to the newsboy, supermarket attendants, and garbage collectors, and by law you give a yearly Christmas bonus to the maid, gardener, and any other employees. Since this Christmas bonus is not a gift or a tip but is required by law, an extra Christmas present would be considered thoughtful.

If you are a guest in someone's home where there are servants, it isn't necessary to tip them unless they've done something special for you, such as laundry, ironing, or running errands. If a friend lends you the services of her maid, it's customary to tip and to pay for her taxi or bus fare home. Hotel chambermaids like to be tipped just as they do back home.

GREAT COFFEE Some of the best coffee in the world grows on shaded mountain slopes in Costa Rica. These exceptionally rich-tasting beans are in demand by coffee wholesalers, particularly those who boast that their products are "Mountain Grown." To substantiate such a claim, at least 60 percent of the coffee has to come from mountain farms in places like Guatemala, Colombia, and Costa Rica. Curiously, Costa Rican coffee is exceptionally low in caffeine; sellers have to use high-caffeine (and cheaper) beans from Brazil and Africa to bring the jolt up to what coffee drinkers expect. In Costa Rica you have the advantage of brewing coffee from 100 percent Costa Rican beans. If you need more caffeine, drink another cup! We sometimes purchase coffee beans direct from the roaster and take them home while they are still hot. The use of instant coffee (a barbarous practice) hasn't caught on here. A *café con leche* with just a dash of sugar makes a wonderful starter for breakfast and is useful for washing down savory *gallo pinto* and warm tortillas.

Costa Ricans have an interesting way of making coffee that gives a characteristically rich flavor to the brew. Instead of using a percolator or an automatic coffeemaker, Ticos use a wire or wooden stand holding a cloth strainer bag that hangs over a waiting cup. They place two tea-spoons of coffee into the bag and pour boiling water over the grounds, letting it drain into the coffee cup below. For each additional cup of cof-fee, another teaspoon of ground coffee is added. The result is a flavorful, velvety drink that grows richer with each cup made. The grounds aren't discarded until the sack is full of grounds or until the end of the day—whichever happens first. "The aroma and essence of the coffee is much better if it isn't boiled," explained a Tico. "We call our coffeemaking sys-tem a *chorreador*. It brings out the flavor without acid bitterness. This method requires more coffee grounds, but since coffee is inexpensive here, we use nothing but the best."

COOKING **AT HOME**

For those staying for longer than a vacation, an apartment or house with a kitchen is a wonderful way of enjoying Costa Rican cooking and exper-imenting with the unusual tropical ingredients available in the markets. Around the San José area, every neighborhood has at least one super-market, supplemented by weekend *ferias*, or open-air markets. Every neighborhood also has its little *pulpería*, or convenience store, where you can buy items you forgot at the other markets.

Major supermarket chains are Auto Mercado, Periféricos, Pali, and Mas X Menos. (The "X" in Mas X Menos is pronounced as it would be in an equation, as in 5**x**8. Costa Ricans would say *"cinco por ocho."* Therefore, the store is literally pronounced Mas **por** Menos, meaning "More for Less." Open-air markets are held on weekends, the major ones being Saturday in Escazú, on the south side of the main square; Saturday in Pavas, about 5 blocks from the main shopping center; and Sunday in Zapote, next to the Bull Ring. Heredia's farmers' market, also on Saturday, is perhaps the best known of all, with local families selling produce raised in their backyards. Heredia's main market, open daily, is a wonderful place to browse for food, clothing, tools, furniture—whatever you can imagine.

Costa Rica's selection of fruits and vegetables is sometimes bewil-dering for us North Americans. In addition to delicious pineapples, straw-berries, melons, and other things we are used to, you'll find *chayotes*, *pejebayes*, *palmitos*, *plátanos*, and other strange-looking items that will soon become standard parts of your menu. A common substitute for potatoes, the yucca root, in my opinion, tastes much better than ordinary spuds. Exotic tropical fruits such as *guayabas, tamarindo,* and *carambolas* are exciting to experiment with and make delicious *refrescos* (blended drinks). One of my favorite *refrescos* is made by blending fresh cacao nuts (the source of chocolate) with *horchata* (a rice-flour and sugar drink). My wife prefers a *batida* of fresh papaya, milk, and ice, whipped to a milkshakelike consistency.

Some fruits are so exotic that they border on fantastic—with shells, spines, and barbs—looking like something from a science fiction book cover. Especially interesting is the *marañón* fruit, the source of the common cashew nut. The nut itself grows at the end of an edible orange or yellow fruit that can be eaten raw or, more often, made into a *refresco* by blending with sugar and ice cubes. The cashew nut itself is encased in a rubbery shell that is primed with cyanide, making it bitter and somewhat poisonous. I have to marvel over the wonderful way nature designed this fruit as a way to disperse its seeds. In the wild, monkeys, parrots, and other creatures pluck the fruit and carry it away to be consumed. When they finish eating the sweet fruit, the bitter-tasting seed is discarded, dropped on the ground to produce another tree.

Since Costa Rica is a cattle-growing country, steaks and roasts are quite lean, with the flavor that only grass-fed beef can have, and they're inexpensive. You might be surprised to discover that pork and chicken are sometimes priced higher than filet mignon. One reason is that commercially raised pigs and chickens require large amounts of protein in their diets, which isn't available in bananas or other cheap tropical foods, so imported protein supplements bring prices up. Still, the quality of pork and chicken here is excellent. Eggs are delicious, having a brighter-colored yolk and a better flavor than we're used to up north.

With an ocean on both sides, Costa Rica, of course, enjoys a wide selection of seafood. And since shipping distances from either ocean involve just a few short hours, the sea harvest arrives fresh. Almost any kind of fish and shellfish you can imagine is available, plus some you can't imagine. You might want to try some of the shellfish and conch that thrive only around the Costa Rican shores.

Imported foods are expensive. Partly because of shipping costs and partly because of foreign exchange differentials, North American and European products can be costly. Central American substitutes are often as good and locally grown—fresh foods are always much better than something canned or packaged.

FURNISHING **YOUR HOME**

It used to be that when foreign residents received their papers, they had the right to import household goods duty-free. This was a valuable consideration, since high import duties make electrical appliances, televisions, video recorders, and the like expensive in Costa Rica. The rules were that after the goods had been in your possession for three years, you could legally sell them, possibly turning a profit on the transaction, and then buy new ones.

To the dismay of incoming *pensionados*, this benefit was repealed several years ago. The anguish and wailing over the loss of these privileges rocked the North American resident community to its heels. After a series of appeals, the new laws were not applied to those who already had their pensionado status or those whose applications were pending.

Even though tax breaks are a thing of the past, you should be aware that duty-free imports on household goods aren't nearly as important as they once were. At one time demand for furniture outstripped the capacity to produce it. It was cheaper and more convenient to ship your used stuff from Miami than wait several months for the factory to fill your order at exorbitant prices.

Today supply has caught up with demand; you'll have no problem finding a wide variety of furniture at reasonable prices—usually less than you'd pay back home. The amount of money you'd have to pay to have that bedroom suite and living room furniture shipped from Des Moines, Detroit, Denver, or wherever would go a long way toward furnishing your new home in Costa Rica. Furniture stores have great selections, and you can visit small, family-operated factories and have pieces custom-made for about what you'd expect to pay retail.

Household appliances such as refrigerators, washing machines, and TVs can be purchased from a local dealer without waiting for months, as was the situation before. But these prices will include very high import taxes. For example, a few months ago we purchased a popular U.S.-make washer and dryer; we paid more than $600 for the washer and $525 for the dryer. We could have bought them for 40 percent less in a U.S. appli-

ance store. Our Tico neighbors, by the way, were astounded that we would waste money on a dryer when we could simply hang the wash on a line and let the sunshine dry it in an hour for free! But being spoiled gringos—too impatient to wait for the sunshine and too often forgetting about the drying wash until after the next shower wet the clothes down again—we felt we couldn't live without an electric dryer.

Yes, it hurts not to be entitled to pensionado discounts, but Costa Ricans have been paying full price for years. What's so terribly unfair about having to pay the same for goods as your Costa Rican neighbors do? You can be sure this special treatment was a source of irritation and resentment among the Costa Rican community. Perhaps they didn't blame foreigners for paying less, but they did fault their government for taxing them more.

HOUSEHOLD SERVANTS   The notion of housemaids and gardeners seems a bit wild for most of us when we first move to Costa Rica. (The last time we hired a cleaning lady in the United States, she charged $14 an hour and wouldn't do windows.) But in Costa Rica servants are affordable. With the going wage for domestic servants about $250 a month—including all benefits—it makes sense to hire a housemaid and a gardener, at least on a part-time basis. Ticos are generally hardworking and honest, and if you can afford it, you can have someone working around the house who won't complain about doing windows.

Most North Americans report that they pay more than minimum wages; doing so keeps their employees happy and loyal. Although servants are affordable, you must be aware of the laws covering their benefits. By law, not by custom, you are responsible for things like vacations, Christmas bonuses, Social Security, and severance pay. Wages are indexed twice a year, according to inflation. You are responsible for knowing about the benefits and paying them on time. These rules are discussed thoroughly in Chapter 12. Don't hire a servant until you've read the rules!

TELEVISION **AND OTHER MEDIA**

A few years ago, in order to watch baseball or football games, you had to wait for a videocassette to be mailed from the States. Today there are six cable TV services in the San José area alone, plus satellite dishes throughout the country. Costa Rica's modern television system offers six channels, some of which can be received in remarkably out-of-the-way places. On our San José cable system, we enjoyed abundant programming direct from the United States: two TV stations from Denver, one from Atlanta, and one from Chicago. Several international channels delivered programs coming from South America, France, and Germany as well. We found that watching CNN, CBS, and NBC nightly news on our cable TV made up for not having a daily newspaper delivered to our door.

Note that I describe our TV cable system in the past tense; where we live now, on the Pacific Coast, normal reception is confined to two weak channels. (That's the price you pay for not living near the big city.) The answer for those who want to watch CNN, the World Series, and late-run movies is the satellite-driven Direct TV, with an almost unlimited choice of channels. Installation prices have dropped, from $1,500 to less than $100 for a complete installation. If you feel that it is worth the extra money, you can have TV anywhere in the country.

In San José and most of the surrounding cities, you'll find stores selling English-language paperback books and magazines. In addition to the essential *Tico Times*, you can buy daily editions of the *Miami Herald* Latin American edition, the *New York Times*, the *Washington Post*, and the

Wall Street Journal. These papers are a bit expensive—they arrive by airplane—but at times North Americans become starved for a big-city daily newspaper. However, it's easy to keep up with major newspapers and very likely your hometown newspaper via Internet. Every morning, with my coffee, I read the front pages of the *New York Times*, the *Washington Post*, and the *San Francisco Chronicle* (including the comics). Several Costa Rica daily newspapers are online, so I browse *La Nación*, *Diario Extra*, and the *Tico Times* for Central America news.

In San José a dozen theaters show first-run and recent English-language films, mostly from Hollywood. Tickets cost about a third of what they cost back home. The dialogue is almost exclusively English, and Spanish subtitles are printed over the lower part of the screen. This provides an opportunity to improve your Spanish skills by reading Spanish and listening to English at the same time. In many countries where almost no one understands English, the sound is turned down to a whisper, and the audience chatters away, making comments about the movie or whatever. But in Costa Rican theaters the soundtrack runs at a normal volume so that the many Ticos who know English can listen. They enjoy sharpening their English by listening and reading subtitles. The end result is that the audience is quiet and all enjoy the movies.

San José boasts nine legitimate theaters, mostly in Spanish, offering entertainment for those who are well along in their study of the language. One ongoing production is about the history of coffee in Costa Rica, tracing its arrival from Arabia, plus legends and beliefs about the wondrous substance. It is half in English and half in Spanish, with discounts for Costa Rican citizens and *residentes*. Two little-theater groups produce plays in English.

Two *folklorico* troupes regularly present traditions from various parts of the republic, one at the Herradura Hotel and another at the Melico Salazar Theater. Also, there are regular concerts by the National Symphony Orchestra. Sponsored by the government Ministry of Culture, Youth, and Sports, many visiting musicians from other countries add to the quality of the presentations. At the time of writing, more than 25,000 Costa Ricans filled the National Stadium in San José's La Sabana Park to hear Luciano Pavarotti in concert. The facility was filled to capacity.

MONEY **MATTERS**

Costa Rica's currency is the colón. As with many other foreign currencies, the colón's value fluctuates against the U.S. dollar according to supply and demand. For years rates have remained fairly stable, rising with inflation, and the currency has not been over- or undervalued. For example, in 1992 the rate was 138 to the dollar; twelve years later, in fall 2004, the colón's value was 450 to the dollar. That's a devaluation rate of about 12 percent a year—not much, when banks pay as much as 25 percent interest on colón certificate of deposit accounts. Most financial experts predict that the colón will remain stable, with devaluations paralleling inflation.

Some people feel uneasy when inflation continually deflates a nation's currency. The important point is whether the exchange rate between Costa Rican colones and U.S. or Canadian dollars is in line with reality and not overly managed by the government (a practice that always leads to disaster in other Latin American countries). Many people, even some economists, tend to assume that when the exchange rate is stable, inflation is under control and all is well. It ain't necessarily so! When exchange rates are steady, yet prices of goods and services rise in the host country, your dollar loses value every day! Just because a currency holds its own against the dollar isn't a sign of a healthy economy; it could be an artificial manipulation of currencies that masks serious problems.

A perfect example of confusing inflation and currency exchange rates is the recent collapse of the Argentine peso, which had been pegged to the U.S. dollar for ten years. At first the economy did just fine. But since inflation rates vary between Argentina and the United States, the peso became overvalued in relation to the dollar. This caused Argentine goods to be expensive on the world market, and foreign goods cheaper than domestic products. Then suddenly, the peso fell to a value of 33 cents for each dollar. The result was a disaster for the country and citizens.

Yes, mild inflation has been going on in Costa Rica for decades, paralleling the inflation in the United States. But since the colón adjusts for this inflation as prices and wages rise, there's no appreciable change for those who own dollars. For example, prices and wages in Costa Rica today are twice as high as they were eight years ago, yet we North Americans receive twice as many colones for our dollars as we did eight years ago; for those of us with dollar incomes, it's a wash. There's no fore- seeable reason to expect that exchange rates will vary in any significant way in the future, other than a steady adjustment to world currencies, totally in line with reality.

DEALING IN DOLLARS When buying dollars, or when bringing dollars into the country, be sure to inspect each bill carefully for rips or tears. Banks refuse to accept any foreign currency if it's torn ever so slightly. Never mind that the 1,000-colón bill you get in return looks like a dog's breakfast; if that $50 bill you have isn't pristine, you'll end up taking it back to the States with you. One scam is for an unscrupulous waiter or shopkeeper to take your good $50 bill, then return with a torn bill and ask you for something smaller, hoping you won't notice the tear.

A continual problem is the importation of counterfeit $100 bills from Colombia—so many that shopkeepers are sometimes reluctant to accept your big bill. One place where you might get stuck (so I've been told) is at a gambling casino because in the unlikely event that you win big, the house tries to get rid of the phony bills they previously got stuck with by giving them to happy gringo winners.

INTEREST RATES In mid-2004 a nice rate of interest was being paid on time deposits of colones, from 12 to 14 percent. (Dollar accounts pay about the same as CD rates in New York.) While 12 to 14 percent sounds like a terrific return on your investment, you must consider the inevitability of the colón losing value against the dollar. You are gambling that the colón will devaluate less than expected, in which case you come out somewhat ahead. If the rates fall at the expected rate, you'll do fine. But if for some reason the colón's value falls more quickly than the expected 10 percent, you could lose money. My guess (and it's only a guess) is that deflation of the colón will be slow and steady, as in the past.

It is important to remember that nongovernment banks sometimes don't have good track records. It's difficult to discern which are safe, because when they fail, it is without warning. Some private banks, Scotia Bank for example, seem to have good reputations. The situation to be leary of is extraordinary high interest rates offered by some private investment companies. Until recently, some were paying 3 percent per month to investors; that's 36 percent per year! Many expats were living on the income from their savings; $100,000 invested brought in $3,000 a month—a tidy income here in Costa Rica! Tragically, the bubble burst when the largest investment company became snarled in a government investigation, and the other companies folded with it, disappearing with investors' savings. Some hold out hope of recovering at least some of their money, but it looks rather bleak at the moment.

BANKING

In many ways Costa Rica is a modern and efficient country, but for some inexplicable reason a visit to the bank is an Alice in Wonderland experience. It takes forever to do a simple transaction such as exchanging dollars or traveler's checks into colones. Although each bank handles things a little differently, it sometimes involves standing in two or three lines while the clerk checks your passport, examines the bills or checks, fills out forms in triplicate, and pounds everything in sight with a rubber stamp. Then you move to another line and wait until a second clerk fills out more forms in quadruplicate and does more rubber-stamping.

Banks are also where you can usually pay traffic tickets and utility bills and make Social Security payments for your maid and gardener. Since each transaction requires a flurry of forms, rubber stamps, and calculations, you can count on spending a lot of time in Costa Rican banks. Because of the time-consuming process of dealing with banks and government bureaucracy, some Ticos make their living by standing in line for you, by knowing whom to contact and when. They are called *tramitadores* (from the verb *tramitar*, meaning "to transact," "to take legal steps"). Your friends and neighbors can recommend a reliable *tramitador* to make your life easier. Many people become close friends with their *tramitadores*, dining with them and exchanging presents at Christmas.

Criticize the banking system as I do, the fact is that government banks are financially sound. Not long ago BancoAnglo, one of the big three Costa Rican banks, was forced to close its doors because of mismanagement and reckless speculation. The situation closely paralleled the savings and loan debacle in the United States. Costa Rican investors didn't panic; they simply took their passbooks to one of the other national banks and exchanged them for new passbooks from that bank. Nobody lost a nickel; contrast that with the U.S. shenanigans. By the way, the Costa Rican bank officials responsible were immediately arrested. Now just consider how many U.S. savings and loan wheeler-dealers were even scolded, much less shown the inside of a well-deserved jail cell. Costa Rica went one step further: The government decided that those who *borrowed* money and didn't pay it back were equally guilty. It was surprising how quickly many "bankrupt" businesspeople found millions of dollars to repay their loans rather than go to prison. Is there a lesson here?

Not all banks are government-owned. Many private banks deal with the public, usually in a much more efficient manner, at least as far as the amount of time you spend in line in front of a teller's cage. But there are two problems with private banks. One is that deposits are often backed only by the bank's reserves. In some cases, limited government funds are available in the event of default. The second problem is that some private investment companies that *appear* to be banks are outrageously fraudulent, their reserves siphoned into private accounts in the Bahamas. Before you invest in a private bank, investigate its past performance and talk to your neighbors about its reliability. If the bank just opened last March and the main office is a post office box in Haiti, you just might be suspicious.

Until recently only nationalized government banks were permitted to offer checking accounts in both dollars and colones. Now some private banks have equal status with government institutions in this respect.

Local residents and business owners recommended a private bank to me: Banco Internacional de Costa Rica (BICSA). It has a branch office in Miami and operates under Florida's laws and regulations. I haven't used it yet, but this seems to be the most convenient way to transfer or wire funds from the United States and Canada. If it makes you more secure, you can keep most of your money in a dollar account and transfer dollars to the colón account to write checks and cover bills.

Bank accounts can be in either colones or dollars. But an unpleasant bank practice is holding dollar checks from foreign banks for up to twenty-two days before crediting them to your account. (This was supposed to change as a result of the bank reform laws of 1996, but the last time I checked, they're still holding checks before crediting them to the account.) Another quirk is that the banks often do not have enough dollars on hand to cash a large check. You have to take a cashier's check instead. This is OK if you are making a local purchase with the money, since the party to whom you are giving the cash will probably deposit it in his or her account anyway. But should you need several thousand for a trip home, you'd better plan ahead.

KEEP YOUR HOME BANK ACCOUNT For a variety of reasons, most people keep their home bank accounts when they move to Costa Rica. For one thing, the U.S. government will not direct-deposit Social Security or pension checks to a Costa Rican bank, and you certainly don't want those checks floating around Costa Rican post offices. Furthermore, your checks will be tied up for a month or more until the funds are available. With your money deposited in a U.S. or Canadian bank, you can use your ATM card almost anywhere to withdraw cash as you need it. Some expatriates don't even bother with a Tico bank. Local businesspeople who know you will usually take your checks; they know they will be good and they don't worry about the long wait because there's always a balance in their accounts anyway. Our local grocery store cashes our checks for $100 any time we want them to.

CRIME AND **PERSONAL SAFETY**

I'm always surprised when friends visit us in Costa Rica and express surprise when they see wrought-iron bars on our windows. "Is crime so bad here," they ask, "that people must live behind bars?"

This question surprises me because bars on Costa Rican windows seem as logical and natural as window screens in Atlanta or storm windows in Cleveland. Maybe that's because my family moved to Mexico City when I was a youth, a place where homes traditionally have bars on their windows, so I suppose I grew up with the custom. The fact is, in every Latin American country—from the Río Grande to Tierra del Fuego—a home isn't considered complete without a set of decorative wrought-iron bars. To me a Latin American home looks naked without them, like a Cape Cod home without shutters or a Southern mansion without a portico and columns. When the first Spanish colonists came here five centuries ago, they brought iron bars with them. Roman settlers brought window bars to Spain 2,000 years ago; for all I know, the Romans picked up the custom from the Greeks, or maybe the Egyptians.

My wife and I recently spent a few weeks traveling in Spain, southern France, Italy, and Malta. I made a point of observing the various residential neighborhoods we encountered in our journey. Without exception, every home we saw had either heavy window shutters, bars, or both on the windows. After all these centuries, security is still fashionable in Europe.

Do window bars deter professional burglars? Not really—not any more than door locks keep out burglars back home. Bars and locks simply keep out honest people. But I think they make the house look finished—plus they discourage amateur burglars and remove temptation from neighborhood kids. Frankly, I feel quite snug and secure with bars on my windows; I sleep much better.

Like any other place in the world, Costa Rica has crime. That shouldn't surprise anyone coming from the United States, where crime and personal safety have become a high-priority concern of the country. Take a look at some U.S. neighborhoods: The bars you see on windows and doors clearly aren't meant to be decorative; they are grim attempts to protect occupants from violent crime. The alternative to bigger and stronger bars is moving to a safer place with lower crime rates, perhaps rural Kansas or small-town Costa Rica (that's my solution).

I personally see crime as another one of those annoyances I have to put up with if I want to live here—an annoyance like potholes. To avoid destroying my car, I have to drive carefully to miss potholes. That's an annoyance. To avoid crime, I have to be careful where I park my car and where I keep my wallet. That's an annoyance. So far I haven't been affected by crime, but potholes have eaten several of my tires.

Of course, there's crime in Costa Rica; but it's of a different nature than that in the United States. It doesn't seem fair to compare the two places in the same paragraph. The difference is the usual non-violent petty crime in Costa Rica compared with frequent brutal crimes in the United States. Criminals don't just rob up north; they savage and maim as well.

Another big difference is the lack of rampant drug addiction among Costa Ricans. You won't find an army of desperate addicts who are forced to steal several hundred dollars each day to support a habit. The law provides a jail sentence of eight to twenty years for anyone involved in drug dealing. Drug use is considered extremely serious, and mere possession of drugs can be interpreted as evidence of drug dealing. By the way, these laws apply equally to native Costa Ricans and gringos.

From time to time the downtown section of San José is bothered by the appearance of *chapulines*, gangs of street urchins who rob pedestrians by grabbing wallets and jewelry. *Chapulines* literally means "grasshoppers," describing the way the kids jump on a victim and keep him or her off balance while one of them goes for the wallet. I believe that incidents of this nature have been somewhat overstated. (I don't personally know anyone who has been bothered.) The fact that each episode made headlines in San José newspapers suggests that such incidents can't be all that common. However, the problem all but disappeared when strict laws were passed, with stiff sentences for juvenile offenders who previously avoided punishment because of loopholes in the law. Recently a San José judge handed out sentences of up to twenty-five years in prison to a band of chapulines.

It's best to take basic precautions when wandering about the center of San José—or any other big city in the world, for that matter. To be fair, having a wallet lifted or a gold chain stolen are crimes that plague tourists not only in Costa Rica but anywhere else in the world tourists go. Furthermore, this kind of crime can usually be avoided by taking reasonable precautions. Residents and long-term visitors infrequently haunt bad areas of downtown San José after dark, and they know how to avoid pickpockets.

The overall rate of burglaries in Costa Rica is much lower than that in the United States. But a high percentage of break-ins are performed on foreign-owned homes. Burglars know that the average gringo has a nice VCR, a TV, a microwave, and maybe a stereo. Here again, a little precaution is in order. Besides a protective set of bars, it's worthwhile to contribute to the neighborhood *guardia,* the watchman who patrols your neighborhood on foot or by motorcycle. Every block has a couple of them. Because of these guardias, most middle-class neighborhoods are often as safe as similar places in the United States, where a police car cruises by once a day—maybe.

LEISURE **PURSUITS**

GOLF COURSES When I first started writing about Costa Rica, golf courses were almost nonexistent. This disappointed many tourists who feel that a vacation isn't complete without a few rounds of golf. For golfers looking for a place to spend a long time or to retire in Costa Rica, the near absence of golf was a severe drawback.

Why the scarcity of golf courses? It's partly a matter of economics. During the rainy months, when golf course maintenance is limited to cutting grass, tourists are few. In the dry season, when lots of tourists are here, sufficient water might not be available. Another factor is that golf is not a Tico tradition. The main sport here is soccer, a team sport, with strenuous running, kicking, and body contact. The excitement is contagious, with everybody cheering wildly for his or her team. Ticos have difficulty understanding golf as a sport. What they see is a few lackadaisical people fooling around with clubs. Someone hits a ball, then rides a sluggish cart to where the ball lands, and then whacks it again. Nobody cheers. Nobody gets excited. There aren't any spectators. It doesn't make sense to Ticos. To them soccer is more like a real sport!

Since only an estimated 400 Ticos play golf, and without enough tourists and year-round gringos to play, investors were hesitant to build new courses. For years the Costa Rica Country Club nine-hole course and the Cariari eighteen-hole layout were the only golf courses in the country, and both were private. So if you were addicted to golf, you were restricted to living in the Central Valley—and you had to join a club.

Because of the increase in long-term foreign residents and the recent revival of tourism, the situation is changing. As of summer 2002 fifteen golf courses were in operation. Some are for members and guests only, but eight are open for public play. Nine more golf courses are under construction.

Developers are enthusiastic about golf's future here. As tourism increases and more and more full-time gringo residents are moving to Costa Rica, more courses will be opening. Following is a partial list of golf courses open or due to open soon in Costa Rica.

Costa Rica Country Club West. In the San José suburb of Escazú; opened 1944; nine-hole; members only and guests.

Cariari Golf Club. General Cañas Highway, near San José; eighteen-hole, par-71 championship course; hotel guests, club members.

Los Reyes Country Club. San Rafael de Alajuela, near San José; nine-hole; members, guests of certain hotels.

Tango Mar. On the tip of Nicoya Peninsula; nine-hole, tough executive course, par 31; hotel guests only.

La Roca Beach Resort & Country Club. North of Caldera on the Pacific Coast; eighteen-hole, par-72 championship course; members and public.

Meliá Conchal Golf Club and Resort. Playa Conchal, Guanacaste; nine-hole, with another nine holes scheduled; par-72 championship course; hotel guests and public.

Parque Valle del Sol West. San José suburb of Santa Ana; nine-hole; additional nine holes could be added; public at present.

Los Sueños Marriott. *Playa Herradura;* opened December 1999; eighteen-hole, par-72 championship course; hotel guests and public.

Tulin Resort. South of Jacó Beach; eighteen-hole, par 72; members and public.

Cacique del Mar. Playa Hermosa, Guanacaste; eighteen-hole, par 72; under construction; members and guests only.

Monte del Barco. Resort north of Liberia, Guanacaste; under construction; eighteen-hole; members and public.

Resort Rancho Mary La Cruz. A half-hour north of Liberia; nine-hole with another nine holes planned for the near future. It will be an eighteen-hole, par 72; members and possibly the public.

Future courses. Several are planned or under consideration near Flamingo, Tamarindo, and Playa Tambor, as well as near the community of Atenas, a half-hour west of San José.

GAMBLING CASINOS For those addicted to the sound of a roulette ball bouncing along the wheel, or to the riffling sound of cards being shuffled, you'll find no lack of action in Costa Rica. Most gambling casinos are in the San José area, with casinos in hotel lobbies. Sometimes it seems like a miniature Las Vegas. Occasionally gambling casinos are found upstairs over nightclubs or restaurants.

While I sometimes like to gamble, I also like to have a chance of winning. I have the distinct feeling that gaming in the average Costa Rican casino is not really gambling, merely donating to the profitability of the establishment. House rules make it highly unlikely that you will break even, much less win. The games aren't standard ones that can be easily understood even though they might seem similar to poker or blackjack. Play is similar to Las Vegas or Reno, but the rules and payoffs are different—sometimes confusing—stacking the odds in favor of the house.

Another disquieting thing about gambling in Costa Rica is that there is almost no government regulation. I doubt very much that the house cheats. It doesn't have to cheat, since the odds are so much in its favor, but there is little or nothing to prevent cheating from happening.

Having bad-mouthed Costa Rica gambling casinos, I now have to admit that several friends disagree with me. They claim that the odds and your chances of winning are pretty much the same here as in Las Vegas or Atlantic City. I'll suspend further judgment until such time as I win something.

WHAT DO YOU *DO* **IN COSTA RICA?**

Whenever a Costa Rican resident goes home to the United States or Canada to visit friends and relatives, one of the most frequently asked questions is, "What in the world do you *do* all day in Costa Rica?" The question is accompanied by the same look of pity I might give a friend who is hopelessly addicted to soap operas or *Family Feud* reruns.

For some reason people picture our lives in Costa Rica as total boredom. They see us sitting in a jungle and killing time by counting army ants, or snoozing the day away in a hammock tied between two coconut palms. There's nothing wrong with these pastimes—only I never was good at numbers, and I seldom have time for luxuries such as hammocks.

When asked this question, my inclination is to return a look of pity and inquire, "What do *you* do all day long in that boring place where *you* live?" However, I usually contain the sarcasm and simply reply, "It isn't what I *do*—it's what I *don't* do. I don't mow lawns, fix plumbing, or wash the car. My wife doesn't do laundry, make beds, or wash windows. We pay $2.50 an hour to have somebody take care of those chores so that we can do things we *want* to do rather than chores we *have* to do."

The following is an example of a typical day in my life in Costa Rica. This is what I *do* all day:

5:15 A.M. A band of howler monkeys happen to have bunked down for the night in the trees behind our house. With incredibly loud roaring calls—sounding like wounded jaguars—they warn neighboring bands where they are. Answering growls and roars come from all directions; there are at least a half-dozen troupes in our vicinity. My wife does not notice; she's used to garbage collectors making noise back home; she can sleep through anything. During my working career early rising was part of the daily routine. So naturally, now that I'm retired, the first thing I do when I wake up every morning is roll over and take a little nap.

6:00 A.M. Time to get up and enjoy another leisurely day in paradise. Since our usual bedtime is 9:30 P.M., we've had plenty of rest. Coffee on the veranda is next on the agenda. The rich aroma of Costa Rican coffee finally awakens Sherry. While waiting for the coffee to finish brewing, I go outside to water the papaya plants and ferns; the gardener won't be coming this week because of his mother-in-law's birthday.

6:15 A.M. We settle back in the wooden rockers we bought in Sarchí and enjoy our steaming coffee. Parrots scold one another as they chatter and flit about the forest, only a few yards from our veranda. Chacalacas, motmots, and other mysterious birds add their voices to the morning serenade. When sunbeams begin striking the forest floor, the monkeys finally shut the hell up and start leaping from tree to tree along their "monkey trails" as they move toward today's feeding area. It could be a ripening fruit tree, flowering vines, or whatever else is on their seasonal menu. On the ground below our veranda, pizotes and armadillos scurry about as they scrounge breakfasts of insects and fallen fruit on the forest floor. Another sunrise in paradise.

6:30 A.M. Over our second cup of coffee, we start planning our day. "Today for sure," we resolve, "we'll go to the beach to jog and swim a little." Since the beach is only 100 yards from our house, that doesn't seem like such a radical resolution. But somehow the unexpected always happens. We haven't been swimming in weeks. But come what may, today we play in the surf!

6:45 A.M. Miguel, the teenager who picks up extra money by doing chores around the house, knocks at the door. I put on my sandals and go to the bodega to get paint and brushes so that Miguel can get started painting the wall and iron gate of our garage. They don't really need painting, but he needs work.

7:00 A.M. By now the local bakery is open, so I jump in the car to score some hot croissants for breakfast. Before I can get home with them, a friend flags me down and informs me of a property owners' meeting at 9:00 A.M. This is bad news, because I'd volunteered to teach a computer class at noon, and meetings often go past that time. So much for the beach this morning. OK, then, this afternoon.

7:10 A.M. When I return with the croissants, my wife reminds me that I need to put gasoline in the car because she plans on going shopping in Santa Cruz this afternoon. That's when I remember that the mechanic is expecting me to bring the car in at 7:30 for an oil change and tune-up— important in the dry season, with dusty roads. In Costa Rica you keep your appointments with *el mechanico* and *el dentista*.

7:25 A.M. After a hurried breakfast I drive the car to the gas station–garage for fuel and maintenance. While I'm waiting, my contractor stops by to discuss the new bedroom and bath we're adding to our house. "You must go with me to Santa Cruz tomorrow," he informs me, "to pick out the floor tile." Hmm . . . that means I'll have to cancel tomorrow's appointment with the insurance agent and find someone to take over tomorrow's computer class.

8:15 A.M. The mechanic discovers he doesn't have an oil filter for my car—too late, because he damaged the old one removing it. "On my mother's grave," he swears, "I'll have a new filter before noon." Sure. But this is Costa Rica, and I happen to know that his mother lives in Heredia. Noon tomorrow is more likely.

8:45 A.M. I hitch a ride to the residents' association office with the driver of a dump truck. He extracts a promise from me that I'll help his twin sons with their English lessons this afternoon; there's an exam tomorrow, and they're worried that they aren't prepared. The only time I can do this would be at 1:30, after the computer class. I arrange to meet them at the library then. Looks like I skip lunch again.

9:00 A.M. I arrive at the association meeting, but we have to wait for a quorum before we can transact any business. In the meantime the association president and his wife extend an invitation for cocktails at sunset—at 5:30. (The sun goes down early in the tropics.) I accept the invitation, with the provision that we can be excused by 7:00. We've agreed to meet friends for dinner at a new Italian restaurant on the beach.

11:00 A.M. The meeting over early, I catch a ride to the garage with one of the committee members. Miracle of miracles, my car is ready! On my way back to the house, I encounter a friend who explains that his car won't start and asks whether I could possibly drive him to his house for a toolbox. Of course.

11:30 A.M. I arrive home, hoping to have time for a quick shower before going to the library, where the high school kids will be waiting for their daily one-hour computer session. But Sherry informs me that the hot-water system isn't working. That means I'll have to find out where the electrician is working this afternoon and ask him to help us. Reluctantly, I take a cold shower.

11:50 A.M. Just enough time for Sherry to drop me off at the library. On the way she tells me that our maid invited us to attend her daughter's confirmation on Sunday and that the Wentworths want us to come to their ranch to see their newborn colt on Sunday afternoon. That means no beach time Sunday either.

Noon. I arrive at the library on time, but to my dismay one of the computers is having an intermittent hard-disk problem. That means I'll have to stay after the tutoring session to isolate the trouble; we can't afford to lose one of the library's seven computers.

Then I remember—I had promised to stop in and see an invalid friend this afternoon. Somehow I have to find time today, because tomorrow is accounted for, as well as the day after. Maybe I can stop by after I fix the computer and still make it to our friends' house for sunset cocktails—provided my wife finishes with her shopping and picks me up at 4:00 P.M. as she promised.

I firmly resolve that Monday, come what may, we're going to the beach to jog and swim. Then I remember: Monday's the day the homeowners chose for their semimonthly beach cleanup get-together. Oh, well, at least we'll be on the beach.

But to get back to the question, "What in the world do you *do* all day long in Costa Rica?" The answer is, "We wake up in the morning with absolutely nothing to do, and by noon we know we'll never catch up!"

MISCELLANEOUS **INFORMATION**

ELECTRICITY The same as in the United States or Canada—110 volts alternating current. Short power failures are common. Keep candles and matches in a place where you can find them in the dark.

TIME Costa Rica is on Central Standard Time, but because the length of the days is virtually unchanged over the seasons, daylight saving time is not observed, therefore time is set back one hour from U.S. time.

HOLIDAYS Sometimes it seems as though every time I go to the bank to conduct business, it's closed for a holiday. Costa Rica celebrates more than a dozen national holidays and uncounted numbers of local fiestas that call for closing the bank. Watch the *Tico Times* for announcements of upcoming holidays, and plan your official business accordingly. The country's biggest celebration starts a couple of days before August 2, when thousands of people walk along the highways in a pilgrimage to Cartago to honor the national saint, the Virgin of Los Angeles. Drive cautiously at this time.

January 1: New Year's Day

March 19: St. Joseph's Day (patron saint of San José)

Easter Week: Thursday through Sunday

April 11: Juan Santamaria's Day (national hero)

May 1: Labor Day

June 29: St. Peter and St. Paul's Day

July 25: Anniversary of Annexation of Province of Guanacaste

August 2: Virgin of Los Angeles Day (patron saint of Costa Rica)

August 15: Mother's Day

September 15: Independence Day

October 12: Columbus Day

December 8: Feast of the Immaculate Conception

December 24 and 25: Christmas Eve and Christmas

RELIGION Costa Rica is predominantly Catholic but also has a sizable Protestant population. In the village near our home, I would estimate that as many as 30 percent of residents are not Catholic, yet they seem to be extraordinarily tolerant and accepting of other religions. Yes, there can be rivalry between Protestants and Catholics in local politics, with the priest trying to get as many of his parishioners appointed to town councils and committees as possible and the Protestant preachers doing quite the same. However, I feel it's more of a prestige thing, because the pressure is low key and everyone works together—at least on the community projects in which I've been involved. Priests often wield powerful political influence in a community, which may dismay some Americans—until they recall that some fundamental Christian leaders refuse to accept a church-state separation back home and are hip-deep in local and national politics.

Common-law marriages are common in Costa Rica, especially in rural areas, and are regarded as perfectly normal. Couples often live together for their entire lives, raising children and grandchildren without any thought of formalizing their relationship. (This practice was originally due to the scarcity of priests to perform weddings.)

INCOME TAX U.S. citizens living abroad must file income taxes. You can file through the U.S. Embassy, and you have until June 15 (instead of April

15). If you operate a business or generate income in Costa Rica, you are entitled to a $70,000 deduction, provided you live outside the United States at least 330 days of the year. (See your U.S. tax accountant for details. Not all can qualify.)

You are also required to file with the Costa Rican government on all income earned in the country; income earned abroad is exempt from Costa Rica taxes. Your attorney can file these forms. You also have to file an income tax statement for any corporation that owns property, even if there's no income. You won't pay taxes, but there is a fine for not filing.

A caveat here: I am not a tax expert. Please check with someone who is *before* making tax decisions. ■

CHAPTER NINE

A HEALTHY **COUNTRY**

Costa Rica is a healthy place to live. The United Nations recently noted that Costa Rica is in first place in Latin America for development of preventive and curative medicine, ranking with the United States and Canada among the twenty best in the world. Infant mortality is lower in Costa Rica than in the United States, and the average life expectancy is longer. This is not happenstance; the Costa Rican government spends a great deal of money on health care.

For example, in many Third World countries you play a game of Russian roulette when choosing a restaurant. A dining room can look wonderful, with white tablecloths, gleaming silverware, and tuxedo-attired waiters, but the kitchen can be a virtual cesspool. Not so in Costa Rica. If a restaurant looks good, then its kitchen will probably be just as nice. I've found very few places where I would hesitate to eat, and I've never been served spoiled food. (I can't say that about some restaurants in the United States.) This is due in some measure to the high quality of the underground water supply but also to the Ticos' natural inclination toward neatness and order. The level of cleanliness of Costa Rican restaurants is remarkable.

Another factor in restaurant safety is the relative scarcity of houseflies in most parts of the country Costa Rica. Since this is the tropics, you might expect to see more insects than you would in the temperate zones of North America, and you do, but in balance. For some reason you'll see remarkably few houseflies, true villains in spreading disease. In San José and other towns on the Central Plateau, you can eat outside at a sidewalk cafe without sharing your lunch with flies. This seems strange to visitors from North America's Midwest, where the fly population blooms in the summer to a plague. Yes, an occasional fly might drift past, curious as to what you are having for lunch and hoping to join you, but nothing like you expect back home in the summer.

The same thing goes for mosquitoes: In the dry season they are often as scarce as houseflies. In many areas of Costa Rica, people don't use window screens. (I wouldn't advise this, because you never know what might fly into the bedroom at night.) However, when in an area where dengue fever is known, mosquito repellent is essential. Mosquitoes can carry this flulike illness, which has also appeared in the southeastern United States. So far it's affected only a few parts of Costa Rica: around Puntarenas and Cañas. A continuing campaign to wipe out the particular mosquito that carries the virus is under way.

YOU CAN DRINK THE WATER! As part of its commitment to serving the public, the Costa Rican government has spent large sums of money on water and sewage treatment. Unlike the case in most Mexican and Central American cities, safe drinking water is found in San José and other major towns around the country. Most smaller towns have excellent-quality water, as do most hotels, where drinking water comes from safe wells. The government strictly monitors these water systems, even private ones used by a handful of people. Every two months, at a minimum, tests are made for purity.

MEDICAL **CARE**

The U.S. health care system, with its exclusion of nearly forty million citizens from the ranks of the medically insured, is a major reason some folks think favorably about living in a country where health care is not only available but affordable. In a typical U.S. hospital, for example, patients

with Medicare coverage usually pay more—just for the deductible share of an operation—than the total surgical and hospital bill would cost in Costa Rica!

Should you visit an emergency room in the United States, you would have to provide proof of a hospitalization plan or a personal credit card. If you have neither, you could be told to get lost. If you have Medicare, you will find many doctors who won't accept it. When one goes to an emergency room in any government hospital in Costa Rica, there is no mandatory charge for resident, visitor, or even someone in the country illegally! If you can pay, they appreciate it, but you will never be turned away. This affordable medical system is another of the benefits Costa Rica enjoys because there is no military or defense industry to absorb resources. Statistics show that the general level of care is equal or superior to that in the United States—and it's available to all citizens, not just those who can afford premiums.

Obviously, the level of health care and facilities cannot be the same in rural and isolated communities as in the metropolitan area of San José. Yet the government tries. To ensure that most villages have medical backup, a system of mandatory medical service sends newly graduated doctors to remote or rural settings for a one-year period. The new doctors have to work for minimum wages for this time as a way of repaying the country for the education received in state universities.

Why is quality health care inexpensive in Costa Rica? A prominent physician (in private practice in San José) explained it this way: "Here, our government considers medical care a public service and obligation, just as it considers education and highways a public responsibility. The government builds hospitals and trains medical specialists to serve the people, not as a business. But in the United States, medical care is a profit-making industry, a big business where profits are maximized to the highest point people can pay. Here, a doctor working for a government clinic earns between $800 and $2,000 a month. In the USA, where doctors work for profit, $20,000 a month is more common."

The doctor went on to say, "Where there is no competition, medical specialists can charge what they like. But here in Costa Rica, we have competition between our free, public hospitals and private clinics staffed with private doctors such as mine. We private doctors must keep our fees in line or we lose our patients to free clinics."

MEDICAL BILLS In San José a routine visit to a private physician's office costs between $35 and $50. As of summer 2004 a day in a first-class private hospital costs about $150. (Hospital food is excellent, by the way, not the skimpy, tasteless food we're used to in U.S. hospitals, but delicious and usually more than you can eat.) That $150 rate is at one of the country's most expensive hospitals—for a private room, a private bath, and a color television, plus an extra bed and meals for an *acompañate*, or companion. (It's customary for a family member or friend to spend the night in your room after an operation or when you are in serious condition, at no extra charge.)

If you are willing to put up with sharing a bath with the room next door and can do without your own private phone, the cost drops to almost half. A day in a first-class hospital in Costa Rica costs about the same as a moderately priced hotel room! Compare these prices with those in your community. In the United States if you can get out of a hospital for less than $1,500 a day, just for the room, consider yourself lucky.

CHOOSING A **DOCTOR**

Foreign residents can "buy into" the Social Security system (*Caja*, as it's called in Costa Rica) by paying $40 to $50 a month and then going to government hospitals for treatment. However, since medical care is free, it isn't surprising to find the public system well used and crowded. When people don't feel quite up to snuff, they traipse off to the hospital to see a doctor. Of course, for emergency treatment there is no problem—you are seen immediately—but for an ordinary office visit with a government doctor, you could find yourself standing in line or sitting in the waiting room for a long while. For elective surgery you can expect a wait of several months for your turn.

However, there is a better way: Choose a family doctor who is in both public and private practice. See him or her as your private doctor by making an appointment whenever you have a minor problem and paying for an office visit. But if something expensive ever comes up, such as a major operation, your doctor will check you into the government hospital for free treatment—by the same doctor.

Even if a patient chooses a private doctor and uses a private hospital, costs are ridiculously low compared with those in the United States. For example, in San José the typical bill for a gallbladder operation is $2,500, and for an appendectomy, $1,200 to $1,800.

Again, for those with Medicare, be aware that you're not covered outside the United States. However, those under seventy years of age can buy a health insurance policy from the National Insurance Institute (INS). The last time I checked, the premiums were approximately $500 annually per adult and $250 annually per child. Individual premiums are based on several factors, including age and health history (just like any insurance policy). Several clubs and organizations offer insurance with a group discount (usually 10 percent). Among these are the Association of Residents of Costa Rica (ARCR), the American Legion, and the Canadian Club; sometimes a property owners' association can obtain the discount. An example of medical insurance for expatriates: You can enroll through the Residents' Association ARCR, and take advantage of their special arrangement with the National Insurance Institute for about $37 to $58 monthly per family. Of course, you have to belong to ARCR, with an annual membership fee of $50 to $100 per year. (Remember that as a member of the Residents' Association, you are entitled to many other benefits that have nothing to do with health insurance.) Some plans allow you access to any doctor, hospital, clinic, lab, pharmacy, or provider of medical goods and services of your choice. Under other policy plans, you are given a list of affiliated providers.

With a typical policy, 80 percent of medical costs are covered to about $14,000 or $20,000 per year. (This may sound low, but for Costa Rica it's usually sufficient protection.) Covered are costs of a private room, postoperative care, medicines, lab tests, X-rays, CAT scans, cardiograms, therapy, home care, and support systems. For surgical fees the policy pays 100 percent, up to the maximum set level. As is the case with similar policies in the States, you choose from among the hospitals, clinics, and physicians recognized by the plan. When you join you receive a book listing medical providers, which is updated yearly. The list offers a choice of almost 500 physicians, 15 clinics or hospitals, and almost 100 pharmacies. Dental and eye care are *not* covered. After you've been insured for a year, 80 percent of prescription drugs are covered.

All retirees we interviewed swear by the quality of Costa Rican medical care. I can tell you my personal experience: I went to a doctor with a bad case of the flu, severe back and neck pain, and a fear that I had pneumonia. The doctor decided that I was going to be OK, but he suggested that I go to the hospital for a checkup and a rest. "It costs less than a hotel," he explained.

I requested a shared room, but since the hospital wasn't full, they did not put another patient in with me; essentially, I received a private room for a two-bed ward rate. After three days of tests, medication, and tender loving care (plus great meals), I was presented with a bill that made me feel even better. The entire cost of three days in the hospital, including electrocardiogram, blood tests, and X-rays, was less than if I had stayed in a moderately priced hotel and dined in ordinary restaurants for those three days!

DUAL SYSTEM After graduating from medical school, many Costa Rican doctors go to universities in the United States for further study and to do residencies. This is particularly true for specialists; since Costa Rica is such a small country, there aren't enough patients with the same problem to give a doctor the opportunity to see the wide variety of patients needed to get experience in his or her specialty.

I asked a physician from the United States who had retired to Costa Rica some years ago, "Why would a Costa Rican doctor who does a residency in the United States or Canada return here to work for Costa Rican medical earnings?"

"You have to understand," he replied, "that most doctors only work half-time for the government. The rest of the time, they work for them-selves. Take the case of a cardiologist who charges $50 an office visit. If this doctor sees five patients a day, that's $250 a day, or about $50,000 a year, plus his salary from the government. When you consider that income taxes and the cost of living are far less here, and that high mal-practice premiums aren't necessary, a huge percentage of the doctor's earnings are available for savings or investment. Even though Costa Rican doctors earn a fraction of what U.S. doctors do, they live here just as well or better, and they can live in Escazú instead of Kalamazoo!"

HOSPITALS IN **SAN JOSÉ**

Three large Social Security system hospitals provide San José with round-the-clock emergency care—with regular hours for laboratories, X-rays, pharmacies, and doctors' appointments. These are the Calderón Guardia, San Juan de Díos, and Mexico. Some private hospitals are the Clinica Santa Rita, the Clinica Biblica, and the Clinica Catolica, all excellent hospitals—the Clinica Biblica being the newest and most modern—that offer the same services as the government hospitals but with no waiting for elective medical care. Note that the term *clinica* usually indicates pri-vate hospitals or clinics, available to anyone.

Next to the Clinica Biblica is the Clinica Americana, an office complex with a group of English-speaking doctors, most of whom did residency in prestigious U.S. university hospitals. The KOP Medical Clinic in Escazú specializes in treating foreigners, with a staff that speaks English, French, Spanish, and Japanese. They offer a wide range of services, including obstetrics, gynecology, pediatrics, and dermatology.

Some emergency rooms specialize; for example, Hospital Mexico specializes in heart problems, and San Juan de Díos has a burn center. All towns of any size will have a hospital, and those that are too tiny often still have a doctor or paramedic and emergency equipment.

The latest and most impressive addition to Costa Rica's medical care system is Hospital CIMA San José, which is located in Escazú. This is one of the largest, most modern facilities in Central America, offering com-plete clinical laboratory services, radiology—including the only open MRI in Central America—and a full range of medical and surgical specialties. The hospital is affiliated with Baylor University in Dallas, Texas.

MEDICINES AND LIFE **EXPECTANCY**

Most prescription drugs cost slightly less in Costa Rica than in the United States, but for Costa Ricans, prescriptions are horribly expensive. Note that Americans commonly spend more for hypertension and cholesterol-lowering medications and other drugs every month than the average Tico *earns* in a month. Costa Rican physicians are reluctant to prescribe drugs unless the patient absolutely needs them, such as antibiotics to halt an infection.

However, according to 2002 statistics, the life expectancy in the United States was 76.9 years. In Costa Rica the life expectancy was 76.22 years. That would indicate that after spending thousands of dollars a year for the latest pharmaceuticals and availability of the most ultimate in high-tech medical treatment, the average American lives only *eight months* longer than the average Tico! Go figure!

REST **HOMES**

Care for infirm elderly patients is excellent in Costa Rica, with the cost paid for by the government. However, I believe that this is something available only to long-term residents who become infirm after becoming *pensionados* or *rentistas.*

A government facility probably won't be suitable for a foreigner because of language and communication problems. But several private full-care facilities are able to address the needs of non-Spanish-speakers. (At least one of these offers specialized care for Alzheimer's patients: Golden Valley Hacienda in Alajuela; also in Alajuela is the Villa Comfort Geriatric Hotel, which specializes in folks who are not bedridden but who need care in everyday living.) The cost is about $1,500 a month for round-the-clock care.

A facility in Los Yoses, the Hogar Retiro San Pedro, was given high praise recently by an American woman for the care there. Another facility is the Hogar para Ancianos Alfredo y Delia González in Heredia. This one is in the process of starting something new in Costa Rica: a residence-development of individual cottages for senior citizens who do not require full care. Housekeeping services and meals will be provided, as will recreational facilities and physical therapy services. In addition to medical care, the facility will have recreational, hobby, arts, and travel programs for its people. Residents must be over sixty-five and able to purchase a cottage. A catalog can be obtained by writing to Apdo 138 in Heredia.

Since the last edition of this book, several new private facilities have opened, thus reflecting the growing expatriate population in Costa Rica. The Web page www.geriatriaonline.com/internacionales/costarica.htm lists nine nursing care facilities. If the patient is not fluent in Spanish, my recommendation is to personally check out the facility and speak to the employees to see if indeed they can communicate. Management can exaggerate the English-speaking ability in order to gain a new patient.

DENTISTS

The University of Costa Rica trains medical specialists of all kinds, including highly skilled dentists, periodontists, and orthodontic surgeons. Like medical care, dental care in Costa Rica is affordable. I go to an English-speaking dentist in Pavas who has a very modern clinic. After he received his degree in Costa Rica, my dentist did postgraduate work in the United States.

When asked about Costa Rican dental prices compared with those in the United States, the dentist replied, "Depending upon where you live in the United States, dental care there can be three to six times as expensive. For example, in Costa Rica the standard price for a porcelain cap is $135. In Los Angeles the same work costs from $600 to $700. A bridge typically costs $375 here, but a similar job in Los Angeles would cost at least $1,800. I've had patients who fly here, pay for their hotel, food, and airfare—and still save money."

What about quality? "Dental work in Costa Rica is equal to that done in the USA," he replied. "There is absolutely no difference in the competency of the dentists. However, the quality of dental laboratory work is usually better here in Costa Rica. Don't misunderstand, the USA also has excellent dental labs, but because they can get the work done cheaper in the Philippines, many dentists routinely send bridgework and dental caps overseas to low-cost laboratories. The quality just isn't up to the standards of Costa Rican or American labs. If I were to have caps or bridgework done in the USA, I'd certainly insist that my dentist use an American dental laboratory."

Charges for dental work vary widely, depending on the part of the country in which you live and on the financial status of the dentist's clientele. You'll pay more in the more affluent suburbs of San José and less in small cities in the provinces. Many smaller towns and few villages have no dental services other than visiting dentists who are sent in by the government to take care of schoolchildren's teeth.

Along with cosmetic surgery, cosmetic/restorative dentistry is becoming a big business here, with huge savings over the cost in the United States or Canada. People have reported savings of $6,000 to $18,000 over prices quoted in the United States and Europe. They've reported satisfaction with the treatment and quality of the dentists.

PLASTIC **SURGERY**

Costa Rica has gained worldwide recognition for another of its medical services: reconstructive surgery, commonly known as plastic surgery. San José is becoming known as "Beverly Hills South" because of the number of people coming here for body renewal. Several excellent surgeons specialize in face-lifts, liposuction, breast reconstruction, and other corrections of nature's mistakes. Not only are Costa Rican plastic surgeons ranked among the best in the world, but their fees are based on Costa Rican medical standards: in a word, inexpensive.

Why would Costa Rica be so popular with those wanting to rid themselves of wrinkles? Besides affordable costs and quality surgery, it turns out that San José is a perfect place to slip away to have an operation because of its climate—never hot, never cold—which makes recuperation faster, safer, and more comfortable. Since the healing process takes three or four weeks, many patients find this a great time to learn Spanish in one of the many "total immersion" schools around the city. These schools provide for homestays with a Costa Rican family and have small classes or even individual instruction if you prefer.

Another attractive thing about Costa Rica as a base for cosmetic surgery is that many folks feel embarrassed about having their friends and family know they are going to have it done. Therefore, a growing number of them vacation in Costa Rica, where they are unlikely to run into acquaintances; they have the operation; and they return home a month later, when all traces of the surgeon's handiwork have disappeared.

What does all this cost? Happily, the cost of a face-lift, a breast job, or a tummy tuck with liposuction—including surgery, postoperative care, and hospital stay—is less than one might pay just for three days in a hospital in the United States! For example, a complete face-lift costs from $2,000 to $4,000, plus $1,100 for the operating room and two recovery days in the hospital. The same operation in New York or Los Angeles would be $22,000, plus a lot more for the hospital.

San José's leading plastic surgeon is Dr. Arnoldo Fournier, who did his residency in reconstructive surgery at New York's Columbia University and who has the oldest established plastic surgery practice in Costa Rica. Dr. Fournier charges $800 to $1,200 for an eyelid operation when done separately. Nose surgery or liposuction to abdomen and thighs costs about $1,500 to $4,000, compared with U.S. rates of about $15,000 for the same procedures.

How safe is it? Costa Rican hospitals are excellent, with all modern equipment. Personnel are highly trained. Dr. Fournier points out, "Most of my surgery is done under local anesthetic and sedation. The patient is given some pills a couple of hours prior to the operation, and intravenous medication is given by an anesthesiologist during surgery. This is much safer than using a general anesthetic. Some patients just stay one night in the hospital and then check into a bed-and-breakfast for a few days. Others prefer to stay awhile, since hospital rooms don't cost any more than a first-class hotel." For information about plastic surgery, go to www.drfournier.com/ing. ■

CHAPTER TEN

THE REAL **ESTATE GAME**

Most North Americans feel at home in Costa Rica's city and suburb middle-class neighborhoods throughout the Meseta Central. They don't feel the need to group together—living in compounds or sealed-off neighborhoods as expatriates do in many other foreign countries. Because Costa Ricans and North Americans are so similar in personality and world views, most expats feel right at home with their neighbors. Since juvenile delinquency isn't out of control in residential areas here, and because neighborhood kids are generally well behaved, Americans don't feel threatened as we might in some lower-economic areas back home. For these reasons, the price range of housing in Costa Rica is very wide, with inexpensive housing available in perfectly acceptable neighborhoods and towns to elegant "view" homes on mountain slopes and beach palaces.

Granted, North Americans do tend to congregate in the more expensive areas—nice homes, condominiums, and plush housing developments. But not everyone can afford to live in these neighborhoods, and not everyone wants to live in an English-speaking enclave. Therefore, you'll find foreigners scattered all over the Meseta Central and, in fact, all around the country.

One expatriate who has lived here for nearly twenty years with his family of five said, "We live in a Costa Rican barrio with Ticos who are typical of most Costa Ricans I know. They love their family, neighborhood, and country, and [we] all work together at watching out for one another. Our home has never been broken into, and we don't live in a fortress. We have no walls, pit bulls, Dobermans, or security systems. Five minutes and a crowbar could gain entry."

Not only are foreigners right at home in city and suburban areas of Costa Rica, but they also find that they are accepted without any fuss in rural settings and villages away from the Meseta Central. This is something you'll definitely not find in the rest of Central America or even in Mexico. In other cultures, a gringo family living in a native community would stand out like a pig wearing a toupee. Your neighbors would look at you as more than a little eccentric, and you would feel bewildered and lonely because the culture is so different. Not so in Costa Rica. I know many gringos who enjoy living in rather humble (and inexpensive) lodgings in a picturesque village, and their neighbors are proud that foreigners would like them so well that they'd want to be neighbors.

This extraordinary flexibility as to where it's possible to live presents a wide variety of alternatives. You can live almost anywhere you want to, and you can buy or rent a range of housing that's almost infinite.

RENTING

Real estate values in Costa Rica don't seem to have dramatic ups and downs, rather a slow but steady appreciation over the years. Real estate will climb upward slightly and rest on a plateau for a while. It has recently resumed a gentle upward trend. This is true at least for the Meseta Central. Some hot beach properties will always rent for whatever the market will stand, and rents in these areas fluctuate with the season. A tip: To get the best dollar value when renting in a beach area, make your deal in September or October—the slowest months of the year—when homeowners are eager to have tenants through the rainy season. At that time you have bargaining power.

When you first arrive in Costa Rica, you are likely to want to rent for a while, to get an idea of where you want to live. Neighborhoods vary greatly in quality of shopping, access to transportation, compatibility of neighbors, and, of course, price. There are some areas where you definitely wouldn't want to live—you can usually detect "bad vibes" quickly—and there are other areas that may look great at first, but later you could be sorry you didn't know about another, more interesting neighborhood. Take your time when looking for a place to live, and ask many questions of fellow expatriates.

To get an idea of what you might have to pay to rent a house or an apartment, check the *Tico Times* classifieds for a wide range of rents. The last time I looked—in fall of 2004—houses and apartments were offered at rents ranging from $250 to $2,500 a month (and even higher). While the $2,500 place should be spacious and luxurious, chances are the $250-a-month place could be perfectly livable and just as nice as places back home that rent for twice that amount. Don't rent on price alone, however; check out the neighborhood closely.

For many Costa Rican families, the idea of paying even $250 a month is prohibitive. (Remember, that $250 is a monthly salary for many Ticos.) So if you are looking for the rock bottom in rents, check the classifieds in the Spanish-language newspaper *La Nación*. The ads in that paper are read by local people who do not have the ability to pay higher rents.

Most people, when trying out Costa Rica for livability, don't enter into long-term rentals or sign leases until they are certain they want to settle in for a long time. An ideal way to savor living in the country, particularly on the Meseta Central, is to rent an apartment by the month or the week.

Short-term rentals are particularly useful when determining which neighborhood you'd like to settle in. San José has several *apartotels*, small furnished apartments complete with cable TV, telephone, and cooking utensils—in short, everything you need for a trial of Costa Rican living.

Another excellent way of discovering whether you like a neighborhood or a city is to rent a room in a Costa Rican home. Because of pressure on hotels for tourist rooms a few years back, many private families converted spare bedrooms into rentals for the busy seasons. They're delighted to host North Americans on their visits, to take them into their homes and treat them as part of the family. Another possibility is a bed-and-breakfast located in the neighborhood you want to investigate. The owners can provide invaluable information about the area.

BUYING **REAL ESTATE**

Many if not most countries in the world severely restrict the rights of foreigners to buy property. Some absolutely prohibit it. Not Costa Rica; this is one country where you needn't be a citizen or go through all kinds of legal gymnastics in order to own property. If you're financially capable of buying it, it's yours.

The standard recommendation to visitors is to wait at least six months before buying property. However, many catch real estate fever within the first few days of their initial visit and end up buying something anyway. For a while the buying spree in Costa Rica diminished somewhat, but people from all over the world are still plunking down money to buy something—anything—before it's all gone. At the present time, the dollar is weak against the Euro and some other foreign currencies, down some 40 percent over the dollar's peak rate. This makes Costa Rica properties look very attractive to foreigners who desire to move to Costa Rica and puts an upward pressure on prices. Over the past several years the real estate market has been gradually going up at a higher rate than inflation, but from my point of view, many properties are still bargains. My guess is that the boom will continue, with predictable cycles of frequent selling followed by slack periods, just before another sellers' market.

For twenty years armchair experts have been saying that Costa Rica real estate is overpriced, that the market has peaked and is sure to tumble. Overpriced, compared to where? Clearly, you can buy a home in Nicaragua, El Salvador, or Panama for a fraction of the price in Costa Rica.

If you want to live in Nicaragua, be my guest. These same experts have been predicting the collapse of California real estate for twenty years. Yet prices keep going up, despite the fact that you can buy cheap property in places like Oklahoma, Nebraska, or Kentucky. The reason Costa Rica and California real estate keeps appreciating is a basic principle called "supply and demand." When a surplus of buyers feel they'd rather live in San José than Managua, prices will be higher in San José. Should they prefer Santa Barbara to Sioux City, home prices will rise to meet the demand.

MORTGAGES As an indication of how many foreigners are buying real estate in Costa Rica today, private banks have started financing sales by granting mortgages. Previously, this was unheard of; sales had to be handled by cold cash up front. Of course, the loan will be in dollars, and the interest rates are somewhat higher than you'd pay up north. (A friend is paying 8 percent variable on a fifteen-year loan.) You have to be a resident or your residency in progress or else you may pay an extra 1 percent interest. I hope I'm not making this sound easy, because the few people I know that have received financing had to wade through complicated applications and provide letters from their home bank and/or employer. Obviously, banks are concerned that you can and will pay off the mortgage rather than walk away and leave them with a foreclosure.

TICOS ARE *NOT* NAÏVE! Many newcomers to Costa Rica have the mistaken notion that there are two prices for real estate: the *Gringo price* and the *Tico price.* They believe Ticos are simple, naïve country folk and will ask less money from another Tico than from a foreigner. Therefore, the trick (they believe) is to have a Tico do the negotiating for you. They also believe that bargain real estate can be had by dealing with Ticos, because most Ticos do not fully realize the value of their properties.

First of all, it is more than a little arrogant for strangers to come to Costa Rica and assume that they know more about the real estate market than Costa Rican landowners, who have lived here all their lives and are thoroughly familiar with selling prices. To think they might sell property at less than its value to another Costa Rican is a little naïve on the part of the prospective buyer. When we are talking about desirable properties— those with ocean views, or in pleasant neighborhoods with elegant homes—realize that virtually *all* of these properties are owned either by wealthy Tico families, North Americans, or Europeans, none of whom are naïve or ignorant of the value of their property.

Obviously, land isolated from the city, up in the mountains, accessible by dirt road, will usually be owned by Ticos who have only a vague idea of the value of their properties. Who does know? Certainly not a newcomer to the region. If that's the kind of land you want, having a Tico bargain for you makes sense only because the landowners probably can't speak English. But it is a mistake to think that you can pick up land like this at below-market price because these are simple people.

BUYING A HOUSE FOR INVESTMENT Sometimes people will buy their dream home now, planning on renting it out until the day retirement rolls around. Usually this works out fine, particularly if they find amiable renters who are temporary, and who clearly understand that when the owners need the house, it must be vacated. The key here is to be sure you have "amicable" renters, people you can trust to do the right thing. Like most Latin American countries, the landlord-tenant laws of Costa Rica are tilted to favor the tenant over the landlord. Once tenants are in possession of your home, getting them out can be a problem if they don't want to go. For example, all leases have a minimum validity of three years, no matter if they are written for a shorter term. Therefore a one-year lease could be extended, by the option of the tenant, by another two years. Eviction is a difficult, involved process. On the other hand, the tenant can break a lease simply by walking away and forfeiting the deposit (usually a month's rent). Your rent or lease money should be in dollars, and not in colones, because it's not easy to increase the rents as the value of the colón depreciates. One plus: You enjoy tax advantages on your rental property when you file U.S. income taxes by claiming a loss when you depreciate the home, just as you would if the home were located in the United States. (Consult your tax person about this.)

HOME PRICES Some people are surprised when researching home prices by Internet or looking at ads in the *Tico Times*. There are plenty of places to be found at bargain prices, but you must realize that there are several levels of real estate, from the very cheap to the ultraexpensive. If you're looking for something at the lower end of the scale, Internet and English-language newspapers aren't the best places to look. When property is a real bargain, it won't be on the Internet and it probably won't be in the *Tico Times*. The more affordable properties are usually bought and sold by Ticos, who read *La Nación* or *La Republica*, and who don't have access to the Internet. When the price is much over $60,000, most Ticos and those gringos with ordinary budgets can't buy. The advertisement for these properties goes into places where well-to-do buyers will see it, like on the Internet. The same goes for rents. A house or apartment that rents for $200 a month doesn't need to be advertised in a newspaper or posted on the Internet; word of mouth does it. But a luxury place that rents for $2,000 or sells for $200,000 needs to be exposed to a different market.

LEGALITIES OF **BUYING REAL ESTATE**

Although buying property in Costa Rica should be rather straightforward, it can be tricky if not handled carefully. The following are some points to keep in mind. (For complete details see Chapter 19.)

The first rule: Find a competent, English-speaking attorney to handle the deal for you. This can be a challenge in itself. Inquire around the North American community for recommendations. Some claim that attorneys from one of the "old families" are best, because they know a lot of people in the bureaucracy who can make things easier.

You need a lawyer to be sure the person who is selling you the property actually owns it. This is a common scam: pretending to be the owner of property belonging to an absentee owner and selling it several times to gullible buyers. Your lawyer can also make sure that liens, mortgages, and second deeds aren't attached to the property like warts on a toad.

The second rule: Never count on a verbal contract for anything. A handshake means nothing. You may think you have a deal, but when you return with the cash, someone else owns the place and is moving in furniture. Get everything in writing, after you are completely satisfied that the property is registered and actually belongs to the seller and that the seller is who he or she claims to be. This seems elementary, but you'd be surprised how often buyers don't bother to check!

An attorney told of a client who insisted on buying a piece of view property against the lawyer's advice. The attorney investigated and found that not only was the seller asking twice the value, but he knew the land belonged to someone else, a man who had bought the property twenty years earlier and forgot about it. To complicate matters, the real owner had died and his heirs couldn't be located. That land will be vacant for some time.

Since Costa Rica is so small, the government is able to keep land records in one place, at a central title registry called the Registro de la Propriedad. All liens and attachments must be registered here, and the books are open to the public. Your attorney can look up the *escritura* (deed) and can tell immediately who owns the property, if there are any liens against it, and other items of legal interest. Actually, since the records are open to the public, you can look for yourself by using the Registro's Web site. Always have your attorney double-check you on this, just in case you miss something. (At the end of Chapter 19 you'll find instructions for using the Registro Nacional's Web site.) If you find nothing registered against the piece of real estate, you can safely transfer it to your name. Any outstanding debts or obligations that were not registered are none of your concern. But don't feel smug until you make sure that your lawyer actually registers your new property and the documents are stashed away in your safe-deposit box. Incidentally, another valuable use of information provided by the Registro can be used to check out the legal history of the automobile you are about to buy. You can see who actually holds the title to the car, whether there is a mortgage, and who were previous owners.

The third rule: Do not trust the seller or agent just because he or she is a fellow North American! There's something about Costa Rica that seems to bring out latent tendencies toward larceny in some of our compatriots. An astounding number of confidence men come out of the closet the moment they arrive in Costa Rica. Mostly they are rank amateurs, but since they deal with people like you and me—also rank amateurs in business deals—they can cause much damage before they are finally stopped.

This leads to **the fourth rule:** Make sure the lawyer you hire represents only you, and not both parties! Legally, an attorney can represent both sides; if the first client is a crook—look out.

Brokers and sales personnel aren't regulated in Costa Rica as they are in the United States or Canada. As a result, fast-track wheeler-dealers often get into real estate sales. Some have been known to boost the sales price of property by 50 to 100 percent over the asking price, keeping for themselves the difference between the owner's asking price and the actual sales price. Ask local property owners for broker recommendations, and try to contact the seller personally before closing the deal. When selling property, be wary of a brokerage agreement that doesn't pay you the full sales price less commission! These contracts are known as "net listings" and are illegal in most, if not all, states in the United States, but they are legal in Costa Rica. If the salesperson wants your listing, he or she will agree to a commission-only deal. If not, look for another salesperson.

The fifth rule: Above all, do not be so overwhelmed by the beauty and tranquillity of Costa Rica that you pay the first price asked. Gringos and Ticos alike can display irrational streaks of optimism when valuing their properties. Foreigners, bloodthirsty for profit, can be even worse. Determining the actual value of properties is difficult, because there are no "comparables" to gauge value as we are accustomed to back home, where selling prices are a matter of record. In Costa Rica everyone knows how much is asked for a property, but the actual price is always kept a guarded secret because property taxes and transfer fees are based on the selling price. Incidentally, my attorney tells me that although it's customary to fib a little to tax collectors about the sales price of a property, if you get too creative about your fibs, they can arbitrarily assign a value to the property, no matter how much you paid!

The sixth rule: If you're buying unimproved land, be sure you can bring electricity and year-round water to the property. (Some parts of Costa Rica suffer water shortages every dry season.) Make sure the soil is suitable for a septic system. If sewage can't be absorbed, it will sit around, back up, and make your new home smell like an open cesspool. Another important consideration: electricity. If you have to bring power to your place from the nearest source, it could mean paying for installing many poles and stringing electric lines. The cost could be double the price you paid for that lovely parcel in the mountains.

When buying property, if the title is in the name of a Costa Rican corporation, or *sociedad anónima,* that's good. If not, one of the first things you'll want to do is form a corporation. This may sound strange, but there are several advantages. The section on offshore corporations in Chapter 19 explains how corporations are set up and how they are used in buying property. Although offshore corporations are sometimes used for avoiding taxes, hiding assets, and other marginal activities, there is nothing at all questionable or illegal about using corporations for real estate ownership. The big advantage of property registered in the name of a corporation is the ease of transferring ownership. Instead of going through the expensive and complicated procedure of transferring property to your name, you simply purchase the corporation's stock, take over the books, and you are now the owner.

BEACHFRONT PROPERTY Real estate is booming along both coasts. Prices in some areas are going wild, while other places still have bargains available. The situation is somewhat murky, because some properties that are being bought and sold have tough building and ownership restrictions that you might not be told about until you're ready to start construction. Foreigners are supposedly limited as to ownership of oceanfront property, but they manage to sidestep this law by putting their land into Costa Rican corporations.

Property owners are restricted as to how close to the beach they can build. The most important point to bear in mind is that you cannot actually own beachfront property; it must be leased from the local municipality. Make sure you're comfortable with this concept before deciding on that wonderful stretch of coconut trees and sand.

Chapter 19 discusses beachfront property in great detail, but generally, the law goes like this: The first 200 meters ashore, starting halfway between low-tide and high-tide lines, is the "maritime zone," and it belongs to the municipality. It cannot be sold, but it can be leased. (This lease is called a "concession.") The first 50 meters from the beach is the "public zone," which belongs absolutely to the public, off-limits to construction of any kind.

Construction between the 50- and 200-meter points must have the permission of the municipality. Building permits are sometimes issued only for tourist-related projects. Remember, that $35,000 lot on the beach is not an outright purchase; you actually pay that money for the right to renew a lease every five years. It's yours provided you do everything right—make the lease payments, pay taxes on time, and obey all the rules.

Caution: A seller may claim that an existing building that falls within the first 50-meter mark is legal because it's been "grandfathered." That's possible, but more likely someone in the past ignored the rules and the bureaucracy hasn't gotten around to enforcing the laws. The government could force you to dismantle the buildings and restore the property to its original state, when and if it chooses to do so. Check grandfather clauses with a skeptical eye—and a good attorney.

SQUATTERS

Anyone who has followed the battles between North Americans and squatters in the *Tico Times* is aware of hair-raising stories concerning squatters and legitimate property owners. The popular name for a squatter is a *precaista*. If you're thinking of buying a piece of rural property, you need to be aware of the squatter problem. The problem is with agricultural land, not residential property.

We've all heard stories of North Americans who purchased lovely tracts of forested land with the intention of building a home someday and then, when they returned a few years later, were surprised to find the land cleared and someone farming it.

If the property you are interested in has an extra house and a Tico family living in it, beware. Don't let the seller glibly pass this off as the "caretaker's residence." It could be a squatter's home! "This family takes wonderful care of the place!" the seller might exclaim. "They just never leave the property unattended." The seller should add, "They'll never leave, period!" Make sure you see documents proving that this is indeed a caretaker employee, not a squatter. In order to be an employed caretaker, the employee must receive the legal minimum wage rate, including Social Security, and all other legal benefits. The papers proving all this must be up to date. Insist that your lawyer examine the proof. If someone is paid to simply look over the property on a regular basis, make sure there's a written receipt that he is being paid for this service and is not a squatter himself.

To most of us the idea of someone simply moving in on your property is outrageous; it's trespassing; it's theft! Can this really happen in a law-abiding country like Costa Rica? Aren't property owners protected by the law? Isn't all of this illegal?

Well, it turns out that to an extent, it is legal. There are laws to the effect that unowned or abandoned property is open for homesteading,

just as it was in the early days of the United States and may still be in some western states. These Costa Rican laws were intended to prevent a few wealthy people from hogging land they don't use and don't need. This is precisely what happened in the other Central American countries, where 2 or 3 percent of the people own 90 percent of the good land. One reason Costa Rica is so much better off than its neighbors is that citizens have access to land. The laws are well intentioned and fair. The problem lies in how these laws are interpreted and who is doing the interpreting. Too often the bias is in favor of the squatter.

Just when is a piece of land abandoned? One law, which seems clear, states that after property goes unattended for ten years, whoever has been using the land in a "continuous, open, and peaceful manner" for those ten years may apply for a title. And the person will be successful unless the original owner has a good lawyer and a valid excuse. Another principle of law is that the squatter must show that he had reason to believe the land was abandoned; this means that someone who was being paid to watch your land can be removed if he attempts to take it over for himself. (Remember, you need receipts and canceled checks.)

Typically, the scenario goes like this: A choice piece of unattended property becomes a tempting target for a *precaista*. He'll construct a cabin and plant a crop in the hope that he won't be discovered for a year. If the occupancy is less than a year, it's considered trespassing and is handled by the Ministry of Interior and the courts. If the trespass is less than ninety days, you call the local police, and they are obligated to evict the squatters and "present you" with a paper that confirms that you are the true owner of the property. (If the police fail to act, your lawyer can do something about that.) But let it go a full year and the situation becomes a bit more serious. The owner usually has the option of paying the squatter for his expenses and "improvements" or else going to court. ("Improvements" could be cutting down all your beautiful trees and selling them to make a pasture of your forest.) When the bill is too high—you can be sure it will be padded—sometimes it's cheaper to walk away. Understand, these problems seldom occur anywhere but on agricultural land. Land zoned or used as residential property doesn't fall under the category of this law.

The solution to this problem is a matter of prevention. While you are out of the country, have a friend or a management agent drop by the property at least once every three months. At this point, a simple complaint to the police is usually enough to boot someone off your land. Be sure to keep records of expenses and improvements to the property as proof that you haven't abandoned your land. Paying someone to clear brush once in a while is good enough. Be sure to keep a record of how many hours he worked and receipts for how much you paid him. Any place where there are a lot of foreign property owners, you'll find someone who watches property as a paid service. However, be absolutely sure you know who is caretaking your property, and keep records that he is being paid. My attorney advises, "Hire someone to check on the property, and then hire someone else to check on the person checking on your property." The last thing you want to do is hire a squatter to watch over your property!

Occasionally a problem arises when a foreign resident decides to return to the United States for an extended stay and has to lay off the maid, gardener, or other employees. If the property owner isn't familiar with the laws and neglects to pay workers' benefits such as severance pay, accrued vacation, and year-end bonuses, the employees could feel justified in taking over the land as compensation. Chapter 12 covers this in detail.

However repugnant the idea of squatting may be to you, it is important to operate within the law. After all, *precaistas* have rights, like it or not. One woman who had just purchased some property told me that she had been informed that "the only way to deal with squatters is to burn down their houses," and that's what she intended to do if she ever found any on her property. I was horrified to think of someone on a tourist visa, a guest in the country, taking the law into her own hands! This is the way the problems start, and problems of this nature have been known to escalate into gunfire! Sometimes squatters are well organized and have their own ways of striking back; the best advice is to leave this problem to the law. The law may work slowly, sometimes not at all, but this is better than killing or being killed for a piece of farmland. I have friends who have had no problem kicking the rascals off their land, and the police burned the squatters' shacks themselves.

If you are an absentee owner of undeveloped land and have reason to believe that your property is a target of squatters or property theft scams, you should do the following: Make sure you are the legally registered owner; if you live out of the country, ask your attorney to conduct a title search from time to time to make sure you are still on the title, or at least check the Registro National Web site yourself. Let the neighbors know who you are and that you own the property. Fence the property if possible, and post signs. Have a friend walk the property boundary lines every two or three months and file a complaint against any squatters encountered. If you hire a caretaker or agent to watch the property, make sure you have signed receipts showing that you've paid the caretaker for this purpose. Understand, these precautions are only for undeveloped property that is left untended by absentee owners for long periods.

BUILDING **YOUR OWN HOME**

When my wife and I first visited Costa Rica back in 1972, like all first-time visitors, we began looking for some excuse to stay, some way to earn a living, and we looked at property with dreamy eyes. We fell in love with a marvelous tract of ten hectares of coffee trees perched on a mountain slope overlooking San José. It had a modest owner's home of frame construction and a slightly larger house for the caretaker and his family. The price was only $18,000.

By the time we returned to Costa Rica, two years later, the property had been sold and was back on the market for $26,000. Of course, we just knew that the real estate market had topped at a crazy level, so we reluctantly gave up our dream of owning ten hectares of coffee. However, every return trip brought us a new conviction that we were foolish for not buying something last time, because the market had to be at an absolute top. "It can't possibly go higher!" Today that property would probably sell for $100,000.

This process continued for many years, until we finally stopped kicking ourselves for not buying last time and started seriously looking for property. We found a good deal on a condo near San José, a place with a wonderful view and convenient to everything we needed. But after a while the condo seemed to be frivolous; we found ourselves spending more time away from there, renting places near the Pacific beaches. So a new search began with an exciting possibility: building our own home!

We faced two choices. The first option: a lovely view of the beach—up on the side of the mountain. But this type of lot was a ten-minute drive to the beach; walking was out of the question. The second option was something within easy walking distance of the beach, where we could hear but not see the surf. The bonus was a low price, one-third the cost of a view lot.

On the advice of our lawyer, we decided upon a local contractor rather than one from some other part of the country. The reason: Local people have their own crews and know whom to hire. They also know the local officials and have little trouble cutting through red tape. After interviewing several expats who had experience with local builders, we asked for bids.

The plans were drawn on napkins while sitting at restaurant tables, and ideas were tossed about as to what would be the best design. To our surprise all three building estimates came to the exact same amount, about $40 a square foot for a quality home—sitting 28 feet in the air on one end—of reinforced cement, stuccoed concrete block, and tile. The bonus was that by perching our home on concrete pillars, we would have an eye-level view of monkeys, parrots, and butterflies from our veranda.

When estimating how long it would take to build the house, our contractor wisely said, "I can finish it in three months, *no hay problema.*" But since this is Costa Rica, he promised it would be built in five months. "That way you will be happy if I finish in four months," he said.

A work crew set about cutting just enough trees to lay out the house. I watched over them to make sure they didn't cut too many. They thought this amusing, and I made friends with several of them. They started calling me "don John" (a term of friendship and respect accorded to those older and more wrinkled than you). They still do—long after the house has been completed. As I drive to or from the village, someone is always waving at me and saying, "*Hola, don John!*" I've gotten into the habit of waving at everyone, for fear I might hurt someone's feelings at not being recognized.

Watching over the crew is a good idea, by the way—not because they will loaf, but because when you go away for a few months, contractors have a tendency to take their men and go work elsewhere. You can't blame them, because there is a labor shortage from time to time. They figure they can always get back to your house before you return. It does not always work that way.

As construction got under way, I discovered that we needed some bureaucratic busywork. One required item was a *plano catastral*—a legal description of the property—which was kept at my lawyer's office along with the corporation books for the property. I drove to San José for the required documents. When I announced to the lawyer's secretary that I needed a *plano castrado,* she eyed me with surprise and then explained that I probably wanted a *plano catastral.* It turns out that a *plano castrado* is a "castration plan." I quickly agreed that was not precisely the plan I had in mind! Other requisites were a set of architect's plans and a building permit. *No hay problema,* I was told. What with a little bureaucratic delay, they were delivered to my hands six months after we moved into our house. *No hay problema.*

During the early construction phase, I stayed at a nearby bed-and-breakfast and arose at dawn to hang around the building site and observe the wildlife that is so bountiful at daybreak. Monkeys, coatimundis, parrots, and other animals put on an early-morning show.

Hanging around my building site at dawn brought surprises other than wildlife. I discovered something about the Ticos who worked on my project: Not only did they arrive on time for work, but most were early—quite unlike the case in other Latin countries I can think of. Starting time was 6:00 A.M., and at exactly 6:00 work commenced in earnest. They worked hard, with regularly scheduled breaks, until 3:30 P.M. (a nine-hour day). The famous mañana mentality wasn't apparent on this job. On the other hand, they were well paid by Central American standards and enjoyed a comparatively high standard of living. I'm not saying all Tico workers are like this; I'm only relating my personal experience.

A major problem I feared was that the hubbub of workers, pounding hammers, and general noise, would frighten away the forest wildlife. That would essentially destroy the value of our property, since the forest denizens were to be the showcase of our new home. We were pleasantly surprised when that problem didn't materialize. In fact, during construction an unruly gang of howler monkeys congregated in the trees around the building site and spent hours shouting insults and making caustic remarks in monkey language about my work crew.

Don't misunderstand, our building experience was not all peaches and cream—all expected problems raised their ugly heads, and a few creative problems joined in the fun. We quickly learned a Spanish lesson: the difference between *Hay un problemcito* ("There's a little problem") and *No hay problema* ("There's no problem"). Essentially, it's as follows: *Hay un problemcito translates* "We gotta big problem here, pal, and it's gonna cost big-time dinero." On the other hand, *No hay problema* usually translates "There's a problem, but it ain't my problem!"

However, after four months—a month earlier than promised—we had our dream house in Costa Rica. Would we do it again? Yes, we would. As a matter of fact, we just completed the construction of a new home, after selling our original house. It is about 200 yards nearer to the beach, and a little larger than the other one. However, over the years prices climbed a little higher in our area. Now it's a bit over $40 a square foot for quality construction. That's about what a union carpenter in Los Angeles earns per hour!

REAL ESTATE TIPS FROM LONGTIME RESIDENTS The best advice about how and where to buy property in Costa Rica comes from folks who've lived in the country for some time. They can tell you how much you should pay for property and which attorney would best represent you. They will also know which real estate brokers are professionals and which are beginners or downright unethical.

When José Pelleya of Alajuela was asked why prices sometimes seem to be off the wall, he replied, "I learned in my Contract Law class that the price of a thing is exactly what it will bring. This is especially true here in Costa Rica, because there are no records of buying and selling prices, no 'comparables' at all. People go by word of mouth and rumor about what a neighborhood property sold for. So one crazy buyer paying a crazy price will immediately raise prices all over the area. In the end, most buyers have a price/budget in mind of what they want to pay and can afford; in the end you'll get what you want, you just have to search hard."

Lynn Zamora from Grecia, who dabbles in real estate, made the following comments when asked why the price-per-acre cost of bare land could vary so widely on various sized properties in the same area. Lynn's explanation: "It's a common practice here in Costa Rica to price land depending on how large the entire piece is. For example, a lot that's 600 square meters (approximately one-eighth acre) might have an asking price of $17 dollars per square meter, or $10,200 for the lot (equivalent to $81,600 per acre). To continue the example, in the same neighborhood there is a lot of 1.7 acres. The asking price is $38,000 total (equivalent to $22,353 per acre). Yet an adjoining finca of 206 acres might go for $667,000 (equivalent to only $3,238 per acre).

"There is logic to this method of pricing land. Foremost, the property with the most value here is one with the most street frontage. Therefore the more frontage, the higher the cost. The land way in the back of some large finca, far away from the paved road, is worth much less. Land that has street frontage can be divided into smaller lots for building and sold at pretty hefty prices, as seen in the first example.

"Another thing to remember: Although there's plenty of land for sale here, the great majority of the owners do not really need to sell. They might be happy to sell to some gullible foreigner for double what the land is really worth, because a neighbor once made such a lucrative sale." Then she added, "It is easy to *buy* here but not so easy to sell if someone bought an overpriced property or one that has a problem. And problems are not so easy to spot beforehand, especially when someone comes with an American mindset."

Sheldon Marshall (in a letter to the online newspaper *A.M. Costa Rica*) pointed out the importance of being careful and having the services of a good lawyer. Sometimes bogus salespersons will flash a *plano catastro* (an impressive, authentic-looking plat map that looks as though it could be a deed) as proof that they either own the land or have authority to sell. Marshall warned that "a piece of paper, even covered with official stamps, may be just that—a piece of paper. Anybody can commission a plano catastro. It's just a survey plat, and it proves nothing other than the land in question has been surveyed." He stressed, "If a deal sounds too good to be true, it usually is. If something doesn't feel right, it probably isn't. Don't let the sun and climate go to your head. Keep this in mind, and Costa Rica's a terrific place to be and enjoy." ∎

CHAPTER ELEVEN

BUSINESS **OPPORTUNITIES**

Fifteen years ago, the vast majority of those coming to Costa Rica for long-term stays were traditional retirees. By "traditional" I mean affluent couples about sixty-five years old, just retired after forty years of loyalty to a benevolent company with a nice pension, and looking forward to enjoying their "golden years" and a lifestyle of leisure. Retiring any earlier than sixty-five would have been unthinkable. They pictured a tropical beach house overlooking the surf at Flamingo, or perhaps a stately home perched above Santa Ana with a gorgeous view of the valley and volcanoes in the distance. The goal was a lifestyle that allowed ample time for bridge, cocktail parties, golf with other expatriates, plus an occasional charter fishing trip.

Fifteen years can make a lot of difference. For one thing, the retirement age has dropped—quitting work at fifty is not unusual. For many, retirement isn't voluntarily; that's the age employers like to trim from the payroll. There is no such thing as company loyalty or loyalty to employees today. People are hired for whatever skills needed at the moment—and dropped the minute they're not needed. Many new "retirees" are casualties of the "dot-com" meltdown. Others are simply tired of working for someone else and recall thirty years ago, when

"dropping out" was idealized. In the new millenium, "dropping out" becomes a goal rather than an option.

This creates a restless population of not-yet-ready for retirement people who are itching to do something interesting with the rest of their lives. In fact, the word "retirement" isn't in their vocabulary. These are the youth-oriented activists who in the '60s and '70s used to say, "Don't trust anyone over thirty!" They are determined not to get "old" in the way they perceived their parents to be and are eager to get on with life. They have youthful energy, talent, and workplace skills they don't care to waste by loafing on the beach or swinging in a hammock. If they can't find a good-paying job in Costa Rica, the next option that comes to mind is going into business. And many of them do. Some popular tourists locales have more businesses owned by foreigners than by native Ticos.

A FRIENDLY BUSINESS CLIMATE Many countries severely restrict foreign business investment as a way of protecting their national businesses and industry. Special tax breaks are given to local commerce and roadblocks thrown in the way of foreign investors. There's some justification for this, because many foreign businesses only want to take advantage of cheap wages then ship the products—and the profits—out of the country. But Costa Rica takes a positive attitude toward foreign investment. Outside money is encouraged as a way to spur development, yet labor laws and wage minimums are enforced, giving the average Tico worker enough income that local stores, shops, and businesses flourish.

The end result is that Costa Rica is one of the safest and most attractive countries in Latin America for foreign investment and foreign businesspeople. The government maintains a decidedly pro-American and European slant in regard to financial security and tax laws. One obvious benefit has been the relocation of several high-tech corporations to take advantage of Costa Rica's highly educated and computer literate workforce. This business-friendly climate has earned Costa Rica the nickname of Central America's "Silicon Valley." Companies such as Acer Computers, Microsoft, Abbot Laboratories, General Electric, and Continental Airways have established sizable production facilities here. Intel Corporation's three production facilities here now produce one-third of Intel's computer processor chips, creating thousands of good jobs for Ticos!

Any investment that promotes tourism, creates jobs, and doesn't harm the environment is considered especially welcome here. Another plus: Most foreign investors in Costa Rica live in Costa Rica. For them the whole point of going into business is to be able to enjoy living in Costa Rica. They spend or reinvest profits in the country, further bolstering the economy.

To attract desirable investments, Costa Rica offers generous incentives and tax breaks. Depending on the type of business, there can be a twelve-year exemption from income taxes as well as waivers on import duties. If ecology is concerned—particularly projects involving reforestation—tax exemptions can be forever! Be aware, however, that continuing changes in tax laws may affect some of the tax breaks for tourist-oriented businesses.

Investments of $50,000 or more in specially approved projects qualify the investor for residency and, eventually, a Costa Rican passport. A popular $50,000 investment is in reforestation projects; some businesspeople in Hong Kong are buying these as an insurance policy so that, should the takeover by the Chinese Communists become onerous, they can escape to Costa Rica. With $150,000 the investment can be in any enterprise. To qualify for any of these special investment provisions, you need to proceed with government approval. Your lawyer can help you with this.

Reforestation projects aren't just a matter of deciding to start planting. You need to present detailed plans prepared by an approved forestry technical expert (a member of the Forestry Professionals of the General Forestry Office). If your reforestation project is a good one, you can be eligible for government subsidies (a friend is receiving about $5,000 a year under one of these programs). Once planted, the property can be resold, as long as the purchaser agrees to continue with the reforestation project. In any event, serious questions as to profitability need to be addressed. You must realize that profits, if any, will come a long way down the pike. There's more about reforestation later in this chapter.

GOING INTO **BUSINESS**

Before we delve into the subject of going into business in Costa Rica, you should ask yourself some important questions. Do you really want to move to a beautiful country and spend your time working at a business?

Ask yourself whether you'd be better off bird-watching, swimming, or tanning on the beach instead of doing bookkeeping, tending bar, or changing linens in your bed-and-breakfast. Do you feel up to the challenge of dealing with a quixotic, entangled bureaucracy, in a language you don't entirely understand? And finally, if it's so easy to start the business you have in mind—and make large sums of money from your idea—why hasn't somebody else already filled that niche?

Too often, dreamers feel confident that all that's necessary to become a successful businessperson in Costa Rica is to show up and dazzle the country with entrepreneurship. Well, yes, it happens sometimes, but mostly to those who know what they are doing, employing skills and special knowledge gained from business experience in their home country.

But if you're one of those who needs to be doing something and volunteer work doesn't fill the bill, then you might consider joining the numerous foreign business investors already in Costa Rica.

Many North Americans who go into business in Costa Rica don't bother qualifying under the $50,000 or $150,000 investment laws, since tax advantages accrue to any qualifying business and because a Costa Rican passport isn't an enticement to those already holding U.S. or Canadian passports. Residency papers can be easily obtained under the *residente rentista* provisions of the laws (explained in Chapter 13). Also, your choice of investment doesn't need to be approved by the government.

Since most businesses are registered in the name of a corporation, even a foreigner holding tourist papers can effectively control and manage the enterprise. While it is against the law for a noncitizen to work at an ordinary job without permission, it's perfectly OK to oversee your own business. Discretion is required here, however, since part of the scheme is to create jobs, and if a business owner is doing work that could be performed by a citizen, complaints could arise. I know of one case in which a foreign couple built a small business and managed it entirely by themselves (working very long hours, incidentally) to save the $1.50-an-hour wages they'd have to pay a Tico. Local government officials hinted that perhaps they should hire some help, and the officials were slow in granting permits, as a way of reinforcing the hint, until the couple finally hired much-needed employees.

Some North Americans have done exceptionally well in Costa Rican business ventures. They bring enthusiasm, expertise, and imagination, often re-creating successful enterprises they operated in their home country. One businessman from Illinois, who started a successful beach resort about fifteen years ago, said, "It's interesting to see who makes money here and who goes belly-up. The successful ones are those who come here because of the attractive Costa Rican lifestyle and who go into business as a means of staying in Costa Rica. They usually make money despite themselves. The ones who face one disaster after another are those whose main interest is making a pile of money."

Foreigners often feel they can be successful in tourist-oriented businesses because they understand the wants and needs of other foreigners who visit Costa Rica. That's often the case, and restaurants and bars are popular ventures. However, as in any business endeavor, you should know what you are doing, particularly in the restaurant or bar business; the failure rate in Costa Rica is unusually high.

Real estate sales and development have created fabulous success stories as well as woeful tales of spectacular flops. Too many wheeler-dealer types start developments that look great on paper but never get past the fantasy stage. Be cautious about floating your investments on blue-sky dreams.

You needn't start your own business; numerous in-place enterprises are always available through ads in local newspapers. Of course, just as is the case back home, you need to investigate why the business is for sale. Maybe the reason is too much work, not enough profit, or illness, or perhaps the owner feels it's time to cash in the equity and stash the profit. Don't consider buying a business unless you're competent to handle it and understand exactly why the enterprise is up for sale. What makes you think you can make money at this if someone else failed?

Among the many businesses advertised in the *Tico Times* are bed-and-breakfasts, car rental agencies, pharmacies, travel agencies, and lots of bar-restaurants and discos. Apartment buildings, hotels, and beach resorts are always on the market, as are teak and palm-oil plantations (often not a good idea, as I'll discuss shortly).

Remember, it's just as easy to lose money in Costa Rica as it is back home. For a stranger in a foreign land, it's even easier. You must know what you are doing. Business consultant Ray Nelson says, "My best advice is to come here for six months and look around. Study the existing businesses and find out why some are successful and why others fail.

Above all, don't jump into a business just for the sake of being in business—particularly a business that you don't know much about."

Because of Costa Rica's liberal attitude toward foreign business ventures and sometimes lax regulation, a surprising number of foreigners feel as though they have complete freedom to operate as they wish and that ordinary laws and ethics don't apply. This is probably why Costa Rica draws more than its share of swindlers, crooks, and con artists.

The Costa Rican government does what it can to keep on top of offenders, but it's impossible to do much more than prosecute crooks after the damage has been done. And this rarely happens, because the swindler simply skips the country before the trial date. For this reason look very carefully at any business deal presented to you. All too often ostensibly honest businesspeople surprise everyone by turning out to be swindlers. Make sure you have a good, English-speaking lawyer check with all the proper government agencies and verify the integrity of your deal before risking your hard-earned money.

Popular scams include phony mutual funds, nonexistent banks, and so-called tax-shelter investments; gold mines; hotels and resorts that never leave the drawing board; real estate that is sold to several people or property that didn't belong to the seller in the first place; and teak, macadamia, and jojoba plantations—all the get-rich-quick schemes you can imagine.

After pointing out all the pitfalls of going into business, I have to admit that many people are having fun doing so. You can feel a dynamic sense of progress and excitement in Costa Rica. This is the country of the entrepreneur, of wide-open opportunity, inexpensive land, dependable labor, and relatively honest government. Modern-day Costa Rica is reminiscent of the old frontier days of the United States and Canada, full of success stories about North Americans who've opted to "start all over again." Just be aware that there are failure stories as well.

AGRICULTURE AS **INVESTMENT**

Because of incredibly rich soil and year-round growing seasons, Costa Rica is an agricultural paradise. The country is checkerboarded with crops of all descriptions. Just about anything grows here, with bumper crops the rule rather than the exception. Rich volcanic soil and a rainy season that coincides with the peak growing season makes farming a dream in

Costa Rica. Therefore, agriculture would seem to be one of Costa Rica's best bets for investment. It is, actually, but it can also be Costa Rica's biggest investment disaster for novice farmers and for those who don't understand the ground rules. Just because crops grow well doesn't guarantee you are going to make money.

One longtime agriculturist who has struggled to make a living in Costa Rica said, "Farming is a great way to go broke even if you are an experienced agriculturist. There are too many unknowns and too many marketing problems." He added wryly, "If I had invested the same amount in real estate as I spent trying to get an orange grove started, I would be a rich man by now."

Of course, although growing and harvesting are the nitty-gritty of agribusiness, a third factor, marketing, is truly the key. Without a marketing strategy all your efforts in growing oranges or bananas are in vain and your crops a waste, except for whatever you and your family can eat. One farmer pointed out, "If you don't have a contract, you are banging your head against the wall. What are you going to do with a field full of pineapples without buyers? Local marketing is the only way to move them, but there is only so much local demand. Bananas are the country's top crop, but a little guy can't compete with the huge multinational corporations. Coffee growing is a small-scale operation, that's true, but world prices fluctuate so much that you often can't make money."

One ex-farmer narrated some problems he encountered trying to farm profitably in Costa Rica: "We had some great orchards, with good production, but we couldn't get marketing contacts. Local markets can absorb only so much citrus fruit, and high export costs kept our products out of range for foreign markets. The only money appeared to be in marketing juice. So a few of us citrus farmers decided to invest in a juice extraction plant. But before it could be completed, a government plant went into operation, causing our project to go bankrupt."

Teak plantations have been promoted in Costa Rica for years. According to promoters, raising teak trees is a surefire venture that will pay huge dividends. Forestry experts I've interviewed dismiss this as pure hype. It is true that after an eight-year growth (trees will be about 6 inches tall) they are typically cut and sold for beams or cut into chips to make parquet floors. From what I understand, the profit from this first cutting may not cover the cost of planting and maintenance. Then the trees are allowed to sprout again and left alone for about twenty-five years until they really become valuable enough to use for lumber. The *Tico Times* once ran an interesting series of investigative feature articles on teak as an investment. The controversy is ongoing, so before you invest, do some investigation on your own. You're likely to find investors who feel they've made a mistake and others who are pleased.

Agricultural investors can become enthralled at what appear to be profitable Costa Rican cattle operations. Agreed, some Ticos are exceptionally successful ranchers, but you must realize that they usually inherited the business; and the cost of the land, livestock, and infrastructure are not part of the equation. One longtime resident and entrepreneur in Costa Rican agriculture says that in his experience, "few agricultural operations by newcomers ever become successful. For example, unusual or nontraditional cultivation could be a good idea if you personally are going to run the operation, you really know what you are doing, and you find a unique market niche. But absentee operations run by a "trusted" foreman are more often than not invitations to disaster. If your business will be to produce an agricultural product, you have the know-how to process it into a marketable product (agroindustry), and you are going to oversee all operations personally—maybe you have a fighting chance at success. But this takes more than an amateur."

TOURISM AND **INVESTMENT**

Tourism has become Costa Rica's top industry, bringing in even more cash dollars than the export of coffee or even the number-one crop, bananas. Tourism's importance as an economic resource for the country cannot be overstated; neither can its opportunities for foreign investors be overlooked. Most hotels and tourist facilities constructed in recent years have been financed through outside investment. In recent years, more than 6,000 hotel rooms have been added to the country's inventory. Every week sees new bed-and-breakfasts opening their doors to tourists. Yet despite all this action, we still couldn't find vacancies along the Guanacaste Coast during Christmas week! Instead of hotel room prices dropping because of increased competition, rates edged upward—not drastically, just enough to prove that there is still space for more tourist businesses, albeit with larger vacancy rates than before. Again, do a careful market analysis before adding new rooms to the inventory.

Roy Lent of Escazú has spent thirty-five years in Costa Rica and has an awesome background in business enterprises. During his years here, Roy has been a plant explorer for the Field Museum of Chicago, plant physiologist, plant breeder, high school teacher, real estate broker, graphics designer, black pepper grower, and administrator for a cacao (chocolate) farm. He also has experimented with rubber and raised ornamental plants, hogs, and pejebaye palms. He was once in charge of quality control in a bra factory (really he was). Today Roy does professional Spanish-English translations and constructs Web pages. Below are some of Roy's observations about business opportunities in Costa Rica.

"By far, tourism is the best type of business for the English-speaking foreigner to get into. An exception to this might be opening a high-class restaurant. To succeed in this area, you'd better be a top expert, because activity has a fairly low success rate. On the other hand, fast-food chain restaurants seemingly can't fail! You have to use your imagination. If you can think of an activity that has been successful in other parts of the world but isn't yet offered in Costa Rica, make a study. Don't ask a Costa Rican if he thinks that your proposed new activity will fly. His reaction will be negative almost 100 percent of the time because it's never been done here! (Besides, he's not a tourist.) You decide. If your heart is fixed on having a bar or nightclub in Costa Rica, buy an already-operating place that has all the necessary permits and such. Don't try to start on your own, unless you truly have experience in the field."

ECOTOURISM As pointed out earlier, Costa Rica's environment combines several tourist attractions. Visitors are drawn here to enjoy a unique climate, lovely facilities, gorgeous beaches, and Costa Rica's ecological wonderland. Therefore, with a new awakening of environmental aware-ness on our planet, it's no surprise that Costa Rica attracts large numbers of affluent visitors who insist on seeing these wonders firsthand, sights not available anywhere else on the tourist circuit except in a zoo or a greenhouse arboretum. Tourists go out of their way to come here, to enjoy the sensation of walking through a rain forest hoping to catch sight of a quetzal bird, inhale the odor of tropical blossoms, and hear the bizarre calls of howler monkeys.

Accommodations are a secondary consideration for many of these visitors. If they wanted discos, shopping, and spiffy beachfront hotels, they wouldn't travel all the way to Costa Rica. Most come here for some-thing special. They pay well for the privilege of viewing tapirs, ocelots, beautifully colored butterflies, and magnificent flowering trees, all in their natural settings. This idea of combining vacations with ecological marvels in a tropical paradise is called "ecotourism."

In order to attract visitors, traditional tourist resorts must invest heav-ily in great views, tennis courts and golf courses, luxury rooms, and first-class restaurants. Then after they've sunk a fortune into a project, there's always a danger of someone building an even more expensive resort next door to lure away clientele, making the place obsolete. The facility must be top quality and well maintained to stay even with today's competitive market. Without something special, tourists have little reason to patron-ize a particular resort.

Ecotourism, however, is a game played in a different league. An intriguing feature is that it doesn't always require an enormous investment in land and accommodations. The point is that ecotourists search out facil-ities located away from fancy hotels, discos, and boutiques. The best nature preserves are located on almost inaccessible mountaintops or hid-den away on isolated beach coves far from shopping centers, beauty parlors, miniature golf, and other "necessities" of civilization. It isn't nec-essary to provide nightlife, gourmet restaurants, and deluxe accommoda-tions. In fact, most visitors would be disappointed if they found them.

In addition to getting into business with the lowest possible invest-ment, ecotourism entrepreneurs derive satisfaction from working toward preservation of the environment. If they didn't feel that way, they probably would have gone into some other endeavor. Visitors feel that they, too, are contributing to a better world by supporting environmental understanding and education. That investors break even and occasionally make money while doing what they enjoy is a pleasant side benefit.

The Costa Rican government welcomes and encourages this type of nondestructive development. Every hectare of cloud forest or primeval beachfront used as a living museum is a hectare saved from chain saws and cattle grazing. Some ecotourism projects have even gotten off the ground through grants from U.S. government agencies or from conservationist groups.

EXAMPLES OF **BUSINESS VENTURES**

In the course of researching business opportunities in Costa Rica, I've met many foreigners who've made the decision to become entrepreneurs. Their experiences vary, as do their levels of enthusiasm for being in business. Here are a few examples.

HOTEL-RESTAURANT AND CHARTER FISHING. Patty and Chiqui Yaniz—from Key West, Florida—first visited Costa Rica in the 1980s. "I guess we were looking for a place with the same flavor as Key West had back in the '70s," Patty said. "We fell in love with Costa Rica and liked the way the country was progressing (or maybe the way it was not progressing), so we began returning every year."

Eventually they built a home on Guanacaste's Pacific Coast. Chiqui, a commercial fisherman in Key West, quickly found his natural niche: taking tourists on *panga* fishing trips out of Playa Garza. A *panga* is a small boat that carries three or four fishermen on inexpensive charters. The advantage of pangas over larger boats, according to Chiqui, "You have the full attention of the captain and boatman, who are dedicated to bringing in the fish." His panga is called the *Sushi Loco*.

But Patty missed the sociability of her profession, the restaurant-bar business. So from time to time, she filled in at the Gilded Iguana, a bar-restaurant-hotel on Guiones Beach, tending bar and serving food, something she'd done all her adult life. "Then one day the owner asked if I was interested in buying the Gilded Iguana," Patty said. "I didn't know what to say. I hadn't thought about owning a business in Costa Rica before.

"Chiqui and I didn't have money to invest, but we knew several friends in Key West who had expressed interest in buying a business here.

So Joe Davis and Brent Steele purchased the business and gave me a share for managing the bar and restaurant, renting the rooms, and taking care of all the legal things that need to be done, such as renewing licenses and paying taxes."

When asked what she liked best about doing business in Costa Rica, Patty replied, "I guess it's the learning experience. I speak better Spanish now; I know a lot more about what really goes on in this country, and I've met some wonderful Ticos I wouldn't have known otherwise."

Patty's advice to those considering Costa Rica as a place for business: "Too many people come here on vacation, go crazy over the place, and want to open a business. But it's different when you actually live here. If you have an idea of owning a business and kicking back and relaxing and watching the money roll in, think again! Be prepared to work your butt off. And learn Spanish!"

BED-AND-BREAKFASTS. One of the more popular ideas of going into business in Costa Rica has always been bed-and-breakfasts. It seems like a natural for someone who has little or no experience in business. What's so complicated? You just make beds and cook breakfast, right? There's more to it than that, says José Pelleya (originally from Miami). "The hospitality business—be it a B&B, restaurant, or bar—is a year-round, 24/7 operation. Not only that, you have to be a people person, hands-on, doing a lot of the work yourself or with your family to make it work. If you put the responsibility solely in the hands of employees, you'll die. It is a great business, but you're a slave to it unless you just shut down a week here or there, or a month, and get away."

When asked about the profitability of a bed-and-breakfast, José said, "The money's there, but it's not a get-rich business. I just consider it a great way to live in Costa Rica. And I can definitely recommend the lifestyle of a bed-and-breakfast if you do it because you like to meet people, rather than want to make a lot of money."

José's bed-and-breakfast, the Vida Tropical, is located in a quiet residential neighborhood of Alajuela, yet only a short walk to the Parque Central. One thing that has helped his business is his policy of picking guests up at the airport at any hour of the day or night. Since he is only five minutes away, this makes things very handy for travelers who arrive at 2 A.M. (as we often do).

Also located in Alajuela, not far from the Vida Tropical, is Jim Holley's Pension Alajuela. (Actually, Jim and José are friends and refer guests to each other when rooms are scarce.) Jim says he didn't really plan on going into business when he came to Costa Rica. "I was looking for a place to rest and retire, then I came across Pension Alajuela, which just happened to be on the market. For me, a bed-and-breakfast was a logical choice because it is normally small and I could develop its unique character to suit my ideas of what a good, small, and friendly place to relax should be."

Like his friend, José, he says that small hotels are not particularly lucrative. "You won't get rich, but you'll have control. I find it to be one of the most rewarding experiences of my life, dealing with some of the most interesting and adventurous people in the world. It's wonderful hosting people from all over—Russia, Germany, Japan, Australia, Canada, and the United States—and seeing them enjoy this country that has become my home and livelihood."

The Pension Alajuela is more of a small hotel than a B&B, with twelve rooms and a full-service bar in the reception area, where the day generally starts and finishes. The quaint hotel is located in the very heart of Alajuela, across the street from the "Supreme Court of Alajuela" and close to the Alajuela Hospital. Transportation to downtown San José is easy from Alajuela. There are two bus companies, and buses leave every few minutes for about a half-dollar fare. The Web site for Vida Tropical is www.vidatropical.com, and for Pension Alejuela www.pensionalajuela.com.

ECONOMY CABIN-APARTMENTS. "Gringo" Mike originally came to Costa Rica on vacation with his brother, who really loved it here and was excited to show off his discovery. Mike immediately fell in love with the beautiful countryside and the friendliness of the Costa Rican people. He said, "I decided on that trip that I wanted to come back to this country to live, and began making my plans to return as soon as I arrived home."

When asked how he decided to go into business, he said, "On the trip we visited the town of Jacó, and I was really impressed, not only with the laid-back atmosphere of the town but also with the business opportunities I saw in the area. As I was looking for a change of location and occupation in my own life, I felt I could make a positive contribution to the area by going into business here."

Mike found a small group of *cabinas* for lease and began fixing them up. He installed kitchen facilities in each place and provided free bicycles and Internet connections for guests. Because the cabinas are several blocks from the ocean, the lease was reasonable, allowing Mike to offer exceptionally inexpensive rents.

When I asked my usual question about the best part of being in business in Costa Rica, he replied, "Due to my own experiences here and my love of this country, the best part about my particular business is being able to help other travelers and visitors learn about and experience this country for themselves. I have met hundreds of great people through my business, and I really enjoy knowing that I have been able to assist them and advise them on all the wonderful sights and highlights of this area."

As for the downside of operating a business, he said, "Although Costa Rica is a great country, there is unfortunately quite a bit of bureaucracy and procedures that a person has to go through in order to have a business here. It requires a lot of persistence and patience to not become frustrated with the way business is conducted.

"The advice I would give to someone wanting to go into business here is to take things slowly. Be aware that you will need a lot of patience to learn the systems in Costa Rica, but don't be easily discouraged by them. Also try to establish friendships with other local business owners that can help you learn the procedures you need to go through and can give you advice and encouragement on having a business here." Gringo Mike's Web site is at http://gringomike.com.

OCEAN-VIEW HOTEL. At age forty-three, Robbie Felix decided that the world was much bigger than the United States, so she took early retirement from an executive position with a California high-tech computer industry. She says, "I decided to move to Costa Rica because, after looking into other countries in Central America, it seemed almost a no-brainer! I didn't want to be worried about 'express kidnappings' or having to live a low-profile lifestyle for fear of being victimized. Also, being three and a half hours away by air, a low rate of violent crime, and a country without an army really appealed to me. Another benefit is the tropical climate; since I moved to Costa Rica my arthritis rarely bothers me."

When thinking about going into business, Robbie realized that where she wanted to live, in the Manuel Antonio area, there was nothing of a high-tech nature. But she did have a little experience in the hospitality business, so that's what she decided. She found a lovely ocean-view hotel, the Hotel California, and bought it. She says, "I was relatively foolish in retrospect. Like many people, I thought that the hospitality industry looks easy. Had I known that it looks far easier than it really is, I might have chosen differently!"

When asked about the worst part of being in business, Robbie said: "I would say the extremely poor quality of lawyers in the country and the need for lawyers in numerous transactions. My guess is that many, if not all, foreigners here change lawyers with frequency until they actually find someone who is both effective and honest. It took me three years and a lot of failed and costly attempts to find the lawyer that I have now. You will not find me recommending him to anyone; I want to keep him for myself!"

For advice to those thinking about doing business in Costa Rica, she says, "Learning to speak Spanish opened a lot of potential doors for me, and I would advise people to do their homework! Spend time in the country, talk to people, know the industry you are going to enter and know it well. Many people who have little or no business experience seem to have the tropical dream, and in the end they don't have the skills to make it happen. Even people with a lot of experience in business will find the climate here is different than any other, and most of what they know will be useless! First rule, throw out everything you know and start all over. Everything I thought I knew did not serve me here in Costa Rica."

When asked for the enjoyable part of being in business, Robbie said: "The best part about being in business here is that you can really be part of a community of businesses that truly collaborate, both amongst themselves and with the community in general. My business in the United States was very disconnected from the community at large, but here we play a significant part in local affairs." The hotel Web site is www.hotel-california.com.

Robbie hadn't been in Costa Rica very long when she found herself deeply involved in local affairs by helping handicapped children. She started the Roberta Felix Foundation and began raising money to add to her donations. The foundation distributes diapers, wheelchairs, clothing, orthopedic shoes, educational materials, food, art supplies, toothbrushes, books, toys, vitamins, and many other donated items to the seventy handicapped children and their families that are currently involved in the foundation's programs. "We recently completed construction on a classroom in Parrita that will enable children with cerebral palsy and Down's syndrome to enter the public school system. We also purchased property out by the airport to build a development center for all children with disabilities in the canton of Aguirre. We are designing and soon will be building a center with four classrooms, a special library, and a therapy center. We raised the money in the last year and have enough to complete the construction as well."

Robbie says, "Donations can be made to our projects through the Children's Fund in the United States. The address via Internet is www.childrensfund.org, you need only earmark the donation for our foundation. Or you can fill your suitcase with goodies and bring them down! The foundation Web site is at www.felixfundacion.org.

APARTMENT COMPLEX WITH CABINAS. Rudy and Odette Koster were fed up with Europe's rat race and harsh climate. They were living in Amstelveen (close to Amsterdam), Holland, where Rudy worked as a project manager in construction and renovation, and Odette was a manager of human resources in a big ship repair and conversion yard. Interesting jobs, long hours, plenty of challenge, but it wasn't enough anymore. Wanting to have a chance to actually live and enjoy their lives (and do some scuba diving on the side), they stumbled on Costa Rica. Rudy says, "We fell in love with the country and especially with the Costa Ricans' friendliness and their attitude towards life: *pura vida*. With the right attitude you'll find that here the word *stress* only exists in the dictionary. We found our paradise.

"Being too young and too active to completely retire, we began looking for a way to have an income and share our love of the country. We found it by buying and operating our little apartment complex with studio-apartments (cabinas), where we provide a home away from home to visitors from all over the world." The cabinas all have kitchenettes and air-conditioning; one apartment has a balcony with an ocean view. When asked about the nice thing about being in business, Rudy said, "Although we are all fishing in the same pond, so to speak, we are competitors with a heart. Business owners here tend to help each other, refer clients to each other, help newcomers in town to find their way around. And to be honest: the tax climate does help. On the other hand, no matter how much business experience you have, you'll have to start all over here. What works at home doesn't necessarily work here. That can take some time getting used to.

"My advice to others thinking about doing business here: Use your eyes, use your ears, talk to the locals (be it Costa Ricans or expats), don't rush into a business venture, take your time, get the right information and the right people to get that information for you, and above all, enjoy it!" The Web site is www.geocities.com/casalaloma.

HOTEL AND BARS. Pat Dunn, owner of San José's Dunn Inn Hotel, came to Costa Rica nearly twenty years ago at the request of his father, who wanted to know if this would be a good place for retirement. Pat liked it so well that he decided to move here himself. His father decided to stay at home.

Pat's first venture was a bar in San José. After owning several bars, he found a dilapidated old mansion in Barrio Amón, which at that time was a slightly seedy, old section of town. Pat envisioned a comeback for this once-elegant neighborhood, and he began rehabilitating the building as a tasteful hotel. He was correct, for today Barrio Amón is a popular place for bed-and-breakfasts, upscale hotels, and good restaurants.

"Costa Rica is a virgin territory in some ways," Pat says. "If you're willing to work hard and if you find the right niche, you can make it. Too many come here with the idea that they can dazzle Costa Rica with their brilliance. They soon learn the hard way that it doesn't work like that." Not knowing Spanish proved to be Pat Dunn's biggest frustration. Fortunately, he married a Tica businesswoman who helped him across the rough spots.

One piece of advice he offers to those thinking about going into business in Costa Rica: "Do it straight and right, and don't pay off anyone." He explained that at first he tried to cut corners by paying bribes to get things done quickly. But that turned out to be a mistake. Someone was always ready with an outstretched hand. "It takes a little longer to play by the rules, but in the long run you'll be ahead," he notes. (Note: Pat Dunn sold his business and moved to Ecuador, where he will be going into business.)

WHERE TO GO **FOR BUSINESS HELP**

Listed here are a number of sources for help and advice for those interested in going into business or investing in Costa Rica. These are folks who've been around Costa Rica for a while and who are up on the latest scams.

First, look for the Costa Rican–American Chamber of Commerce's publication *The Guide to Investing and Doing Business in Costa Rica.* They also publish a monthly magazine, *Business Costa Rica.* Phone (506) 220–2200, fax (506) 220–2300, or E-mail am-chamcr@racsa.co.cr.

The Canadian Chamber of Commerce plans to hold meetings every other month to advise countrymen; dates should be announced in the *Tico Times.*

DOING BUSINESS **VIA THE INTERNET**

The Internet didn't exist when I wrote the first edition of *Choose Costa Rica for Retirement.* Even three editions ago, few people had even heard of the Internet, much less knew how to use it. Today we routinely check our E-mail several times a day; we read the *New York Times,* the *Wall Street Journal,* and the *Tico Times* online, no matter where in the world we are. We order books from Amazon.com, connect with the Costa Rica Chamber of Commerce, and can research just about any topic imaginable.

But Web technology goes far beyond convenience for consumers and communication with friends and family. Today's technology permits certain types of jobs and businesses to be located anywhere. Many employees don't bother commuting to their offices; instead they work from home and connect to the office by modem. It doesn't matter that their home computer and the office aren't in the same city, state, or even in the same country.

Eddie De La Cruz, from New York, is a high-tech entrepreneur who produces digital informational products (Menufax Digital Media), creating advertising and commercial DVD/VCDs. He describes a work system he calls economic arbitrage. "It allows me to enjoy the economic benefits of Costa Rica while generating revenue from the United States—or wherever the business is. I use the Internet as a conduit to manage my business affairs back in New York while I live or visit anywhere in the world I can find an Internet connection."

Eddie works from Costa Rica part of the time and plans on opening a permanent office here within a year. His system works like this: "First of all, you use an Internet service like www.gotomypc.com, which allows you to communicate with your home computers anywhere you find an Internet connection. In any Internet cafe, you can log on and pull up the screen of any of your computers as if you were actually sitting in your office. You can send files or get files from any of your computers. This allows you to conduct business without lugging around your laptop or other valuable electronic equipment.

"Next, subscribe to an Internet fax program (such as www.j2.com or www.efax.com). For only $9.95 a month you get your own fax number with any area code you want for receiving and sending faxes, right from your computer screen, without paying international charges the conventional way.

"Finally, you'll need an Internet service to transfer money, pay bills, and collect money from customers by credit card (www.propay.com is one such service). Your clients need never know that you aren't located in Dubuque or Detroit, nor should they care as long as they are satisfied with your service."

Although Eddie works with high-tech, the principle can apply to many other kinds of businesses. For example, I know a woman who transcribes medical records for U.S. hospitals, doctors, and surgeons. She recently moved to Costa Rica and is doing exactly the same work from her home in a San José suburb as she did in Florida. The pay is the same; only the neighborhood is different. "My only restriction is that I must live in an area where a high-speed connection is available," she explained.

The key to successful business by Internet is having a product or service that can be marketed in a country where they're needed—not necessarily in Costa Rica, where there might be neither the demand nor the cash flow to generate profits. Another suggestion for a potential Internet business, advises Eddie De La Cruz, would be to assemble a network of expatriates with Internet-related talent (e.g., graphic design, Web design, Java, Cold Fusion) and market their services to businesses anywhere in the world. He says, "You can low-bid for quality work and build a clientele who never needs to know that the work is coming from Costa Rica, since all communications are done via the Internet."

Casey Halloran, who operates an Internet business in Costa Rica (www.costaricapages.com), says this about his enterprise: "After quite a bit of market research I decided to start an online marketing firm. Costa Rica has many tourism operators who need to reach foreign markets, so I knew there was a need for services I could provide. Following a model that worked for Yahoo!, I started a simple Web directory that I could use to drive traffic to my clients. Three years later, it has grown into a five-person company, a slew of Web sites, one hundred-plus advertisers, and an online travel agency. I am not earning the kind of salary most of my contemporaries make in the States, but I work for myself, set my own hours, and enjoy what I do every day. Certainly my quality of life here far exceeds what it was four years ago in the rat race."

Asked about his general feeling about business in Costa Rica, Casey replied, "This is a land of opportunity. Very few businesses here could not be run better. Very few companies here cannot be beat by working harder or being more professional. Because lawyers and judicial systems do not run this country, honor and a businessperson's word are hugely important. This means that when one delivers what is promised, it is considered special, and consistently being reliable can be reason enough for many people to do business with you. Although weakly enforced business laws make Costa Rica a haven for con artists and contract breakers, it also means that business is not crippled by frivolous lawsuits and unnecessary insurance policies. Barry Goldwater would have loved it here."

INVESTING IN **COSTA RICAN STOCKS**

Investing in Costa Rican stocks is not something I'd recommend, even if I were a competent player in the stock market. I've had my problems with U.S. stocks and bonds and would never encourage someone to jump into something I or they knew nothing about.

The Costa Rican stock exchange (known as the Bolsa) has some unique problems. One is that the most successful companies are privately owned by families and aren't found on the stock market. Unlike the United States and Canada, Costa Rica doesn't have a watchdog government agency looking over the shoulders of corporation officers to ensure business is conducted in an orderly and competent manner to protect stockholders. My understanding is that reporting to stockholders can be erratic and sometimes fraudulent.

This is not to say that the Bolsa in general is not on the up and up. Many knowledgeable investors have money in the Costa Rican stock market, and they seem to be satisfied. The key word is knowledgeable. If you know what you are doing, be my guest.

Check with the National Securities Commission (Victor Chacón or Oscar Mora, 506–233–2840; fax 506–233–0969), or the Costa Rican Stock Exchange (506–222–8011; fax 506–255–0131). Just because a stock is registered doesn't mean it is approved or a good investment, but it does mean that certain minimum standards are met. Other sources of information are the Costa Rican Coalition for Development Initiatives (506–220–0036; fax 506–220–4754) and the Center for Promotion of Exports and Investments (Oscar Ureña, 506–221–7166; fax 506–223–5722).

WORKING IN **COSTA RICA**

A question often asked is, "How can I get a job in Costa Rica?" The answer is, "It can be done, but it's not easy." The Costa Rican government discourages foreigners from competing with citizens for work. In order to work legally, you'll need a special permit, which involves proving that you are uniquely qualified for a job that can't be done by a Tico. Foreign companies are entitled to a percentage of noncitizen employees, but in practice they seldom fill this quota. The reason is simple: They can hire all the qualified Tico employees they need, and foreigners don't want to work for Tico wages.

Since the collapse of high-tech employment and the dot-com meltdown, many highly qualified and skilled software engineers, technicians, and Web specialists are "at liberty," and many are eager to begin life anew in an interesting setting such as Costa Rica. They are aware that the country's computer technology is riding a wave of expansion as business, industry, and government become computerized and enter the Web universe. It's only natural that those recently unemployed and soon-to-be-downsized high-tech people who love Costa Rica will be looking in this direction.

Are there jobs for these qualified people? Maybe not. You have to realize that Cost Ricans also see the future opportunities in the world of digital employment. That's why every other high school student you meet wants to major in Computer Science. At every one of the many satellite campuses of the universities, the most popular classes involve computers. Students come from miles around to take night classes in *computación*. The good news is that many high-tech jobs have been created. The bad news is that Intel and other corporations are limited to 10 percent of their workforce being foreigners on work permits, and they are committed to hiring as many Ticos as they can.

Other jobs that gringos try for are those that require some English—for example as bartenders, desk clerks, and office receptionists. But almost all of these jobs also require fluency in Spanish, and the pay will be at minimum-wage level. Finding a job normally requires some extraordinary skills. One exception is in the field of teaching. Qualified teachers can often find employment, although, again, for minimal salaries. More on this subject can be found in Chapter 14, Costa Rican Schools.

This isn't to say that a large number of foreigners aren't working illegally in the country. Some work in real estate sales, property management, and tourism. A few with special skills work in construction—usually on a temporary or emergency basis. Sometimes foreigners working as contractors are not hassled by the local government—because they hire workers and provide jobs. Unless foreigners are obviously taking work from Ticos, their activities are often ignored. But the bottom line is that working without a permit is illegal, and you can be deported for doing so. After you've had your residency for a time, you can apply for a *carta libre*, a permit to work freely, and can then accept any type of work without restriction. Check with your attorney for the current status of regulations. ■

CHAPTER TWELVE

HIRING **EMPLOYEES**

During World War II the Costa Rican government passed a series of progressive labor laws that remain on the books and are strictly enforced. These laws seek to avoid conflicts between workers and employers by setting out concrete employment rules and a system of wages and benefits. In effect, these laws take the place of union contracts between worker and employer, guaranteeing individual workers benefits they probably couldn't negotiate on their own. If you look at the rules from the viewpoint of the worker, they are only fair—and they're certainly not unreasonable from the standpoint of a considerate employer.

Therefore, hiring a maid, a gardener, or an employee in your business involves more than a simple understanding of wages and conditions as is the custom back home. Because we North Americans aren't used to such formal relations with employees, and because we are likely to be hiring workers, even if just domestic help around the house and garden, the rules need to be spelled out in some detail. Following the laws to the letter prevents unexpected and serious problems.

Briefly, here are some ground rules: The employer is responsible for making Social Security payments for an employee as well as deducting

contributions from the employee's wages. All workers are entitled to paid vacations. After a thirty-day trial period of employment, an employee is entitled to severance pay as well as notice before being laid off. A Christmas bonus is neither a gift nor a nice gesture but instead an obligation mandated by law. The employer is required to give three months of maternity leave at half-pay. All these rules are detailed below and should be studied carefully before hiring any help. One other piece of advice is to purchase accident insurance for your employees, even if they are only part-time. The cost is minimal, and they'll appreciate the extra coverage. You'll also protect yourself, should something horrendous happen to your workers.

GOOD LABOR **RELATIONS**

I once spoke with a woman who was visiting Costa Rica with the intention of starting some kind of business. "When hiring workers," she said, "I understand that the secret is to just hire them for eighty-nine days and then lay them off. That way you aren't responsible for benefits such as severance pay and vacations. Once they work ninety days, you are obligated; so you simply hire new workers every eighty-nine days!"

This upset me, and I told her so. Although her information was incorrect, that wasn't the point. The Costa Rican people work very hard for a fraction of the wages employees receive in the United States or Canada, and the law guarantees them certain benefits. It seems repugnant to me to try to chisel them out of their rightful benefits. Attitudes like this can do nothing but tarnish the reputations of other North Americans. Those who have lived here for a long time generally realize the wisdom of paying their help more than the law requires. "I try to make it so my maid can't afford to quit," said one woman. "She is wonderful, and I couldn't stand to lose her."

Word quickly gets around the neighborhood if you are a good person to work for (or a difficult one). If you earn a poor reputation as an employer, your job applicants will be those who can't hold a job elsewhere. Then you'll wonder why your employees are lazy, don't show up half the time, or have a tendency to steal!

After I gave the newcomer a piece of my mind about her attitude, she explained that she had heard that if you lay workers off after they've

worked more than ninety days, you must pay eight years' salary as severance pay. She heard wrong again. The facts are these: For each year worked an employee is entitled to severance pay of one month's salary— up to a maximum of eight *months'* pay. That is eight *months'* salary, not eight *years'*!

From a worker's point of view, this is only fair. Let's suppose that after eight years of faithful service, it becomes necessary to let your housekeeper go. For eight years the severance pay amounts to about $1,500. Does that sound outrageous for eight years of loyalty and hard work? If it does, then maybe you deserve workers who are lazy, don't show up half the time, or have a tendency to steal.

The owner of a hotel and restaurant in Manuel Antonio told of his experience hiring Costa Rican workers. "It's important to gain their trust," he said. "They don't know anything about you or how you are going to treat them. At first I had trouble attracting the best workers. But I treated people fairly and tried to keep them busy during slack seasons so that I wouldn't have to lay them off. Before long I earned a good reputation. Now I have a waiting list of people who want to join my staff."

CONDITIONS OF **EMPLOYMENT**

1. Length of employment. The first thirty days of employment are a trial period, and either employer or worker can terminate without notice. However, vacation pay and *aguinaldo* (Christmas bonus, described later) must be paid in addition to wages if the employee has worked more than twenty days in that month's time period. Thereafter, for each month worked one day's vacation pay is due, up to two weeks of vacation for a full year's work. Many employees, either by custom or through union con-tracts, receive three weeks' vacation. My understanding is that an employee may work through his or her vacation, provided that the employee receives an additional day's pay for each day worked. (I'm not a labor lawyer, however, so you will want to confirm this point if it arises for you.)

2. Wages. Just about every employment imaginable in Costa Rica has an official job description with a corresponding minimum wage. From taxi drivers to physicians, from clerk-typists to college professors, all are listed in a biannual list of minimum wages that requires several pages. Laborers who work with machetes are listed separately from those who mend fences or work with shovels. In addition, various regions of the country have different minimum-wage rates. My favorite wage scale is for journalists: They have the highest in the country, even above airline pilots! I assume this is because the legislators are afraid of journalists' clout. Their minimum is about $700 a month, compared with an unskilled worker's $225 (approximate), or $260 for a salesperson. (These wages are probably higher now due to regular cost of living raises.)

An interesting facet of the wage structure is that a maid, gardener, or chauffeur who lives in your home is considered to be receiving an addi-tional 50 percent of his or her salary as "payment-in-kind." If, for exam-ple, you pay a live-in maid a salary of $150 a month, the actual salary is considered to be $225, or 50 percent more when figuring benefits. This is important, because the gross salary (salary plus payment-in-kind) is used to figure the *aguinaldo,* Social Security payments, and severance pay. A catch here is that an hourly employee who regularly receives a lunch at your home is also considered to be receiving a 50 percent payment-in-kind, so your Christmas bonus, severance pay, and vacation pay have to be based on this. If you feel that you are already paying the hourly employee enough, you can save money by sending them out to lunch! (To be fair, this is a rather extreme example; few employees would ever put in a claim such as this.)

3. Working hours. The maximum for domestics is twelve hours a day, although almost nobody expects more than eight. The standard is usually an eight-hour day and a five-day week. For regular employees other than domestics, work on Saturday and Sunday is at double-time rates. Often construction workers work a half-day Saturday for a full-day's pay. For those working in businesses or industries that traditionally operate seven days a week, the rules are a bit different; check with your local Social Security office. Although the laws are quite specific, Tico employers often do not follow the laws to the letter, knowing that employees seldom complain. However, I earnestly advise expatriates to follow the rules; you have a high profile in the community, and cutting corners is really a pinchpenny tactic.

4. Social Security. An important obligation for employers, one taken quite seriously by the government, is Social Security. This critical institution pays for health care, sick leave, and disability pensions. You, as an employer, must pay 20 percent of a worker's gross salary and must deduct 9 percent of the worker's wages and pay both portions of the tax to the Caja Costarricanse del Seguro Social. Make sure your workers understand that you are withholding the taxes from their pay. Otherwise their share of taxes could come out of your pocket. Some people pay both sides of the Social Security payments as a bonus for a good employee.

Within eight days of hiring a regular employee, you must notify the local Social Security office. Doing so is vital, because should a worker become ill or injured on the job, you could theoretically be liable for medical bills and 50 percent of the employee's salary for the duration of the sickness (for life, should the disability be permanent). When your employee is covered by Social Security, your liability is limited to the first four days' salary; Social Security takes over from there. To prevent abuse of this law, you, as the employer, are entitled to demand a health certificate from the worker (*carnét de salud*) when the employee is hired and every six months thereafter. This is provided at no cost to the employee by the Seguro Social Hospitals.

Pregnancy is a different situation. Your employee's blessed event will obligate you to some additional employee benefits. Employees are entitled to a month's rest before the baby is born and three additional months afterward—half the salary to be paid by the employer and the other half by the government. By the way, firing a worker for being pregnant is frowned upon, and you might need to validate your reasons for firing other than pregnancy.

5. Christmas bonus (aguinaldo). Sometime between December 1 and 20, employees are due an aguinaldo. For those who have worked a full year prior to December 1, the bonus is a month's pay. For those who

have worked more than the thirty-day trial period but less than a full year, the payment is prorated over the time they have worked. Thus, a person who has worked three months gets three-twelfths of one month's pay. Remember that employees who live in or who regularly receive at least one meal a day get a Christmas bonus based on the payment-in-kind, in addition to their salary, or an additional 50 percent.

6. Notice and severance pay. Workers employed more than ninety days and less than a year are entitled to two weeks' notice before being laid off. After a year, one month's notice is required. If you don't or can't give notice, you must pay the employee full wages for the notification period.

Unless an employee quits, you are obligated to pay severance pay dependent on length of employment: up to three months, none; from four to six months, two weeks' pay; between seven months and one year, one month's pay. Then you must pay an additional month's pay for each year or fraction over six months worked. In no case can this payment be more than the equivalent of eight months' salary.

Again, remember that this is based on gross pay (including 50 percent payment-in-kind, if applicable). It doesn't matter if the worker immediately finds a new job; you still have to pay.

A worker can be fired at any time during the first thirty days for any reason, with no obligation other than the aguinaldo and wages due. Furthermore, a worker who fails to give notice (*preaviso*) before quitting forfeits the aguinaldo.

EMPLOYEE OBLIGATIONS   According to government regulations, workers can be held responsible for damages they have caused, whether intentionally or due to imprudence or "inexcusable neglect." A domestic worker can be discharged without receiving severance if "notorious lack of respect or civil treatment is shown," which should be backed up by witnesses. You had better have good proof, though, because in doubtful cases the Ministry of Labor tends to side with the worker.

When an employee quits or is laid off, it is a good practice to make things crystal-clear by having him or her sign a statement (in Spanish) to the effect that all benefits have been paid. Include the severance pay, vacation pay, Christmas bonus, and any salary due up to the time of separation. Have the employee sign the document in front of a witness. Should the employee be quitting voluntarily, be sure to note that in the document.

ACTUAL VS. MINIMUM WAGES   As long as Costa Rica's economy is booming, with little or no unemployment, you'll find competition for good employees. Consequently, actual wages are usually higher than minimum wages. Many workers earn commissions and bonuses on top of minimum wages, so in reality minimum wages are simply basic starting points. For a realistic figure of what to pay your household or outside labor, consult your neighbors and see what kind of rates they pay. Talk with local businesspeople and see what they consider appropriate.

We always pay a little more than our neighbors for two reasons. First of all, we want to feel like we aren't being cheapskates. Secondly, wages are so low anyway, I always feel guilty on payday, as though we're exploiting people. Yes, we risk the ire of those who accuse us of "ruining it for everyone," but I can easily dismiss that. I can hardly believe that paying our gardener or maid an extra 40 cents an hour will "ruin it" for anyone. Neither can I believe that all this extra money will go to our workers' heads and cause a labor strike among our neighbors' domestic help. We try to be friends with our employees, not bosses. Our maid always gives us both a hug and kiss on the cheek when we see each other on the village street, just as we do with our good expat friends when we meet.

Tico employers tend to be reluctant to pay higher wages than the law requires, but they are often forced to if they want good help. At times construction workers are in very short supply, so they naturally earn more than minimum. In some parts of the country they could earn double the minimum rates. Nicaraguan workers (many of them illegal) will always accept the minimum or less, and are often resented by Ticos who have to compete with them for jobs.

North Americans who successfully operate their own businesses usually agree that paying decent salaries means happy employees who are loyal and hardworking. For an up-to-date list of minimum wages, either visit the local *Surcusal Seguro Social* office, or ask an employee to get a copy the next time he or she goes there. ∎

CHAPTER THIRTEEN

BECOMING **A RESIDENT**

Visiting Costa Rica as a tourist is a piece of cake. Anyone with a passport receives a full ninety-day visa, just for stepping off the airplane! At the end of the ninety-day period you can apply for another ninety days. Because the rules for entering Costa Rica are so liberal, most people who live in the country for six months or less at a time do not feel it is worth the effort of applying for residency. My wife and I fall into this category. We seldom live in our Costa Rica home more than three months at a time, and when we do, we either apply for an extension through a travel agent, or leave the country for a seventy-two-hour stay in Nicaragua or Panama before returning and receiving another visa.

Although the laws seem clear—that you are entitled to one visa extension—many people have spent years in Costa Rica, leaving every ninety days and "renewing" their visas at the border. Many didn't even bother doing that, since the fine for having an expired visa was a ridiculous amount, about $6.00 a month. However, in spring 2002 the government did away with the fines and began cracking down on those overstaying their visas. Several persons were picked up and deported. Since that time, however, there has been little or no action against those who continue to go out of the country every ninety days, those

the government refers to as "permanent tourists." Generally those tourists who are deported are those who are undesirable in the first place. But that doesn't mean that at some point the Ministry of Immigration will not become serious and begin enforcing regulations.

If you are going to stay year-round in Costa Rica, you might as well consider applying for residency. Once your application is in, you don't have to worry about leaving while your residency is being processed.

Even though the rules have tightened somewhat, they are still exceedingly liberal compared with those in most other countries. In the United States, for example, if you stay one day over your visa, you will never be permitted to return! It's embarrassing to contrast the openness of Costa Rica's immigration with the closed-door policy the United States shows Costa Ricans when they want to visit Disneyland or Las Vegas. To receive a temporary visa, a Costa Rican must visit the embassy, hat in hand, pay a nonrefundable application fee, and prove beyond the shadow of a doubt that he or she has every intention of returning to Costa Rica and has no possible motive for staying in the United States. It must be a humiliating experience to be denied a visa because your job doesn't pay a salary high enough to convince an embassy employee that you're sufficiently trustworthy to visit Hollywood and return. A large percentage of those requests are turned down with no explanation. Supposedly, a daughter of a Costa Rican vice president was once rejected because a clerk doubted her character.

For example, I have a Costa Rican friend who won two air tickets for Miami in a raffle and went to the U.S. Embassy for a visa for her and her daughter. Now, when you apply for a tourist visa, among other things you must show a bankbook as proof of your affluence and intention of returning. My friend's husband is a successful contractor and always keeps large sums of money in his account to cover his payroll, materials, supplies, and everyday expenses. So my friend was confident that this healthy bankbook would impress the embassy clerk who was handing out visas. But when he noticed that the account held more than $10,000, he tossed the bankbook back at her, saying, "Drug money!" He motioned for her to step aside so that he could process the next person in line.

Compared with U.S. immigration rules, Costa Rica is very liberal. To enter the country all you need is a passport. To become a legal resident, all you need to do is prove you have between $600 and $1,000 a month income and do not have a serious criminal record. At the moment, the Costa Rican congress is considering raising the income requirements, thinking that they may be unrealistically low. However they've discussed this many times before, and it is questionable if this legislation will pass. If it should, I will report it on my Choose Costa Rica Update Web page at www.discoverypress.com/update.

From time to time the government declares an amnesty; those who've been in the country illegally for a certain amount of time—say, two years or longer—can apply for permanent residence. And those who are operating successful businesses are also sometimes permitted to apply for residence papers. Those who qualify under amnesty rules are particularly lucky, because they don't have to certify that they won't work and therefore aren't restricted from holding jobs.

Understand, I'm not recommending that anyone overstay his or her visa or try to ignore Costa Rican laws. I'm simply reporting how the laws are being enforced at this time and how they are being applied toward foreigners who have the wherewithal to support themselves, who may invest much-needed capital in the country, and who won't be taking jobs from citizens. Those who are indigent or who get into trouble may not find the laws applied quite so gently. Stricter enforcement could occur in the future, as is the case for Nicaraguans and Panamanians who have slipped across the border as economic refugees.

RESIDENCY IN **COSTA RICA**

Many years ago, Costa Rica's government recognized the economic value of retirees entering the country, bringing dollars to spend and deposit in banks. Retirees create jobs by building homes and hiring employees. To encourage foreigners to apply for residency, the government used to offer some enticing benefits to retirees. Retirees received huge exemptions from import duties on household goods, appliances, and automobiles. With import taxes on automobiles in the 100 percent range, you could bring in a new car, drive it for five years, and sell it for as much as you paid for it!

For years these valuable duty-free imports were major attractions for wanting legal residency. As you might imagine, these tax-free imports became a point of contention between Costa Ricans and foreign residents, with the local people complaining that it was unfair for them to pay more taxes than foreigners. Because of complaints from citizens and pressure from the World Bank and the International Monetary Fund, the Costa Rican government canceled these benefits for newcomers in 1992. Those who entered the country before the laws were changed were granted "grandfather" status.

Today, with longer stays possible, the necessity of obtaining legal status is not as pressing as it once was. For someone like myself, who can be satisfied with living half the year in Costa Rica and the other half in my home country, there's no clear advantage to becoming a legal resident. One can own property or a business and can travel about the country with nothing more than a tourist visa. On the other hand, there are restrictions and obligations on pensionados and rentistas—not ponderous ones, but they involve a certain amount of red tape. For example, you must prove that a certain amount of monthly income has been deposited in a Costa Rican bank. On a regular basis, you must provide police certification of good conduct, and you must live in Costa Rica for at least four (nonconsecutive) months of the year in order to hold on to your *residente* status.

For those who will be staying pretty much full-time in Costa Rica or who plan on entering business and working as a manager in the business, the resident option is probably the best way to go. Once you have the papers and as long as you fulfill the residency obligations, you are completely legal and can enjoy all the rights of a Costa Rican, except voting. Becoming a legal resident of Costa Rica doesn't affect your U.S. or Canadian citizenship in any way.

CATEGORIES OF RESIDENTS Immigration and applications for residency are handled by the Costa Rican Tourism Institute. Basically, it recognizes three classes of legal immigrant residents: *Residente Pensionado, Pensionado Rentista,* and *Rentista Inversionista.* After two years of residency under one of these categories, you may apply for permanent residency, and then you have fewer restrictions—for example, you can work without permission from the government.

Residente Pensionado. This category pertains to retired people with pensions of $600 per month or more. Social Security is usually sufficient to qualify for this status. A total of $7,200 a year must be deposited to a colón account in a Costa Rican bank and proof of this shown to the government every year. No law says that you can't take the money out of the bank right away and change it to a dollar account or that you have to spend all of it; you have only to prove that you've brought that amount of dollars into the country. Some people deposit the full amount at the beginning of the year to get the requirement out of the way.

For a married couple the person without retirement income is considered a dependent, and no extra income is required (that is, only one pension per family). Children under the age of eighteen (or under twenty-five, if in school) are also considered dependents. Social Security is sufficient proof of income. This is the option most retired people go for.

Pensionado Rentista. This category is for those who are not old enough to retire or who do not have a pension, yet who want residency in Costa Rica. Applicants must prove $1,000 a month income ($12,000 a year), deposited in colones to a Costa Rican bank under the same rules as regular pensionados. The income must come from an investment such as a certificate of deposit, an annuity, or some other source that guarantees at least $1,000 per month. Younger people and those who want to go into business often choose this option.

For some people, qualifying for this status is difficult because of the large investment needed to return $12,000 a year income. Others would prefer to use the money to start a business or build a home. One way to immediately acquire residency status is to deposit $60,000 in an interest-bearing dollar account in a Costa Rican bank. The bank then pays you $1,000 a month, or $12,000 a year (plus interest), from this account for a period of five years. Deposits in state-owned banks are government guaranteed without limit, and most bank interest in Costa Rica is not taxed by the Costa Rica government.

Rentista Inversionista. People who are serious about going into business prefer this category. It requires a $50,000 investment with an approved tourism or export business, $100,000 in a reforestation project, or $150,000 to $200,000 in any other type of business. If the investment is in an existing company, you need to submit the firm's latest balance sheet and a statement indicating its profit-and-loss situation.

You understand, of course, that you needn't become a resident to own or operate a business in Costa Rica; you can do so on a tourist visa. Many foreigners invest far less and don't bother with residency. However, they are ostensibly restricted to management duties and not permitted to work at ordinary tasks in the business. This is not usually enforced, especially if the person working isn't displacing a Costa Rican worker.

When it comes to investment in a business or a reforestation project, please exercise extreme caution. As mentioned elsewhere in this book, Costa Rica is teeming with sharks just waiting for fish like you and me. Reforestation investments are highly promoted as lucrative investments. You should be cautious of overly optimistic claims; teak promoters have poor track records in fulfilling their promises. Consult a good lawyer first.

WHAT DO YOU GET WITH RESIDENCY? As a resident of any of these three statuses, you have the following benefits and requirements:

1. You have all the rights of citizenship except voting.

2. You can own and manage businesses, but you aren't permitted to earn a salary from a Costa Rican employer or company. You can pay yourself dividends, however. Once your residency is permanent, you can work for anyone.

3. You must reside in Costa Rica the equivalent of at least four months a year, not necessarily contiguous months. Once you have permanent residency, you are expected to visit Costa Rica once a year, for at least one day.

4. You must renew proof of stable and permanent income annually until you have full residency.

THE RED TAPE The question of whether to become a legal resident or to visit using a tourist visa varies with the individual. Some feel that four

or five months is all they want to stay, so why bother with the red tape of papers? Others plan on making Costa Rica their primary home and therefore see benefits in becoming residents. It all depends on your circumstances. One benefit is that residents receive a 50 percent discount on in-country airline flights as well as certain other breaks, such as reduced entrance fees to parks.

To make an application, you can either do it yourself or hire someone to go through the red tape for you. The process requires a deposit of about $100 and about $30 for fees, stamps, and forms. It could take from a few months to a year before approval comes through, depending on how thorough your preparation and who is assisting you. Meanwhile your residency status is legal and won't be challenged.

Ask around the North American community for recommendations of a good lawyer or an experienced *tramitador* (a person who knows which lines to stand in and knows whom to see to get your papers processed promptly). Some people I've talked to have had good experiences with tramitadores they located through classified ads in the *Tico Times*. But be careful; hiring someone who doesn't know what he or she is doing not only takes a lot more time but could be a waste of money if the person does not or cannot follow through.

PENSIONADO **ASSOCIATION**

Yes, some individuals have done the paperwork on their own, but you'll hear sad tales of woe from those who have tried it without knowing what they were doing. Few people enjoy standing in line, facing the indifferent attitudes of some clerks or the hard-to-understand questions and information in Spanish. One way to avoid this is through the Association of

Residents of Costa Rica. Among other things, this organization special-izes in obtaining residencies, and it charges reasonable fees, considering the amount of time you save. A provisional membership is $100, entitling you to apply for residency through the group and to attend social events and meetings. Regular membership is $50 a year.

Further benefits are as follows: The association can make sure your annual papers are up to date, translate and notarize your documents, renew the required Costa Rican ID card, help you get a driver's license and other special permits, and assist you in many other aspects before your move. The organization will also do English-to-Spanish translations and authenticate a photocopy of your resident's *carnét* so that you can leave your original at home.

Members with residency are eligible to receive doctor and hospital care in the National Health Services System, under terms of a special con-tract. This relieves you of the obligation of standing in line each month to make your payments. The organization pays it on a three-month basis and sends you proof of payment for the current month, which entitles you to medical service. The association also publishes a newsletter six times a year. For more information write ARCR, Apdo. 1191–1007, Centro Colón, San José, or call (506) 233–8068 (fax 506–255–0061). The ARCR has a comprehensive Web site at www.casacanada.net.

PAPERWORK In any event, the process of getting your resident papers is best started by you, right in your home country. It's much easier to get these at home than by mail from Costa Rica. The four main items you need are listed below, and in all cases processing must be done through your local Costa Rican consulate. They charge about $40 per document.

1. Income certification. This is the first and most important step; it's often complicated and difficult. Rules and proof of income differ between residente pensionados and pensionado rentistas. Social Security or other government pension money is the easiest to prove. Ask for a statement from the pension source confirming that you have at least $600 a month pension, and have that notarized at a Costa Rican consulate in your coun-try. If the pension is nongovernment, you'll need notarized letters that the pension is for life and two letters from bank officials testifying to the soundness of the company's pension plan.

The guarantee of income for rentistas is $1,000 in interest and divi-dends from banks or investment houses. The decision on whether your income qualifies is made on a case-by-case basis. You'll need statements establishing that this income is guaranteed for at least five years, and you'll need to renew these guarantees every succeeding five years. The Costa Rican consulate can help you with this. Again, it's important to have the notary certification and authentication of the documents done by a consulate in your home country.

2. Birth certificate. This is needed for you and each of your dependents.

3. Marriage certificate. Proof of previous divorce is not necessary.

4. Police certificate of good conduct. Obtain this at your last place of residence, and make it the last document you receive. Have the police certify a set of fingerprints as well; ask the Costa Rican consulate for the necessary forms. Make the good conduct verification your last step, because it's only valid for six months from time of certification. If you get this document first and then spend a lot of time with the other papers, it could expire before your application gets under way. I know of people who've had to return to the United States to get another conduct certification because theirs was more than six months old. You'll also need certificates of good conduct for dependents over eighteen.

Note, too, that if you are traveling with children, some special rules apply. Apparently, these rules apply more for Costa Rican citizens than for tourists, and even though they don't seem to be strictly enforced, it's important that you be aware of them. When a child traveling without both parents stays beyond thirty days, the child falls under the jurisdiction of the Patronato Nacional de la Infancia, a children's welfare organization. In order for a child to leave the country without both parents, it might be necessary to have a permit notarized by the Patronato offices on Nineteenth Street and Sixth Avenue in San José. I've never heard of any tourist being hassled for this, but if just one parent is traveling with a child for long periods, it might be a good idea to have a notarized statement of permission from the other parent. And remember, just having your documents notarized is not enough.

The documents must be taken to the Costa Rican consulate in your country to verify the notary's validity and certification. The notary isn't merely verifying your signature but also that the documents are valid and that they belong to you. Not following each step correctly is responsible for the many delays and obstacles you often hear people complain about.

Other details can be taken care of in Costa Rica at the time you make a formal request for residency. Several certified copies of your passport are required, and you'll fill out a questionnaire of personal information. As a retiree, you'll have to sign a statement that you won't work for pay while in Costa Rica (without authorization) and that you'll spend at least four months a year in Costa Rica. (As stated earlier, the months needn't be consecutive.)

From here on, it's filling out forms, standing in line, waiting for stamps and signatures, standing in more lines to put a deposit in the bank, going hither and yon, to stand in still more lines—most of which can be done by your surrogate, the tramitador. ■

REMINDER: Be aware that there could be changes in the pensionado and rentista income requirements. As mentioned earlier in this chapter, the government is considering increasing the amounts of future pensionados from $600 a month to a possible $1,000 a month and the rentista amounts from $1,000 a month to an unspecified higher amount.

The author's view is that there is a good chance nothing will happen, but you should be aware of the possibility. Anyone who applies for residency or pension status before the law changes will fall under the old regulations.

To keep abreast of any laws affecting potential retirees or rentista applicants, watch our Web page at www.discoverypress.com/update.

CHAPTER FOURTEEN

COSTA RICAN **SCHOOLS**

Because of Costa Rica's high literacy rate and extensive education system, a higher percentage of people speak English here than in any other Latin American country. English is a required course in grade school and high school. But don't expect every Tico you meet to understand English—they forget high school English just as quickly as you forgot your high school Spanish. The fact that most Costa Ricans have at least a smattering of English makes it easier for you who are struggling with Spanish conversation. When a certain word eludes you, you simply toss in the English word and forge ahead with your discourse, knowing there's a good chance the listener will understand either the word or its context. Fluency and learning are greatly enhanced when you don't have the tension of pausing and searching your memory for the proper word. Tension is an enemy of language acquisition.

Surprisingly enough, many North Americans live in Costa Rica for years without ever learning any more words than needed to deal with the gardener or the gas station attendant. But those who do take the trouble to learn Spanish find they are highly respected by their Tico friends and neighbors. Knowing the language opens many doors that would otherwise be closed to you. Being able to communicate with

anybody, instead of only those who speak English, permits interaction with a whole new set of potential friends and acquaintances.

SPANISH LANGUAGE **SCHOOLS**

An excellent way to study Spanish and to learn about Costa Rica at the same time is to enroll in one of San José's many Spanish language schools. Language acquisition is big business here, with at least twenty schools in and around San José offering intensive Spanish classes. (Teaching Spanish is a popular cottage industry here.) Throughout the country you'll find individuals who are eager to give you private, one-on-one Spanish lessons. Some schools keep the class size to three or four students, ensuring each person maximum attention from the teacher.

Most schools offer programs that include living arrangements with a Costa Rican family. By interacting with a local household, you might learn how Costa Ricans cook, where and how they shop, and how to deal with servants, as well as other everyday routines of life that can be so different from back home. Combining classroom study and a homestay with a Costa Rican family puts you in a round-the-clock Spanish environment, speeding up the learning process. Some schools include tours of farms, factories, archaeological sites, museums, conservation projects, national parks, and other places of ecological and cultural importance as part of the curriculum. Some schools will pick you up at your door every morning and return you to your homestay in the afternoon.

An important observation about homestays comes from a former student, who says: "It's best to find a situation where you are the only guest in the home. When three or four students stay in the same house, you'll find yourselves talking to one another in English instead of to your hosts in Spanish."

No matter where you are in Costa Rica, there'll be a language school nearby. You can study Spanish in downtown San José, on the beach in Quepos, in the cloud forest at Monteverde, or even in a typical rural village. The sheer number of schools makes it impractical to list them here. Also, the varying quality of instruction makes it impossible for this book to make recommendations; we just don't know enough about them to vouch for their quality. The *Tico Times*, various tourist publications, and the Internet are full of information about Tico language schools. Your best source for recommendations are from those who have attended a language school in Costa Rića.

YOUR CHILDREN IN **COSTA RICAN SCHOOLS**

A remarkable difference between Latin American children and their North American counterparts is their behavior toward one another and toward authority. Gringo kids are typically boisterous, full of energy, and extremely competitive. On the other hand, Latin American children, especially Ticos, tend to be polite, calm, and well behaved. Bullying other students is all but unknown. Both in the family and school, cooperation is approved and competition discouraged. Classroom discipline is no problem for the teachers, which makes Tico kids a delight to work with. (I can say this from experience, as one who has taught language classes both in the United States and in Costa Rica.)

Your children can select from three types of Costa Rican schools: (1) private English-only schools, (2) private bilingual schools, or (3) free public schools. The farther you live from Meseta Central, the more limited your choices. When you live in an area where private schools are too far to commute, your choices could be a public school or homeschooling.

Most foreign residents I've interviewed about their children's progress in private schools heartily endorse the educational and cultural experience their kids were enjoying. Tuition costs vary from the most expensive private school, with tuition and fees of about $7,500 per year (plus bus transportation), to some of the more inexpensive bilingual schools that offer tuition as low as $60 a month. Again, it's way beyond my scope of expertise to even try to make recommendations. You'll need to interview your neighbors and interview the school personnel.

PRIVATE SCHOOLS Most North American parents prefer an American-credited school with a curriculum equal to that offered stateside. Around the San José area, you'll find a choice of twenty or thirty English-only or bilingual private schools. Some present classes half in Spanish, half in English; others are basically English-language schools. Some offer classes from prekindergarten through high school, others just the first three to seven grades. English-only schools are popular with Costa Rican families who can afford the tuition. They want their children to learn English, and these schools are essential for those preparing for U.S. universities.

At the end of this chapter you'll find a partial list of well-known private schools that cater to North American students. Tuition varies from expensive to moderate, and selections will depend on the location of the school facility and distance from your new home.

PUBLIC SCHOOLS For the most part, Costa Rica's public schools are patronized by expatriate children living too far from the larger population centers to attend a conventional private school. Despite the fact that Costa Rica spends an inordinate amount of money on education, schoolrooms and facilities can be crude and rustic when compared with the average U.S. or Canadian classroom. Often library books are scarce or nonexistent, and the quality of the teachers varies widely.

The daily hours of a public schoolday are usually shorter than those at private schools. Also, when a teacher is absent, classes are canceled and children sent home early. This is partly due to an irrational government policy of assigning teachers to schools based on need, without considering where a teacher's home is located. Schools provide housing for teachers during the week, and they go home every weekend. Of course, teachers look for any possible excuse to cancel Friday-afternoon classes so that they can get an early start on the trip to their hometowns.

Depending on where you live, your only alternatives could be homeschooling or a Spanish-only public school (sometimes both). Parents of kids enrolled in public schools give mixed reviews. Some children are immediately befriended and accepted by the other children and love their teachers. Others feel lonely and ignored. None reported their kids being mistreated, bullied, or teased because they are different—as is often the case in U.S. schools. Much depends on a combination of the individual child's ability to adjust and the particular situation in the school (the attitude of the teachers, the friendliness of the other students, etc.).

I know a couple from Holland whose three children attend an all-Spanish classroom located in a small village on the Guanacaste coast. The youngest (in second grade) absolutely adores the school, the teacher, and her classmates. The next oldest (fourth grade) hates school as much as her sister loves it. The older brother, who has Down's syndrome, enjoys school so much that his parents have trouble making him come home after classes. The students his size encourage him to play soccer (which he loves), and they treat him with extraordinary kindness and respect.

The bottom line is that all children cannot adapt to a public-school setting, and some could do poorly. It seems to be an either/or situation that becomes apparent rather quickly. They either love it or they hate it. Whatever you do, don't force the issue if the child is not happy with public school. When there's no way for the child to attend a private school, the only other solution is homeschooling.

Even when children enjoy going to a public school, it's a good idea to supplement the Tico school curriculum with homeschooling. First of all, a student in an unfamiliar foreign-language environment will have gaps in understanding or grasping class material until he or she is totally fluent in Spanish. Second, Costa Rican schools do not teach subjects on the same schedule or level as North American classrooms do. When students go back to the States for college, they'd like to be on par with others of their age group.

CHILDREN LEARNING SPANISH Whether your children go to public or private schools, you will be astounded at how quickly they become fluent in Spanish (while you struggle and can't seem to get anywhere). It's nothing short of miraculous how kids can absorb a language simply by sitting in a classroom and listening to strange words and mixing with children using these same words. With most adults, it's too late to simply "pick up" the language; you're going to have to work at it.

My favorite example of this instant-learning process comes from Hilary Aeschliman, originally from Kansas City. Her daughter Stephanie had been placed in a very rustic village school on Costa Rica's Guana-caste coast. She started class not knowing a word of Spanish.

After a few weeks, they wanted to purchase Stephanie another school uniform. Hilary says, "We went to this little village store, but despite my Spanish lessons, I couldn't understand a thing the owner was saying. We were just talking in circles—my husband and I in English—the lady who was running the shop spoke only Spanish. We exchanged plenty of smiles and *lo siento's*, but neither had a clue to what the other was saying. After about fifteen minutes we gave up.

"As we were leaving, I said, 'Well that wasn't very productive. I have no idea what she was trying to tell us.'

"At that point, Stef piped up and explained, 'She said that the lady who makes the uniforms is in Nicoya today and for us to come back next week. She'll be here Monday and Tuesday.'

"I could have strangled her!"

UNIVERSITIES AND **FOREIGN STUDENTS**

Students from abroad are welcome at Costa Rica's many universities. There are four public universities and nine listings for private institutions. The largest school is the University of Costa Rica (UCR), with about 35,000 students, located in San Pedro, on San José's northeastern edge. Tuition for Tico students is about $70 a semester; foreign students are charged considerably more, with rates available on request. The other large school is Universidad Nacional. It has about 13,000 students and has several campuses scattered about the country, as does UCR.

Most satellite campuses are rather basic, with instruction geared to Ticos who can't afford to take time off from work to study in the San José area. Most classes are held in the evening and offer studies in computers or bookkeeping or preparatory classes for entering a full university setting. I doubt that many gringos could benefit from attending one of these schools.

Private universities offer programs ranging from MBAs to degrees in theology, tropical agriculture, and conservation. Most accept and welcome foreign students, charging tuition of about $100 per class and $5,600 for an MBA degree.

EXCHANGE-STUDENT OPTION If you're convinced that you'd like to relocate in Costa Rica but just aren't ready for it right now, an interesting idea is to send your offspring here for a school term as an exchange student—or maybe just for a summer vacation class. This gives the youth a head start in learning the language as well as a great cultural experience. And, you will have an interpreter when you do decide to make the move. You can contact the Iberoamerican Cultural Exchange Program and inquire about their various exchange-student programs in Costa Rica. The address is 13920 Ninety-third Avenue NE, Kirkland, WA 98034; phone (206) 821–1463, fax (206) 821–1849.

Christen Kemp, a Spanish and International Business major at the University of Tennessee–Knoxville, tells of her experience as an exchange student in a Costa Rican university where she studied Spanish under ISEP (International Student Exchange Program) for a year. The Universidad Nacional is one of few schools offering an optional fee-paid ISEP Spanish program outside the United States and is designed to provide study opportunities beyond those offered typically only through reciprocal exchange.

Christen says, "I studied at university's campus in Heredia and, though it's not the nicest school in Costa Rica, it was better than I had expected. Some foreign students who studied at other universities claim their schools are better. Apparently Universidad Nacional enrolls many Ticos who can't afford the tuition to attend the better schools. I spoke to one who told me the tuition for a Tico at the school was only about $30 a semester. (I can't help but wonder what happened to the thousands I paid.)

"Technology at this university is not up to U.S. standards. There are only a few computers in the library, and students line up to use them. I found it easier to go to one of the many Internet cafes around town. An hour's Internet connection costs only a dollar. And then there's McDonalds, where you can use the Internet if you buy a Value Meal.

"Registering for classes was quite confusing. They don't use a computer system, so you end up making several trips to classes and the registrar's office. Another big difference is that the teachers are on Tico time. In my first class the teacher was always about forty-five minutes late. The students told me that teachers can be up to an hour late and, unlike the United States, where a class meets for an hour three days a week, at this school a class was held once a week for three to four hours. It's hard to keep focused for that long, but the teachers were actually pretty good. I had an excellent literature teacher from Chile. You do not buy books for your classes—instead your teacher places a packet of photocopies at a designated copy shop and you go there each week and make copies. They are really cheap, like five colones each.

"Living with a Tico host family is awesome. This was probably the best part of my education in Costa Rica. Being introduced to and actually accepted into a traditional family and being part of their religious holiday celebrations was an unexpected gift.

"There are many advertisements for families looking for students. The exchange program from University of Tennessee paid my family $300 a month. For this I received a nice room, three full meals a day, and all my clothes and linens washed and ironed (sheets, pajamas—everything was ironed!). The family had a maid from Nicaragua whom they paid $100 a month to cook and clean five days a week."

TEACHING ENGLISH **AS A SECOND LANGUAGE**

I maintain a very popular Internet Costa Rica bulletin board as a public service to those who want to know more about traveling in or moving to Costa Rica. It's also used by those who have already moved to Costa Rica and want to keep in Internet touch with one another. Nearly 200,000 visitors have visited the bulletin board over the past four years (www.discovery press.com/wwwboard/).

Hardly a day goes by without requests for job information from young people who want to live in Costa Rica so bad they'll work for any amount of money. The most frequent question is "How can I get a job teaching English in Costa Rica?" Many queries come from those who assume that just because they speak English, they are competent to teach English. This obviously can't be true or else people wouldn't waste time in universities earning teaching credentials, studying classroom techniques or the latest ESL (English as a Second Language) methods. Believe me, as a credentialed ESL teacher myself and one who passed courses in these techniques, I can vouch for the awesome magnitude of facing a class of eager faces and hoping they will learn more from today's lesson than I will. (Even though I have university training in ESL, have taken all the requisite classes, and have even coauthored textbooks in language acquisition, I am the first to admit that I am not a very good teacher. I have neither the temperament nor the patience.)

That's not to say that you can't find a teaching position without an ESL degree. Mike Curliss, who teaches ESL at two schools in the San José area, points out that it's not essential to be an experienced English teacher. But you should have some teaching background, he says. "Myself, I have a degree in Business Administration (Accounting major) and teaching experience from the Air Force. I was a classroom instructor in Resource Management School with extensive background training." By the way, many local colleges offer classes in teaching English to foreigners. It will go a long way toward your finding a job if you have some experience before you move to Costa Rica

How to find one of these jobs? Something that ought to be obvious is that you won't find one in the United States or Canada. You'll have to apply in person, in Costa Rica, ready to go to work. Every day schools receive job queries from people 6,000 miles away, and the schools routinely ignore them. Why waste time corresponding with someone who may or may not ever come to Costa Rica—who is very likely just daydreaming about an adventure that will never happen? You'll have to be on the ground, ready to go to work.

Claudia Jenkins, who taught ESL in Costa Rica, points out an exception to the rule of applying in Costa Rica. "One way for an experienced ESL teacher—or one with a master's degree or at least an ESL certificate—to get a job with a Costa Rican language school might be to go to the annual springtime TESOL conference, which is held in different parts of the United States and sometimes other countries. While there, I showed copies of my résumé to two school administrators from the Centro Cultural Costarricense-Norteamericano. They wanted me to start teaching in ten days! I couldn't do it because I was a full-time teacher and only looking for something during my summer vacation. Later I did teach at that school for a ten-week bisemester."

Claudia also points out an enormous drawback to teaching English in Costa Rica: the pay. She says, "At that time (in 1990) my net pay in Costa Rica was $2.00 per hour. My hourly pay in California at the same time was more than ten times that amount! This year (2002) the school is paying $4.00 an hour. And it's mostly part-time work." Today Claudia is a volunteer ESL teacher for an expatriate-sponsored library in Nosara and does

teacher training of volunteer college students who come to Nosara every winter to teach classes for university credit.

Mike Curliss reports on today's salaries, saying, "The pay is not adequate if someone needs to live on the salary. The Pro English school where I work pays 2,000 colones per hour ($5.75), but most classes are two hours a day, two days a week ($23 a week). Where I teach in Cartago they pay by class size. For example, a class of six to nine students pays 40,000 colones ($114) a month; twelve or more students pays 50,000 colones ($142) per month."

Why such low wages? Obviously it's because of the excess of applicants for the jobs. This is one of the few jobs foreigners can obtain without a work permit being absolutely necessary. Technically, one would think that schools would demand work papers, but they get around this by hiring their teachers as *servicios profesionales,* or independent contractors. Technically, they aren't really working for the school. Mike Curliss says he is aware of only one school at the moment requiring working papers: Berlitz. Apparently they had a problem a few years back with people without work permits, so they are somewhat fussy about it.

Claudia Jenkins says, "Teaching adults at a private school in Costa Rica is simply a wonderful experience. The students pay a lot of money, by local standards, for the classes, so they are motivated to learn. Since Ticos like to *quedar bien,* even the most disinterested adult student would never be disruptive in class!"

Many Americans and Canadians earn extra money by tutoring in English in their homes. Sometimes a lack of formal training isn't that much of a handicap because the students merely want an opportunity to practice their fluency in one-on-one conversations.

LIST OF PRIVATE **ELEMENTARY AND HIGH SCHOOLS**

A full list of private schools is far too long for this book, and I have no way of evaluating them. Below are a few of the more popular and prestigious schools that have come to my attention. As in any educational situation, you'll need to ask other parents for recommendations and personally interview school personnel before making any decisions.

- **Country Day School** is a prestigious institution in Escazú, with classes from prekindergarten through the twelfth grade. It is Costa Rican accredited and has 650 students, with classes all in English. There is also a Country Day School in Flamingo. Tuition is moderately expensive. Phone (506) 289–8406; fax (506) 228–2076, E-mail codasch@sol.racsa.co.cr; Web site www.cds.ed.cr.

- **Costa Rica Academy** is another popular school and charges similar tuition. It is accredited by Costa Rica and in the United States by the Southern Association of Colleges and Schools. It's located in Ciudad Carari, west of San José, on the way to the airport. Phone (506) 253–1231; fax (506) 225–9762.

- **Lincoln School** in Moravia is the largest, on the northeast side of San José, with 1,600 students. Tuition is somewhat less than the above-mentioned schools. Phone (506) 247–0800; fax (506) 247–0900; E-mail director@ns.lincoln.ed.cr; Web site www.lincoln.ed.cr.

- **Escuela Britanica** teaches half in English and half in Spanish, kindergarten through eleventh grade. It's located in Santa Catalina on San José's west side and has 800 students. Tuition is very affordable. Phone (506) 220–0719.

- **American International School** is located in Cariari. This is a coeducational dayschool and college-preparatory school, with classes prekindergarten through twelfth grade. Phone (506) 239–0376.

- **Marian Baker School** in San Ramon de Tres Rios offers a United States and Costa Rican based curriculum to prepare students for colleges and universities in the United States and Costa Rica. Phone (506) 273–3426; fax (506) 273–4609; E-mail mbschool@sol.racsa.co.cr; Web site www.marianbakerschool.com. ■

CHAPTER FIFTEEN

IMPORTING YOUR
BELONGINGS

Public transportation in Costa Rica is more than adequate, and many folks here do perfectly well without an automobile, yet having your own wheels is a luxury some refuse to forgo. Since car rentals cost between $800 and $1,200 a month, after a while the savings involved in owning your own car become quite evident. The equivalent of a year's rent would purchase a nifty used, four-wheel-drive vehicle.

An additional benefit of driving your own automobile is not having to worry about collision insurance deductibles. You see, rental cars come with $750 deductible insurance, or $1,500 if the car is stolen or totaled. Every scratch they can find or invent goes on your bill. I firmly believe that some rental companies make more money charging customers for tiny scratches than they do on car rentals. Nowadays you can buy full-coverage insurance for a few dollars a day. If you have your own vehicle, you can take the scratches as learning experiences, and fender-benders are covered by your personal insurance on the car.

There are places in Costa Rica where it just isn't practical to visit without a vehicle. True, buses make it just about anywhere you can imagine—some places I'd hesitate to take a four-wheel-drive vehicle—but after you get there, then what do you do? If you have to walk 5 kilo-

meters to the nearest store or restaurant, you are stuck. Without a car your choice of hotel accommodations is governed by where the bus stops. With your own transportation you can shop around for the best place to stay and then use your wheels to select the best restaurants or hunt out the nicest beaches (which are usually a long way from a bus stop).

BUY OR **IMPORT A VEHICLE?**

Chapter 17 gives details on driving your vehicle down from the United States. That's an option for the hardy, one not to be undertaken lightly, but it can be fun, too. If you don't choose to drive, you are left with the alternatives of buying a vehicle in Costa Rica or shipping one down from the North. There are advantages to both options. Which option is better depends on several conditions in effect at the time you need a vehicle.

There are two schools of thought about buying vehicles in Costa Rica. One side claims that cars here are maintained in excellent shape because they are so expensive; folks protect their investments with loving care. The other side claims that Costa Rican roads are so full of bumps, that cars age quickly beyond their years.

No matter which school of thought you favor, take my advice: Never buy a refurbished taxicab! Taxis in Costa Rica go through absolute hell, driving all day and all night, cruising over rough streets—stop and go, stop and go—the worst kind of wear. How can you tell if a car is a rebuilt taxi? Don't ask me; you need to find an expert mechanic you trust and have him inspect the vehicle. I know a mechanic in San José who restores taxicabs for a living. He has a great body-and-paint man and has a skilled upholsterer on his staff. I've seen vehicles limp in looking hopeless and strut out looking brand-new. I've studied these cars in minute detail, and I swear, each looks showroom fresh!

HIDDEN COSTS Custom duties are responsible for the sky-high prices of new and used cars in Costa Rica. At one time taxes were more than 100 percent of the vehicle's value. They are a bit lower now but still range from 60 to 85 percent of the appraised value, depending on age. Tax rates keep changing as the Congress and Ministry of Customs vacillate on how to apply customs duties. Decisions change every year or so.

I know, this sounds like highway robbery (excuse the metaphor), but the government presents two arguments for high customs duties. One, of course: They need the money. Ticos dodge as many taxes as they can, but they can't avoid customs on that new Mercedes because it's collected before they get their hands on the steering wheel. The other justification is that high prices discourage people from adding more vehicles to already overcrowded streets and highways. This strategy doesn't seem to be working, at least not the last time I tried to drive to Paseo Colón.

It doesn't do any good to argue about the value of your vehicle with the customs people, because they go by a printed list of market values. If your vehicle is in bad shape, they may deduct for that. But you won't be bringing a junker here in the first place. My recommendation is to hire a customs agent or a tramitador who knows how to get things done and can tell you exactly what you'll need to pay in taxes.

SHIPPING YOUR VEHICLE Cars can be shipped from either Atlantic or Pacific ports to Costa Rica. But the cheapest and fastest way is from Florida or New Orleans. Most people say they paid $400 to $800, depending on the shipping line and availability of space. From California costs are higher: I paid $1,300 from San Francisco. From Florida the destination port is Limón; from California it's Puerto Caldera (near Puntarenas). The shipping line will prepare the documents stateside and take care of details once you deliver the car. Don't fail to ask for full-coverage insurance; it's not terribly expensive. You will also need to obtain a smog certificate from the state of origin of the car before shipping it to Costa Rica. This is important!

Once the car arrives at the port, you have the option of picking it up at the port or waiting until it arrives at the main customs house in San José. In either event, you then have the decision of taking possession and going through customs yourself or hiring a Costa Rican customs agent to handle the paperwork for you. If you speak a bit of Spanish, you can do it yourself, but I'd advise asking a Tico friend to walk you through the hurdles of red tape and forms in triplicate. The friend needn't be an expert, just someone who speaks good Spanish and who can ask which line you must stand in—and which line after that.

MY PERSONAL EXPERIENCE I chose the option of shipping my first automobile to Costa Rica rather than buying one there. I realized that it was going to cost a small fortune, but I figured it was worth the trouble; the car was in exceptional shape and had exceptionally low mileage—a 1967 Volkswagen Bug that had spent sixteen years of its life in a garage.

We began the process by calling shipping companies in nearby San Francisco, shopping for the lowest cost. Estimates ranged from a high of more than $2,000 to the bid we accepted of $1,300. The difference was that for $2,000 you got a container for your vehicle alone and for $1,300 other merchandise was included in the container.

The shipping line (Maruka) handled most of the paperwork for us and gave us a date to deliver the car to the docks. We said good-bye to our little car, apprehensive of its voyage, despite the full insurance that was covered in the fee. We were told that the car would arrive twenty days later at Puerto Caldera, near Puntarenas. So we flew to Costa Rica to be ready to greet our Bug when it arrived.

After our anxiously calling Puerto Caldera every day, the ship finally arrived fifteen days late. We found out that three days one way or another is average for cargo ships on the West Coast. A Tico friend and I hurried to the port and began our first inquiry of a long day of asking questions, standing in line to fill out papers, getting signatures, and standing in line for more papers and signatures. We also had to drive into Puntarenas to purchase three months' worth of liability auto insurance. This cost only $20, one of the lesser amounts for the day.

The most expensive cost was $85, to open the container. Another gringo was trying to get his car at the same time, and when he complained about the $85, he was told, "You don't have to pay it. If you'd rather, you can wait until the container arrives in San José and wait until the customs officials get around to opening it. That could take a month or more." He paid the $85.

I highly recommend taking a pleasant-mannered Tico with you if you go through this process. My friend handled things very smoothly. He joked with the clerks, he patted them on the back, and we bought soft drinks for a couple of helpful workers. Not once did anyone suggest a bribe, nor did we offer one. The result was that by the end of the day, we had a bevy of friends in all corners of the huge customs office. (In fact, when the ordeal was over, one of the clerks came out and towed my car to get it started when I discovered the battery was dead.)

Finally, with fifteen minutes to go before the customs office was ready to close for the day, I was told, "All you need now are four copies of each of these documents, and you can pick up your car."

I eagerly rushed over to the copy machine and stood in line. Ten minutes to go, and my turn was next! But to my extreme dismay, the clerk shrugged and said, "Sorry, the machine is out of toner. You'll have to come back tomorrow."

This is where our friendships paid off. One of the clerks we had been joking with rushed over and took the documents from my hands. "Wait here," he commanded. "I'll copy these in my boss's office." He came running back with the copies with four minutes to spare.

When I finally got my VW started, I drove to the exit gate and handed the guard a stack of documents that weighed almost as much as the car. He looked through them carefully, handed me the originals, tossed the rest into what looked like a wastebasket, and motioned me on. Now I believe I know what they do with all those duplicate and triplicate forms.

At this point the car was in the country legally, but only for ninety days. In order to make the car a naturalized "Tico," it had to go through the main customs warehouse in San José. Supposedly, this is a simple matter requiring two days in the warehouse while papers are filled out, the car inspected, and license plates issued. Unfortunately, the government was in the middle of a campaign to cut the number of warehouse workers, so employees were protesting by working "by the book," as slowly as possible. In Costa Rica this can be very slow.

"When can I get my car?" I asked hopefully.

"Ordinarily, it would be two days, señor, but with this slowdown, it will take two weeks. God willing."

I called my customs agent to complain. He calmed me down by saying, "I'll talk to the chief. We can get your car in a week. God willing." I returned to the customs warehouse in two days to see if I couldn't hurry things along, and I arrived just in time to hear the chief explain to another gringo that his car would be out of hock within a month. "God willing."

I was going to ask how long God had been involved with Costa Rica customs, when the chief saw me and smiled broadly. "A miracle! The papers came through on your car just an hour ago." To be fair about all this, I must point out that the strike was an untimely event, and apparently God only works part-time for customs. Most people tell me they've had to wait no more than the expected two days for their car.

I drove away in ecstasy, thinking that my problems were over, that my car was a genuine Tico now, entitled to all the freedoms of the road of any other Tico automobile. Not so. Next I had to go through a safety inspection in order to get papers that could then be presented to another office for clearance to get a piece of paper that was pasted on the windshield until my license plates were ready.

At this point I gave up and turned the papers over to a *tramitidora*, who went to work. She knew exactly where to go, what line to stand in, and whose bread to butter. Three days later my VW Bug was a naturalized citizen of Costa Rica! After waiting a year and a half for my license plates, I found someone who earns a good living by making plates in his garage, so for an additional $25 I now had license plates. Eventually, I assumed, they would have the plates for me, God willing. However, I sold the car three years later, without an official license plate.

SHIPPING YOUR **HOUSEHOLD GOODS**

Although many will disagree, I wouldn't bother shipping my household goods and belongings to Costa Rica, unless they were items that I couldn't replace or couldn't live without. Just about anything you can think of to import into Costa Rica can be purchased for about what you would pay in the United States or Canada—except, of course, things with huge import duties, such as refrigerators and washers and dryers. However, by the time the customs guys slap you with duties on these items, you won't be saving much. And remember that you will have to pay for shipping—and you will have used appliances. For the same cost or less you could make a trip to Golfito or to the Panamanian border and buy your appliances—duty-free in Golfito and $500 per person duty-free at the border (a couple gets $1,000, and they can do this every six months). A recent development: I've been told that the government decided that automatic washers and dryers are no longer luxury goods; they've reduced if not eliminated import taxes on them. That would bring prices down to U.S. levels.

Many of you will go ahead and import everything but the proverbial kitchen sink. Some have probably brought that, as well. If so, you will need a shipper in the United States to make sure things are packed properly and stowed away on a ship. When your cargo arrives, you will need a customs broker to handle things on this end. You can get your personal items out of customs yourself, but I'm convinced that an experienced hand—someone who knows whom, when, and where to schmooze—will save you money.

Some people I know have shipped by air, as long as it wasn't too much weight, because the cost is about a dollar a pound. The cost is much less by cargo ship, and unless you have an inordinate amount of stuff, your things will share a container with other merchandise. Shipping from Florida or New Orleans is much less expensive than from the West Coast.

A problem with cargo ships is they are seldom on schedule. This makes it difficult to arrange a definite date to meet the ship and usher your belongings through customs. You'll have to wait until the unpredictable day when the ship finally docks in Costa Rica. As noted previously, when we shipped our car from San Francisco we were told it would arrive within a three-day spread. Would it surprise anyone that the ship was fifteen days late? We called every day, and they promised it would be there within two more days, God willing. (God was most unwilling during those two weeks.) By the way, shipping from San Francisco was three times more expensive than it would have been from Tampa.

Packing your goods correctly will save them from damage when tossed around in the loading process. Labeling them properly will help keep duty down. Marking boxes USED HOUSEHOLD GOODS and NOT FOR SALE will also help. Some people take grease pens and mark USADO on the items themselves: to make it clear that they aren't going to be sold. Duty assessed can be rather erratic, depending on the mood of the customs official, so this is where your suave customs representative can earn his pay. I will say that I've always been treated with respect when dealing with customs, with one exception: I was bringing in a computer that the customs official wanted to mark on my passport as my exempted duty—after a shouting match (which I won), we both apologized.

You are entitled to import a certain amount of items for personal use tax-free (as well as $500 per person of normally taxable goods). The amount of duty you pay on additional items can be minimal or very high—according to a highly involved and subjective combination of import duty, consumption tax, sales tax, and other miscellaneous charges. These are multiplied by the value of the item (a combination of estimated cost plus freight plus insurance). Depending on the article, there could be a 37 percent tax or, sometimes, no tax at all.

I've heard different experiences from people who've brought a lot of things into the country by automobile, and they've been mostly favorable. My own experience is that when entering Costa Rica from Nicaragua—the back of our station wagon stuffed to the max with household goods, power tools, and who knows what—the only inspection we got was from a Costa Rican guard, who asked whether we had electronic items such as TVs or VCRs. When we said no, he waved us on. Maybe we were lucky. By the way, one thing you don't want to get caught bringing in without proper papers is arms and munitions!

BRINGING PETS TO **COSTA RICA**

Those of you who refuse to relocate anywhere without your faithful furry companions will be pleased to know that there is no legal problem bringing them to Costa Rica. You will, of course, have a certain amount of paperwork.

You begin the process with a visit to your local veterinarian for a complete examination of your pet to make sure that your companion is free from all infectious and/or contagious diseases and that all vaccinations are up to date against rabies, distemper, hepatitis, parvovirus, and leptospirosis. The rabies shots should be at least thirty days but less than one year old at time of departure. The examination report will identify the pet's name, breed, sex, and color, as well as the owners' name and address. This health certificate must be signed by a licensed veterinarian.

The papers are supposed to be good for ten days after issue by the consulate, but customs people say thirty days is okay. Many travelers report that they weren't even asked for papers when they arrived in Costa Rica, but it makes sense to shoot for the ten-day deadline if possible.

I have a friend who doesn't bother with papers going in either direction; she just tucks her toy poodle into her large handbag and marches aboard the airplane. That's taking a chance, but she claims that if there's a problem she has a thirty-day grace period to straighten things out. (Presumably, little Fifi could be incarcerated in a doggy jail in the meantime.) I highly recommend getting all the proper documents, with precisely crossed i's and correctly dotted t's—or whatever.

Some unusual animals—especially endangered species—require special papers, from both the U.S. and Costa Rican governments. Another friend's son insisted on bringing his pet Tasmanian Monitor Lizard (or some such thing), and although she had the proper papers, the freaked-out customs inspectors at the San José airport refused to allow the large reptile to enter until a veterinarian certified that it wasn't venomous.

Yet another friend wanted to bring Oliver, her daughter's blue-and-gold macaw into the country (akin to carrying coal to Newcastle). After three months of paperwork in both the United States and Costa Rica, paying fees and duty and such, Pam made a special trip back to the States—only to spend a lot more time cutting through red tape. "The only hassles I ran into were in the States!" she said. "When I arrived in Costa Rica, the customs guy peeked into the large carrier, glanced at my paperwork, and sent me on my merry way, never asking to see the health certificate or declaration papers that cost me so much time, effort, and worry!"

Once you have your pet's papers, you still have to figure out how to get the animal to Costa Rica. I find it difficult to give advice in this area because airlines keep changing their policies. Some airlines (and maybe all) are currently refusing to carry pets in the cargo holds in summer because of possible heat danger to the animals. Some airlines are refusing to accept animals, period; others are more pet-friendly. The last I heard, Delta was the most friendly, still allowing small animals to be carried into the passenger cabins (although they could balk at accepting a large Tasmanian reptile). With the current uncertainty about rules and regulations, you'll need to check individual airlines to find the right carrier. I'll try to post current info on my Web page for the book update (www.discoverypress.com/update).

To leave the country, your pet needs an exit permit, just like human residentes. For this you'll need a health certificate from a Costa Rican veterinarian (well actually *you* don't need it; your pet does). The vet usually accepts your original papers as valid and fills out the proper Costa Rican exit permit without having to personally inspect the animal. The vet can do all the paperwork, obtain the proper stamps, and pay fees. Some people arrange this by fax; the vet or an assistant then meets them at the airport with the necessary permits. Call your vet or contact the Departamento de Zoonosis, Ministerio de Salud, Apartado 10123, San José; (506) 223–0333, extension 331.

Costa Ricans love their pets, but they tend not to keep them on leashes or in their yards, as most North Americans do. So be careful; your free-wandering pooch or kitty could be at the not-so-tender mercies of the big watchdogs that swagger about the neighborhood, always ready to bully. The worst offenders and most dangerous are often not Tico dogs but gringo-owned rottweillers and Dobermans allowed to run free. I know of one set of gringo-owned dogs who not only killed a dozen other pooches but became bold enough to attack humans. A Tica died from her injuries before the animals were finally chained.

Contrary to the situation in some Latin American countries, pet food is readily available at most Costa Rican supermarkets and sometimes in the local *pulperia*. Veterinarians are numerous, with at least a dozen practicing in the San José area. Some will even make house calls. Actually, few villages are without a veterinarian, but most of the village vets specialize in treating large animals such as horses and cattle. They have little experience taking care of pets and some don't like to be bothered with them. Those vets with small-animal practices are often reluctant to travel 30 or 40 kilometers to your beach village home just to give a distemper shot to Fido or to neuter Miss Pussycat. Expats sometimes bring their pets together and have a "veterinarian party." They'll have a dozen animals ready for the vet to work on when he arrives for his monthly visit. The party guests enjoy themselves, eating *bocas* and sipping cocktails, while the unfortunate *animalitos* are experiencing the business end of needles—and possibly losing some precious parts of their anatomy. ∎

CHAPTER SIXTEEN

GETTING TO **COSTA RICA**

The most practical way to get to Costa Rica is by airplane. Most people travel this way, even though fares are scandously overpriced. For the exceptionally hardy, automobiles and even intercity buses are alternatives. It's theoretically possible to travel as far as Guatemala City by train, but the logistics of doing this are best left to wild adventurers who are willing to put up with incredibly uncomfortable and unreliable facilities. Ship travel is all but impossible, too. Cruise ships touch at Costa Rican ports, but it's difficult to book a one-way passage.

CENTRAL AMERICA **BY AIR**

The quickest and easiest way to get to Costa Rica is by air, but this, of course, restricts the amount of belongings you can take—things you may need for a long-term stay. Those of us who live here full- or part-time always enter with as much luggage as we can get away with, packed with personal things we need from home and items difficult to find in Costa Rica. We send "wish lists" to our friends to carry in their luggage when they visit. They bring everything from paperbacks and videotapes to bedding and automobile parts.

A number of airlines schedule regular service to Costa Rica—American Airlines, United, and Continental, among others—and inexpensive Canadian charter flights fly from Vancouver and Montreal. Mexico's Mexicana Airlines flies to Costa Rica, as do several other Central American airlines, such as TACA, Aviateca, COPA, and SAM, which fly from Miami, New Orleans, Houston, San Francisco, and Los Angeles.

Costa Rica used to have its own airline, LACSA, but now it is part of TACA, an El Salvador line. Occasionally LACSA beats the price of other airlines, but generally all carriers keep their prices within a dollar or so of one another.

Getting the best fare may involve shopping around a bit. My experience with travel agents is that not all of them can find the least expensive way to travel. You can often save money by calling the airlines yourself and shopping for their best rates and either making your own reservations or requesting that your travel agency make them for you (costs the same either way). I once saved $160 on Costa Rica tickets this way. Check directory assistance for airlines' toll-free telephone listings. You'll spend time on the phone, listening to boring music while waiting for a clerk, but you could save dollars. Be sure to ask about special promotions, which can save you a bundle. Sometimes the clerk won't know until a month in advance just how much, if any, of a discount will be available. And don't overlook the Internet. Web-savvy individuals can surf the Net for the best rates.

COSTA RICA'S MAIN AIRPORT Totally renovated and ultramodern, the Juan Santamaria Airport, near San José, has streamlined its arrival and departure procedures and is almost a pleasure to use. They've added to the departure tax, to pay for this: to the tune of $26. Customs inspections is relaxed yet professional. Airport taxis to downtown San José are plentiful and prices competitive. The standard price to downtown San José is around $15. Drivers readily accept dollars. By the way, some airport taxis aren't supposed to go to more than one hotel or address per trip, so if you share a cab with someone, make a deal with the driver, if necessary, perhaps a tip for the extra stop. Also a bus stops on the main road in front of the terminal, with buses for downtown every few minutes.

When returning from Costa Rica, paying the departure tax is different today. Instead of buying stamps for your passport from hawkers on the sidewalk, you now have to stand in one of two lines in the terminal and

the airport and pay at special desks. You can use colones, dollars, or even a credit card. Again the tax has gone up to $26. I hear lots of complaints about this tax, but consider that U.S. airports charge a hefty tax, it's just that it's included in the price of your ticket.

A new international airport near the northwestern city of Liberia is finally open for business. It had been completed and ready to open for some time, with the first official inauguration held twenty years ago and several other grand openings since, each time with service predicted to begin shortly. At each inauguration ceremony officials from the tourism ministry, travel agencies, and businesspeople all celebrate the impending opening of this new facility. This time they are finally open for business. LACSA flies several times a week from Miami, and charter flights from Canada are landing now. Delta and American have added flights to Liberia's Daniel Oduber International Airport, and other airlines are said to be planning on initiating service. The management of this airport seems to be somewhat inefficient, with long lines both arriving and leaving. Last time I was there, I noticed a really slow-moving passenger line while security personnel appeared to be searching everyone's luggage for explosives—*after* they disembarked from the flight! With the Liberia airport in service, Guanacaste's Pacific Coast towns and resorts will boom.

The economy here is already healthy, but this will boost it even higher. A friend flew in from Miami the other day, with about two and a half hours' flight time and two and a quarter hours' drive time from Liberia to a Pacific beach resort—a total travel time of less than the drive from San José to his destination!

CENTRAL AMERICA **BY BUS**

For those with lots of time, patience, and a sense of adventure, it's entirely possible to travel from the Mexican border to Costa Rica by bus. As a matter of fact, my wife and I did exactly that during our first visit to Costa Rica, thirty years ago. We didn't do it to save money (although it's a cheap way to travel); we just enjoy bus travel in foreign countries and happened to have unlimited time for our vacation. With somebody else driving you get to see the countryside and enjoy visiting the cities in a much different way from flying over at 33,000 feet. Like driving to Costa Rica, however, a bus trip is something you need to think over carefully. It takes a stalwart traveler with a highly developed sense of adventure and lots of free time to enjoy this trip. Friends related the following itinerary for the trip they took a couple of years ago.

My friends caught the Ticabus at its San José terminal and headed to Guatemala City; tickets cost less than $50 for the trip. The bus stopped at the Nicaragua–Costa Rica border for customs inspection. The total border cost for both Costa Rica and Nicaragua was $8.75.

The first night they spent at the Ticabus terminal in Managua. They stayed in the small hotel at the bus station, humorously called the "Ticabus Hilton." Rooms cost $6.00 per person and were modest but clean. The bus left early the next morning and stopped at the Honduras border for passport stamping and $4.00 for exit and entry fees. (An alternate route stops over in Tegucigalpa, Honduras, instead of San Salvador.)

Going through Honduras was fairly fast. The bus's next stop was at the El Salvador border, and exit stamps again cost $4.00. Entering El Salvador requires a visa that you can get from an embassy by mail, at no charge. If you don't have a visa, you'll have to pay $10 for a tourist card.

The bus stopped for the night in the city of San Salvador. At the nearby San Carlos Hotel, the room rate was $10. The bus left at 6:00 A.M. At the Guatemala border another stop was made for exit from El Salvador and entry into Guatemala. The costs were $2.00. The bus arrived in Guatemala City at about noon.

In Guatemala they caught a bus that went to Tapachula, Mexico, for a fare of $21. The line was Galgos Bus line, also comfortable and providing very good service. From Tapachula to Mexico City, they traveled on the Cristobal Colon line—the best bus on their entire trip. The ticket cost was $40. The bus had hostesses and plenty of room to stretch out and enjoy the sixteen-hour trip to Mexico City. From Mexico City the twenty-four-hour trip to Juárez (on the border across from El Paso) cost $80.

Even though Mexican first-class buses are OK—often having a bathroom, stereo music, and sometimes even an attendant serving coffee and soft drinks—this was the longest, most difficult leg of the trip. Because of the long distance between the United States and the Guatemala border, the numerous bus changes and long hours made for an uncomfortable trip. (An alternative might be to fly from Tapachula or to break up the trip with stopovers for sight-seeing in Mexico.)

The total cost per person for bus fare and fees came to about $222. This is not a trip for the fussy or overly fastidious, because hotel accommodations are basic to rustic, and you'll feel constrained to stay near your hotel and/or the bus station. I don't advise exploring the cities of San Salvador or Managua during the overnight stops, except in the company of other bus passengers—preferably Central Americans who know what they are doing.

The fun part of this bus trip is making friends with other travelers. Those passengers who live here are eager for you to enjoy their country, and they'll point out landmarks and highlights as you cruise along. While having lunch at the rest stops, passengers make plans for having dinner together at the next overnight stop. By the time my wife and I reached San José, we had made many friends and received several invitations to visit Costa Rican families. ■

CHAPTER SEVENTEEN

DRIVING TO **COSTA RICA**

One of the first questions folks ask when thinking about spending a long time in Costa Rica is, "Can I drive my car there?" The answer is, "Yes, but it ain't easy."

My first Pan-American Highway experience happened many years ago, when my wife and I drove our 1967 Volkswagen Bug from San Jose, California, to San José, Costa Rica. We thoroughly enjoyed ourselves. It was an interesting experience, one we wouldn't have missed for anything.

For a while civil war in Guatemala, El Salvador, and Nicaragua brought tourist automobile travel through these countries to a virtual standstill. But even then some intrepid tourists insisted on driving, merely changing the route somewhat. They traveled the Pacific coastal route through Guatemala, avoided El Salvador by detouring through Honduras, and then carefully skirted trouble spots in Nicaragua. I tried to get through in 1983 but returned to Mexico after tiring of gun barrels being pointed at my forehead at every military stop. Today, with the return of peace to the region, automobile travel is once again routine.

Our last adventure took place in 1997. The actual driving time from the Arizona border at Nogales was about eight or nine days. But not

being in a hurry, we spread the trip over a full month. We stopped to visit friends in Lake Chapala, Oaxaca, and Guatemala City. We also detoured to spend some time at the marvelous Mayan ruins in Copán, Honduras.

It was an unusually pleasant drive. From the time we left Nogales until we reached our home in Costa Rica, we encountered not one military stop, saw no military presence, and were halted only a few times for routine checks of the car—presumably, to make sure it wasn't stolen. At none of the borders did they inspect our luggage or do anything other than glance in the back of our station wagon. Please realize that this good experience could have been due to an unusually lucky series of circumstances and may not be typical. Also, we were careful not to do anything stupid, like driving after dark. So don't think I'm suggesting that everybody will have a breeze. It's a long, hard trip, with some bad roads as well as good ones. Sometimes the accommodations are awful; sometimes they're delightful. If you can speak some Spanish, it would be helpful, but we encountered other travelers who spoke very little yet were making out OK.

With the exception of the amazing and efficient toll roads in Mexico, the Central American portion of the Pan-American Highway today consists of low-speed pavement—sometimes pockmarked, occasionally smooth with dual lanes—with infrequent stretches of gravel. Nicaragua had the worst pavement of all, with more potholes than blacktop left on the highway. Nicaragua's pavement has recently been improved considerably, so this is no longer a problem.

Mexico, however, offers new four-lane divided pavement, with 75-mile-an-hour speed limits. The tolls are expensive, so expensive that often we were the only vehicle in sight. But the price was worth it. We set our cruise control and zipped along as fast as we cared to. The downside is that you see little of Mexico other than fields, cows, and backcountry.

Every day on the road was a new adventure, a new challenge, full of photo opportunities and stimulating encounters with other travelers and local people. The most annoying part of the journey was the delay and inconvenience while crossing borders. Sour-faced officials examine your papers with suspicious eyes, then hand out a sheaf of forms to be filled out in triplicate. Then they rubber-stamp everything in sight. (Oh, how they love rubber stamps!) You go from one official to another for what seems an eternity. Finally, you are allowed to leave the country, only to drive 50 feet into the next country and start the process all over again at the next customs office.

I recall that during the Somoza regime, the Nicaraguan border was absolutely the worst. The personnel were arrogant, corrupt, and sadistic as they bullied travelers. One particularly nasty customs inspector searched through my book bag, looking for subversive literature. Since he read little English, he demanded to know what each book was about. His face turned livid when he found a sociology textbook among my belongings, with the word *sociology* prominently displayed on the cover.

"Socialism!" he shouted in a grim voice. "This book is about socialism!" I tried to calm him down by explaining that sociology is something like psychology. But when he opened the book to the first chapter, which was titled "Revolutions in Social Theory," things hit that proverbial fan. The book stayed behind at the border, though I was permitted to enter the country, albeit with some suspicion. Another man had a khaki-colored field jacket expropriated because it was "military equipment."

Ironically, when the Sandinistas first took over in Nicaragua, travelers reported that the only easy border crossings were in and out of that country. Apparently, Sandinista customs inspectors were somewhat laid-back, casually waving Costa Rica–bound tourists through, saying, "Have a good trip!" (Maybe General Somoza took the rubber stamps with him when he left. He took everything else.) But the new Nicaraguan border guards soon learned the ways of bureaucracy; traffic today flows with the same consistency of cold molasses as the other crossings.

Since writing the preceding words, a miraculous change has come over the Nicaraguan border crossing to Costa Rica. A tremendous amount of money was spent to replace the ramshackle old buildings with their dirty walls and no bathroom facilities. Today the border crossing is brand-new and modern, and the system has been streamlined. This is important for those who choose to spend a few days out of the country to renew their visas. Crossing into Nicaragua is now easy—and there are taxis waiting to take you to the beach!

One of the worst borders to cross is into Guatemala. There I made the mistake of waiting with the car, as the tramitador suggested, and giving him the money to pay the fees. Wrong! I soon figured out that I needed to go with him and pay the fees myself. After that no problem. No *mordidas* (bribes) of any consequence at any border crossing—even when I offered a bribe in order to get through quickly. The easiest border stop was Costa Rica, where it took less than a half hour and where border officials actually smiled and joked with us. (I hope this story doesn't get anybody fired!)

Even if you speak good Spanish, I highly recommend that you hire a tramitador to help you through customs, especially at the busy crossings. (Costa Rica is an exception.) There are always kids hanging around who, for a fee, will run your passport and car papers around to the places where they will be rubber-stamped, have stamps affixed, and signatures scrawled upon them. It's difficult to tell which are legitimate charges and which are *chorizos* or mordidas. Which of the kids to hire? I always pick one who is a little older and looks aggressive. He will not be shy about elbowing others aside to get to the front of the line so that the officials can look at your papers first. If you speak good Spanish, you might do OK without a tramitador, but you might also spend a lot of time in line. If you don't speak Spanish, don't try it alone. One recent traveler reported that the border officials wouldn't deal with him until he hired a tramitador. The cost is usually $10, but you can bargain. Get the price fixed *before* you start.

We didn't drive through El Salvador, though not because we wanted to avoid it; our visit to Copán, Honduras, happened to route us around El Salvador. The border crossing from Guatemala to Honduras at that point is exceptionally easy and painless.

The secret to stress-free traveling in Central America is to "hang loose" at the customs stops—try to laugh at the process. Handing out a few $5.00 bills from time to time helps smooth over the problems.

This is perhaps the most difficult part for Americans: paying money for people to do the jobs they're already paid to do. To us this is wrong, it's blackmail, it's theft, and it's humiliating. If you insist on looking at it this way, the border-crossings are going to be bad experiences. You need to look at the process from the viewpoint of the border-crossing employees. To them accepting money in order to help you is a perfectly natural and legal process. The government pays customs and immigration workers minimal wages with the full knowledge that they'll make it up in tips from travelers. So the tougher they make it, the more travelers will be willing to pay. Like it or not, that's the way it works, and nothing you do will change the system. The customs workers see absolutely nothing wrong with the process and can become highly frustrated when confronting a stubborn, belligerent tourist who tries to single-handedly change the system by refusing to pay for quicker service.

Driving the Pan-American Highway isn't easy, mind you, but then it never was a journey to be taken lightly. We're talking mile after mile of marginal highways, poor hotel accommodations, frustration, and red tape at every border crossing. Yet I've interviewed a dozen travelers who made the trip between 1993 and 2000; all shrugged off these inconveniences. They felt the important thing was that they got their vehicles and belongings through intact, and they had fun doing it. Most described their trip as an adventure they wouldn't have missed for anything.

ON THE **ROAD**

From the U.S. border at Brownsville, Texas, to Costa Rica, the drive is 2,300 miles. From Mexicali the distance is 3,700 miles. Your car should be in good condition, with new steel-belted tires, a spare, an emergency tool kit, road flares, and flashlights with extra batteries.

Always get out of the car and supervise the gas station attendant while he services the car. Attendants have been known to accidentally put diesel fuel or leaded gas into a car requiring no-lead fuel. And make sure they turn the pump back to zero before they start so that you don't end up paying for gas you don't get. (I've never had this happen in Costa Rica.) You might carry a hand calculator to make sure you are paying the correct amount and getting the right change, too. Even if you don't know how to figure this out, the attendant will think you do, and he won't cheat. Another trick that station attendants in Mexico will try to pull on you (cabdrivers do the same): When you hand them a 100-peso bill, they quickly switch it for a 50-peso note, to make you think you made a mistake. The cure for this is to carefully hand them the note and say, "*Billete de cien pesos*" ("Hundred-peso bill").

Don't forget car insurance. Your U.S. or Canadian policy isn't recognized south of the border, but carry it with you anyway, as proof that you have a valid policy, just in case. You need to buy a special insurance policy for Central America. Before you cross into Mexico, contact Chris Yelland of Sanborn's Insurance at (210) 686-0711 (fax 210-686-0732), or write to P.O. Box 310, McAllen, TX 78505-0310. This company can write Central American policies by telephone and will take credit cards. For a fifteen-day policy (which should be more than ample time to drive all the

way to Costa Rica), the cost of full coverage on a vehicle valued at $12,000 would be $201. For fifteen days of liability-only coverage, the cost would be $49. Ask for a *Travelog* with detailed directions, maps, and hotel/restaurant listings for Central America (free with insurance).

Also remember that you should have your smog certificate before driving into Costa Rica.

THROUGH MEXICO The first country to cross is Mexico. You will be issued a tourist card at the border without hassle, or you can obtain one in advance at your nearest consulate by showing your passport. If your vehicle is financed, you'll need a notarized statement from the bank or finance company with permission to take the vehicle out of the country. Best have it notarized at a Mexican consulate, if possible. Mexico has been closely checking cars coming into the country to combat a rash of stolen automobiles. Rules are in a state of flux at the moment; you may have to pay a small fee and post a bond to ensure that you don't sell the car in Mexico. (You must use a credit card for this bond; no cash changes hands.) When you exit the country, they'll cancel this bond. The Mexican crossing is easy; you don't need a tramitador, and you don't have to tip anyone.

If you are carrying household goods or items you will need in Costa Rica, make sure you let customs officials know you are "in transit," and they'll so note on your car papers. Don't let them try to place you in an escorted caravan to the Guatemalan border. You'll have to stay where the police escort says, you'll have to eat where you're told, and the whole thing is rushed and expensive. That's not how you want to travel through Mexico.

Unless you want to visit places like Puerto Vallarta, Acapulco, and other spots on the West Coast, the best route is one of Mexico's new high-speed toll roads. Driving through Mexico on the nontoll highways will add a day or so to your travel time, but you'll see more of Mexico. Figure four or five days to make the trip to the Guatemalan border. You ought to take at least an extra week and enjoy a minivacation, visiting Mexico's recreational and historical sites.

Keep your eye out for speed limit signs and slow down to the posted limit; that way you won't be bothered by cops. They won't stop you unless you're breaking some traffic law. This is pretty much true anywhere in Central America. *Important:* Never drive at night—in Mexico or anywhere in Central America. Mexican and Central American highways are generally in fair condition, but they are built as cheaply as possible. The road definitely ends at the edge of the pavement; when there are shoulders, it's purely by chance. In the dark you have no idea what lies alongside the pavement—a stretch of gravel, mud, or a 10-foot drop-off. You might even find a bull sleeping on the pavement. Repeat after me: Don't drive at night! (I have to admit that I violate this rule when using Mexico's toll roads; they are wide and safe, and they have almost no traffic, even in daylight.)

GUATEMALA The recommended place to cross into Guatemala is near Tapachula, Mexico—at the Guatemalan town of Tecún Umanán. Good overnight accommodations can be found in Tapachula, so you'll be ready for the Guatemala run in the morning. Start early, since the border sometimes closes for siesta from 1:00 to 3:00 P.M.—sometimes earlier if personnel feel in need of a nap.

A typical border crossing was described by Karen Bonis, remembering when she and her husband, Scott, drove their motor home into Guatemala:

> From the center of town, we followed a steady stream of taxis filled with customers, heavy trucks, and cars down a potholed highway to the border a few miles south. We crossed a little river and immediately were deluged with young men wanting to

change money and lead us through the maze of admittance procedures for Guatemala. We exchanged a few dollars and hired a young man, who led Scott into a small building to pay the bridge tax. They were gone an interminable amount of time, during which I tried unsuccessfully to stop several young men from washing our windows with oily rags, while telling young beggars they weren't going to get any dollars from me. Finally, Scott and the young man returned.

We moved another hundred yards to a modern building where a large sign said: FUMIGACIÓN. They were in this building even longer. Occasionally they would reappear at the rig, clutching even more papers. Eventually someone sprayed the tires and underside of the motor home, and then we were confronted by customs inspectors. They weren't happy about the two TVs, didn't like the cellular phone, and were adamant about not allowing the CB radio into the country. It turns out that CBs were illegal in Guatemala because they don't want rebels in the hills to get them.

It was now well into siesta time, but fortunately, no one seemed to take a break. The inspectors grabbed lunch from various food stands lining the road and continued working. Scott disappeared into the building and was gone for well over an hour, negotiating with customs. He returned smiling; we would be allowed to move in just a few minutes. But the inspector returned to look at the car we were towing. Another problem. Only one vehicle per driver allowed. After showing the inspector my license, offering to drive the car across myself, and solving a few more problems, we finally received permission to enter Guatemala. It was a short haggle over the price with our young man who helped us, settling on $5.00 U.S., which Scott felt was worth the price. The total time spent crossing: four and a half hours.

ALTERNATE ROUTES **TO COSTA RICA**

From Guatemala City to Costa Rica, you have two choices: through Honduras or through El Salvador (which includes a few miles through Honduras). The shortest, quickest route is through El Salvador, yet until the cessation of the civil war here, most drivers preferred the slow, safe route through Honduras. Nowadays travelers describe driving the El Salvador leg as uneventful. By the way, Honduras must have found a lot of extra money somewhere, because the highways are new, wide, and marked with a line in the center—and they actually have shoulders!

The drive from Guatemala City to the city of San Salvador takes about six hours, depending upon the delay at customs at the border. At present the roads through El Salvador are almost as bad as those in Nicaragua, but at last report officials are repairing them rapidly. From El Salvador another early start will get you across a short stretch of Honduras and into Nicaragua. Try to have a full gas tank before entering Nicaragua; gasoline shortages here aren't unknown. It's only a 190-mile trip from the Honduras border to the Costa Rican border. For an overnight stay in Nicaragua, you might consider the beautiful colonial city of Granada.

My favorite way to drive from Guatemala City to Costa Rica is through Honduras, bypassing El Salvador entirely, but it is slower. This route takes you through the town of Copán, where you *must* pause to visit the most fantastic Mayan ruins of all. Although this involves driving several kilometers of dirt road to the Honduras border crossing, there's usually only one customs guy there, so it's a snap to cross. The road was in good shape—for a dirt road—the last time I traveled it, in 1999. It may not be passable in the wet season, however. Make sure the border official knows you're going as far as San Pedro Sula and not just visiting the ruins for the day; otherwise, the official will give you temporary papers and no transit visa. Spend a day or two exploring the ruins, then go on toward San Pedro Sula, turning south to the Honduras capital city of Tegucigalpa. From there you cross into Nicaragua on Highway 3 and head for Chinandega and León.

The other route through Honduras is through Agua Caliente and on to Nueva Ocotepeque, where you'll find satisfactory accommodations if you need them. Understand that all of these border conditions change from day to day; on some days you'll slip through like water through a sieve, whereas on other days it'll be more like molasses. Controlling your temper and putting on a pleasant face will help. But also remember the saying "You can get a lot more with a smile and a $5.00 bill than you can get with just a smile."

By the time you've reached the Nicaraguan border, you'll probably be eager to get to Costa Rica. Driving the length of Nicaragua can be done in a few hours, so there's no real need to stop over there, although you might be tempted to linger in one of the colonial cities or stay at a beach hotel not far from the Costa Rican border. Nicaragua is sometimes plagued with strikes and protests, which can slow traffic down, so try to make the earliest border crossing possible.

Once in Costa Rica, be sure to make copies of your papers and your passport—and keep them in a separate place, just in case you lose the originals. Be sure to copy the passport page with the entry stamp for the date you entered the country.

Remember that the car permit and your insurance are good for ninety days. Unless you choose to apply for a Tico title and license plates, you'll have to take the vehicle out of the country for seventy-two hours and reapply for admission for another ninety days. There has been talk of clamping down on reentering with a car after the ninety-day period. The plan is to allow a short time to place the car into customs for processing or remove the vehicle from the country permanently. Be sure to check with customs when crossing the border and find out the current policy.

Remember: Don't drive at night! ∎

CHAPTER EIGHTEEN

TOURING **COSTA RICA**

Every nook and cranny of Costa Rica has something special to offer, something to dazzle the eyes or gratify the other senses. Newcomers are never satisfied until they have seen it all; longtime residents tend to repeat their travels, to see everything again and again. Fortunately, getting around the country is easy. Within a few hours you can visit just about any section of Costa Rica you choose, and you usually have several modes of transportation available to you.

AIR **TRANSPORTATION**

The quickest way to travel about the country is by SANSA, Nature Air, or charter flights. Planes fly regularly, serving San José, Quepos, Golfito, Palmar Sur, Barra del Colorado, Nosara, Tamarindo, and Sámara. Ticket prices used to be inexpensive, but in the past few years they have become costly, and service often leaves much to be desired. Charter flights cost only a few dollars more and are much more reliable. SANSA offers a 50 percent discount for residents with *cédulas*, but it's still five to ten times as expensive as bus travel. Flights to anywhere in the country take far less than an hour, including stopovers. Check with

travel agents or Web sites for schedules. They can change overnight or be canceled entirely.

Because flights are popular, and the planes small, they are frequently booked solid. Make reservations well in advance, and be sure to reconfirm your reservations even though you have tickets. Someone else could end up with your boarding pass if you show up at the airport without reconfirming twenty-four hours in advance and arriving early.

Because regular service can be erratic or crowded, "air taxi" or charter flights are popular. These five-passenger planes will take you any place in the country with an airstrip. What's nice is you can have a driver waiting your arrival, who rushes directly to your charter flight, and you don't need to overnight in San José. (Pause for cheers and whistles.) Sample fares: to Carrillo or Nosara, about $80 one way (minimum of two passengers), or $280 for five passengers to Tortuguero.

What if you are a pilot and would like to rent a plane and fly yourself? Not so easy. Even if you are a certified pilot with a license from another country, you can't rent a Costa Rican plane until you've earned a Costa Rican license. You need to show proof of your total air hours logged in your country as well as log a certain amount of time in Costa Rica. If you own a plane, it can be kept in the country for up to six months without your having to pay taxes, after which time it must be removed. However, there seems to be a question as to how many six-month permits an individual can obtain. You'll need to check this out with customs and with local pilots to see how the laws are currently being enforced.

TRAINS **AND BUSES**

Guidebooks sometimes rave about the scenic wonders of the country's train system. Especially tempting are descriptions of a spectacular railroad trip from San José to the Caribbean city of Limón. However, when you read about train trips in Costa Rica, you know the book is a bit out of date. Since the earthquake of 1991, passenger trains no longer journey to Limón or anywhere else, for that matter. Sad, but true. Some roadbeds and a few ancient bridges slipped downhill—common occurrences in Costa Rica earthquakes—but this time the government decided not to rebuild. The lines were losing money anyway.

It's possible that service to the Pacific port of Puntarenas could be resumed sometime in the future, with a private company taking over the operations. In early 2000 a test run to Puntarenas had people sleeping overnight in line to get tickets. Two hundred disappointed would-be passengers watched the train roll away without them. The train to the Caribbean Coast, however, definitely appears to be history. The cost of repairing the bridges and tracks would be prohibitive.

Buses are another story. In addition to excellent city bus service, eight intercity bus companies provide frequent service to just about any place you'd care to go. Unlike the situation in the United States, where monopolistic intercity bus fares sometimes border on extortion, tickets between Costa Rican cities are downright cheap. A four-hour ride from San José to Limón, for example, costs little more than $4.00.

San José has no central bus station; bus lines depart from separate terminals, ranging from a new, full-service terminal to a curbside parking place in front of a small ticket office. For example, to go to Quepos and Manuel Antonio, you take the buses that leave from the "Coca Cola" terminal. (The Coca Cola terminal gains its name in a typical Tico fashion: There used to be a Coca-Cola bottling plant in the neighborhood.) Buses for Limón, Cahuita, Puerto Viejo, and other Caribbean destinations have their own terminal on Calle Central, 6 blocks north of the Metropolitan Cathedral. Often reservations need to be made a day or two in advance. The better tourist guidebooks list the bus terminals, destinations, and travel times.

A number of smaller bus companies (often with only one or two buses in the fleet) carry passengers to all imaginable sectors of the country. Few towns or villages in the republic lack bus transportation of some sort. Often while I was negotiating impossible backcountry roads, bouncing through deep potholes, skirting boulders in the trail, and wondering whether my rental car could ever make it back in one piece, a passenger-laden bus would appear from out of nowhere, sound its horn impatiently to move me aside, and then rumble past as it hurried on its way.

These country buses tend to be of an older, rattletrap variety, usually secondhand school buses bought at surplus in the United States. Sometimes the owner-drivers don't bother to change the paint, and the bus finishes its transportation career bouncing along dusty trails in Costa Rica with the legend MAPLEWOOD UNIFIED SCHOOL DISTRICT still painted on its side. Sometimes you'll be pleasantly surprised by an air-conditioned vehicle of late manufacture, which makes the backcountry surprisingly luxurious. Of course, there's nothing to guarantee the driver will actually turn on the air-conditioning, which draws power from the engine. And since Ticos open the windows from force of habit, the air-conditioning is redundant.

Since the distance between San José and any destination in the country is not very far, bus trips don't take too long. From San José to Quepos, a popular tourist destination, bus travel time is less than four hours. By air it is only twenty minutes or so, but by the time you get out to the airport an hour early, wait for the plane to leave (always a half-hour to an hour late), and then wait for a bus to take you from the airstrip to town, you haven't saved all that much time. Plus you've missed a lot of interesting scenery. However, be aware that different bus lines have varying schedules. For example, travel from San José to Puntarenas takes two hours on one bus line but four hours on another line.

I knew Costa Rica had a lot of competing bus companies, but for a while I was astounded at how many different bus lines there appeared to be in and around San José. It seemed that the bus lines' names were very creative. Then I discovered that the name painted on a bus's side or on the back wasn't the name of a bus company at all but, rather, an imaginative name given to the bus by its driver as an expression of his individuality.

The *Tico Times* ran a feature article on these names, at which point I realized that the Papa Lolo bus that passed by my house every morning as I waited for my ride was not owned by the "Papa Lolo Bus Lines" but driven by a driver with the nickname "Papa Lolo." Some buses are named after family members; other names are exercises in imagination. Additional names the article noted were Desert Storm, Krakatoa, El Principe Azul (the Blue Prince), Mil Amores (Thousand Loves), the Dancing Queen, and El Guerrero del Camino (the Road Warrior).

TAXICABS **GALORE**

Costa Rica enjoys an excellent system of taxis, with about 7,000 drivers zipping along the streets of San José and suburbs—double what there were in 1990. Almost all cabs are late-model Japanese imports, usually Toyota or Nissan. Occasionally you'll see a Volkswagen or a Volvo. By law taxicabs are painted bright red. You can't miss them.

Not only is taxi equipment usually in good shape, but fares are inexpensive. In San José, you can go practically anywhere in the city from downtown for about $3.00. Between 10:00 P.M. and 5:00 A.M., drivers are permitted to charge an additional 20 percent. Drivers don't expect tips, but I always round the bill up to the next 100 colones, and they drive away happy.

All San José taxis are supposed to have meters, and most do. Ticos refer to a taxi meter as a *maría*. Why *maría*? Some years ago Costa Rica's president decided that taxis should have meters, rather than have drivers and clients haggle over the price of each ride. So he ordered a batch of taximeters from a company in Argentina for a trial run. The company's name contained the word *María*-something-or-other. But with typical Costa Rican bureaucracy, customs officials in Limón refused to allow the contraptions into the country until all the proper papers and forms were filled in. By the time all the tax stamps had been fastened, quadruplicate copies made, and signatures affixed, the meters—which were mechanical (as opposed to the electronic ones they use today)—had rusted in Limón's damp climate and had to be trashed. Ticos thought this so funny that they adopted the word *maría* for taximeter.

Avoid cabs parked in front of hotels or discos. The drivers will tell you that they don't have to use meters, because they pay more insurance, or some other baloney. The truth is, they charge from two to four times the normal rate. When in doubt, ask, "*Hay una maría?*" If the driver claims the meter isn't working, don't enter the cab until you've established a price (provided, of course, that you know about what the price should be). If the driver quotes a ridiculous price or if you haven't any idea of the correct fare, take another cab with a meter. At certain times of the day, drivers are reluctant to turn on the meters, because they know they can get all the customers they want and don't want the cab's owner to know exactly how much was taken in.

Occasionally you'll find cabs without meters, known as *piratas*, or "pirates," private autos illegally operating as taxis. Usually the fares quoted by these nonmetered cabs are about what you'd pay in a legally operated vehicle. The problem with piratas is that some of them aren't in safe operating condition. And unless you know what the fare should be and you know enough Spanish to negotiate, I'd recommend waiting for a cab with a meter. All in all, I think Costa Rican taxi drivers are fairly honest. Rarely have I been overcharged, and that was during times of heavy rains or rush hours—when the extra cost was worth it to me.

Although the law says that taxicabs must use meters, bear in mind that any trip over 12 kilometers is exempt. A trip from the airport to San José, for example, should cost between $12 and $14, depending on what part of the city you are going to.

Why are most cabs new? Because one side benefit of owning a taxi is that it can be purchased free of import duties, as long as it is used for three years before selling it as a used car. This means that after three years of generating income, the vehicle can be sold for almost as much as it cost in the first place.

Up to this point we've been discussing taxicabs around the Meseta Central. Taxis aren't only for city folk; you'll find them all over the country, sometimes in places so isolated that they would seem implausible. Not all villages will have a taxi, but most have access to one from a neighboring village. Away from the city's paved roads, four-wheel-drive taxis are the norm—and in the rainy season, a must. Four-wheel-drive trucks commonly serve as taxis, with the truck bed used to transport furniture, appliances, or more passengers. In rural areas, where buses and taxis are rare or non-existent, private autos and trucks often provide free rides to local people walking from one village to another. I do the same and find that locals appreciate rides—the hospitality enhances their opinion of foreigners.

TAXI CHAUFFEURS Driving a car around San José or through the narrow roads in the immediate countryside isn't exactly a relaxing pastime. I sometimes find myself so involved with traffic and confusion that I see very little. My passengers see even less, since they spend a great deal of their time praying, cursing, or shouting at me: "Watch where you're going, you dummy!" For that reason I rarely drive in downtown San José, even though I own my own car. It used to take me ten minutes of sweating and cursing to get from our condo to the center of town, whereas it takes only five minutes of sweating and cursing in the average taxi.

There is a better way to explore the Meseta Central: Rent a cab! Taxi drivers much prefer the idea of one fare for the entire day, instead of wandering all over town waiting for someone to flag them down. One fare isn't nearly as hard on the cab, since passengers always want to stop, get out, and spend time looking around, giving the taxi and driver a deserved rest.

Not only is it convenient to let someone else drive (someone who knows what he's doing), but renting a cab costs about the same as renting a car for the day. A competent, English-speaking cabdriver will chauffeur you around the Meseta Central for five or six hours for about $50. A rental car for one day, with insurance and gasoline, would cost almost $60—and $1 million worth of tension. In other words, after you buy the driver's lunch and give a small tip, you're about even. Most any cabdriver will rent hourly for about $10 per hour, but you're better off making prior arrangements with an English-speaking driver.

Taxicab rental will also save you hours of time and frustration when checking out neighborhoods for real estate. The driver can whisk you to a half dozen suburbs in less time than you can stumble onto one. This is also a great idea for sight-seeing trips around the Meseta Central. Instead of four people paying $25 to $45 per person for a five-hour commercial tour, a cabdriver can show you the same sights, with individual attention, for much less. Some drivers will even take you on longer trips, any place in the country you care to go—Monteverde or Manuel Antonio, for example—as long as you also take care of their hotel and meal expenses.

Not all drivers are willing to rent by the hour, and not all can speak English well enough to explain what you are seeing. To find one who does, check with your hotel clerk or a travel agency. Many English-speaking drivers are available and eager to show you around the Meseta Central.

RENTAL CARS **IN COSTA RICA**

Renting a car is by far the most convenient way of touring the country. When you get serious about looking for a place to live for a few months or for the rest of your life, renting a car for a week or two allows you to travel about freely in search of your dream location. You don't have to bother with bus schedules; you can check out side streets or country lanes, and you can stop whenever you find a particularly interesting view. With a car you needn't worry about hotel reservations; chances are, if one hotel is full, another will have room. You can drive around, checking out FOR SALE or FOR RENT signs. You can investigate for yourself instead of being under the control of a salesperson, a rental agent, or others with a vested interest in showing you only their own properties.

At present automobile insurance is a government monopoly, and it's mandatory that your rental car insurance be purchased through the government agency. This could change soon, bringing much-needed competition to the field. The way it is now, there's a hefty $750 deductible in case of an accident. Should the car be totaled or stolen, the deductible is $1,500. Since auto theft of rental cars is common, this calls for keeping your rental car in a safe place at night. Nowadays you can pay extra and have full collision insurance, and pay a little more and insure against theft. The insurance isn't cheap, but if you have a "Gold" or "Platinum" credit card (such as Visa or American Express), it should cover the deductible in case of an accident. Check with your credit card provider to be certain. Be sure to report a mishap to the credit card company within twenty days, even if the rental agent assures you that the other driver's insurance covers the repairs.

Accessories such as antennas, radios, tires, and mirrors aren't covered by rental insurance; if they are stolen, you are liable. The answer to the insurance problem is to keep your car in a guarded parking lot overnight when in the vicinity of San José. Auto accessory theft is not common in smaller towns, but in San José and other large cities, be aware.

Important: Unless you purchase full-coverage insurance, before you accept a rental car, check the car for dents, scratches, and blemishes in minute detail! Make sure the rental car employee notes each of them on your contract—no matter how tiny the scar. Unscrupulous employees in some agencies work a scam by charging for the same trivial scratch over and over. If the damage is there but not duly noted, you'll have no recourse but to pay. I've had better luck in this respect with the larger rental companies. Discuss the issue before you sign a contract.

Finally, insist on good tires. A sharp rock can penetrate a tire if the tread is thin and the sidewalls weak. If the tire is destroyed, you're liable for that, too. Insist on another car if the tires are not in good shape. If the car rental agency gives you trouble about this, consider finding another agency.

ON THE **ROAD**

Your regular driver's license is perfectly legal in Costa Rica for ninety days from the time you enter the country. After that you need a Costa Rican license. For residents or for those awaiting residente status, a license is relatively easy to get: Simply apply at the local office of the Ministry of Public Works ("MOPT," for us gringos; ask a friend to help you find one locally) and present a certificate of health from one of the doctor offices nearby. The license is issued while you wait.

However, as a tourist you are not permitted to drive after ninety days on your home country's license. You'll have to leave the country long enough to get a fresh stamp on your passport. Take this warning seriously. The rules for foreigners applying for driver's licenses by presenting their passports change from time to time. For a while it was difficult, if not impossible, because of a ruling that only legal residents could get Costa Rican driver's licenses. How strict this ruling was observed is another question. Some MOPT offices issued driver's licenses to nonresidents; some would not do so. However, the advantages of having a driver's license are nebulous unless you are a resident or have made application for residency, since it's illegal to drive if your ninety-day visa or extension has expired.

Always carry your passport when driving; there's a fine for not having it. A photocopy of the passport is acceptable, provided you have a copy of the page showing the date you entered. The original passport is much preferred. Photocopies of your driver's license are not acceptable.

The first rule of driving in Costa Rica is one that should be followed in any country: Do not leave anything stealable in the car, even out of sight. A favorite trick of thieves is to monitor the car rental desks at the airport and watch who rents a car and fills the trunk with interesting luggage. They then follow the car to the hotel, and while the passengers are inside at the registration desk, the thieves open the trunk and help themselves to the luggage, extra money, cameras, and so on. This does not happen often, but why take chances? If possible, leave someone in the car during that crucial first stop. Once you are outside of San José, the chance of something like this happening is almost nil.

Driving through the Costa Rican countryside isn't difficult; it's just slower. With all that gorgeous scenery, who wants to travel fast? Be especially careful when passing. Make sure you have time to get around safely, and be cautious near hills and curves. Always drive as though you expect trouble. That's just common sense in any country, but particularly in Costa Rica; too many drivers have a daring, gambling attitude that urges them to pass on hills and curves. For this reason accident rates in Costa Rica are unusually high. Drive defensively—and keep an eye on the speedometer. Americans, used to high-speed, paved highways, sometimes have difficulty keeping their speed under 65 miles per hour; it doesn't seem normal to drive slower. But you must realize that 65 miles per hour is about 110 kilometers per hour, an illegal speed anywhere in the country. Most highways have a 75-kilometer-per-hour limit, unless posted with an 80-, 90-, or an occasional 100-kilometer-per-hour limit.

Watch for oncoming drivers who flash their headlights off and on. That means trouble ahead, usually a radar speed trap or perhaps an accident. Another sign of danger is a tree branch or piece of shrubbery lying across one lane of the pavement. That signifies that an accident, a washout, or some other nasty surprise could await you ahead.

Driving in city traffic anywhere around San José can be frustrating. As you get the knack of it and learn the system, it gets easier. Theoretically, finding your way around San José should be easy, because downtown city streets are logically organized on a north-south, east-west grid. *Calles,* or streets, run north to south, and *avenidas,* or avenues, run east to west.

However, nothing in Costa Rica is as simple as it sounds. For one thing, street signs are often missing. Sometimes they'll be posted on the corner of a building or perhaps on a signpost, but just when you need to know exactly where you are, you won't be able to find a clue. Furthermore, most downtown streets are one-way traffic, often without arrows to indicate which way! Perhaps you know that Avenida 9 is a one-way street going west, but how do you know the street you are looking at is Avenida 9 when there are neither street signs nor one-way signs? All you can do is wait to see which way traffic is flowing. If no cars are coming either way, you don't dare take a chance.

In the surrounding towns of the Meseta Central, traffic is lighter than in San José, but the problem of missing street signs becomes even worse. Some streets are one-way and others two-way, but too often there aren't any signs to clue you in as to which is which. An arrow painted on the pavement should indicate which direction is permissible, but sometimes the arrow isn't there. It's especially disconcerting to be driving along what you believe to be a two-way street and suddenly notice that all the cars parked on both sides of the street are pointing in your direction. Since parking on either side of the street is OK in Costa Rica, you have no way of knowing if they just happen to be facing your direction or if you are traveling the wrong way again. When in doubt, park and wait for a car to drive past, then follow suit.

Away from the cities and major highways, you find bumpy roads that demand slow driving. Going too fast over rocks can cut tires, marooning you several kilometers from a repair shop. You may have to change a tire yourself! When this last happened to me, I stood around looking perplexed until two young men stopped to change the spare for me. They refused to accept money. Next I drove to a sort of auto repair place where two kids fixed my tire in a jiffy using strips of an old inner tube, some kind of glue, and what appeared to be a steel crochet needle. They didn't even have to take the tire off the rim, as I expected. They charged the equivalent of $1.50; that included putting the repaired wheel on the car and stashing the spare in the trunk.

TRAFFIC COPS **AND SPEED TRAPS**

I often hear reports of tourists being harassed by Costa Rican traffic cops. No doubt these things happen; as is the case anywhere else in the world, a few bad guys can get on the force. Yet after driving many thousands of miles and receiving numerous traffic tickets (all deserved), I have found the overwhelming majority of Costa Rican traffic police to be courteous and rarely stop someone without due cause. With all the crazy drivers in this country, cops have little reason to stop somebody for "nothing at all." Let's face it: Issuing a ticket for speeding, illegal passing, no safety belt, or the like is not "police harassment." In the United States it's known as "law enforcement." Tourists aren't exempt from traffic laws, even if they don't thoroughly understand them. Why should they be?

Yet you'll continually hear gringos complain that "the cops only stop rental cars. Why not Tico cars?" This is partly true, because Ticos know a little secret: When they see a speed limit sign of 60 kilometers per hour (38 miles per hour), they slow down because they know there's a good chance that there's a radar gun ahead. Tourists, used to 65-miles-per-hour highways, blissfully pass the slowpoke Ticos in front of them. And guess what?

Most Costa Rican highways have maximum limits of 75 kilometers per hour (about 48 miles per hour). This may seem ridiculously slow, but Ticos know that those occasional long, straight stretches of good pavement are also favorite places for radar guns. Maybe it seems sneaky, but when 75 kilometers per hour is the maximum, you're asking for trouble by going any faster. I've come to love those speed traps; if it weren't for them, all Ticos would be traveling 90 miles an hour! The fine for speeding is about $40 for ordinary violations, or $100 for *velocidad temerario* (120 kilometers per hour and above).

Allow me to offer some advice for when you're stopped by traffic police (I've had lots of experience in this department):

1. **Be calm, cool, and courteous.** After all, a ticket is no big deal. Until you're officially a resident, a traffic ticket doesn't affect your driving record or insurance. I've escaped several well-earned tickets simply by joking with the officers.

2. **Do not get belligerent or raise your voice.** Shouting won't help; it only makes things worse. When a cop feels he's being harassed for doing his job, don't be surprised if he retaliates in kind. I suspect this is where many cases of true police harassment originate: A tourist isn't aware that he's done anything wrong and becomes angry and abusive. The cop loses his temper, too.

3. **Don't offer a bribe.** Even the best cops will accept money if you force it on them. This encourages a bad practice. The department has been undergoing a rigorous campaign of professionalism. Wages have been doubled, crooked cops are being dismissed, and intensive training programs are under way.

4. **If the cop suggests that it would be easier to pay him than have to go to some distant place to pay your ticket, just politely decline and calmly wait for the ticket.** Don't even discuss it with him. Again, tickets are no big deal, and you can pay at any national bank or simply save them up and turn them in to the rental company with your car. The agency will pay them for you and add the fine to your credit card. Ticos routinely save their tickets and pay them once a year, just before it's time to renew their auto license plates. If a cop tries to insist on a bribe, make a good mental image of him and report the incident to the Ministry of Public Works (MOPT) at (506) 227–2188 or at the MOPT office on Calle 9 between Avenidas 22 and 23.

I might add that since I've grown accustomed to watching the speedometer, I haven't received a ticket in more than five years, even though I make frequent 400-mile round-trips to the Nicoya Peninsula—past a dozen speed traps—sometimes with California plates, sometimes in a rental car, sometimes with Tico plates. Having no speeding tickets in five years is a Central America record for me.

Traffic tickets used to be so ridiculously cheap that drivers routinely ignored traffic laws, preferring to pay the occasional ticket rather than drive safely. This contributed to an appalling accident rate. Speeding tickets were less than $6.00, so why worry? Even with today's $40 fines, people still keep traffic cops busy.

FINDING HOTELS **AND LODGING**

The tourist bonanza over the past few years made the hotel situation somewhat tight at times. To compensate, new hotels were constructed and private families converted homes into bed-and-breakfasts as quickly as they could. Many North Americans joined this bed-and-breakfast boom, partly financing their retirement by renting out spare bedrooms. In smaller communities hotels and ecotourism facilities raced to accommodate demand. Today you can often find a room in isolated places where camping was the only choice before. This trend seems to have caught up with demand, at least temporarily, because now there's an oversupply of rooms.

The tightest hotel room market in Costa Rica is during the Christmas–New Year's weeks. Not impossible, just tight. During the rush season making reservations before you leave for Costa Rica, even if only for the first couple of nights, is a good insurance policy. After you arrive, you can check around and locate something suitable to your taste and/or the size of your pocketbook.

Around San José, hotels come in all sizes and flavors, with expensive rooms costing $100 a night and up and cheap rooms under $15. For medium-priced hotel rooms, expect to pay from $45 to $65 a night during the tourist season. I looked at one room for under $10 recently, but shivers ran down my spine when I peered into the gloomy-looking room, with dirty linen on the bed, and in a ramshackle wooden building that looked like a firetrap. For my personal tastes a $30.00 room would be my bottom choice, yet many of the younger set and the backpacker brigades believe that anything over $8.00 is far too expensive. My wife's preferences fall into the $60 range or above.

If you're on a budget—as we long-term travelers usually are—don't expect too much in the way of luxury. You may find an affordable rate for a room with a private bath, only to discover that the shower is plumbed for cold water only. When a hotel advertises hot water, you'll often find one of those rinky-dink electric heaters attached to the showerhead. This contraption, known as a "suicide shower," has a lever that can be set to one of three positions. The position that says OFF is the only one that works all the time. This encourages short but exhilarating showers, ideal for anyone considering celibacy. The secret is to let the water flow at its lowest possible volume, in the hope of coaxing warmth from the heating element.

Really inexpensive hotels sometimes use low-wattage light bulbs, so weak that you have trouble reading in bed. The solution is to carry a seventy-five-watt bulb in your luggage and substitute it whenever you feel like reading. (Make sure you aren't into a twelve-volt system!) Other items you might keep in your bag are a drinking cup, a roll of toilet paper, and some nylon string and clothespins so that you can wash out undies. *Very important:* Pack a set of earplugs; I've suffered several nights made impossible for sleep by inconsiderate people partying all night or standing outside my door making plans for the next day's trip—at 2:00 A.M.! One additional item is insect repellent; one buzzing mosquito can make sleep difficult, a dozen of them can make sleep impossible. Understand that most of the foregoing advice is geared toward the low end of the hotel range. Ordinary places are much better.

Should you be stranded out in the country, unable to find a place to stay, your ace in the hole is the local *pulpería*. This is the Costa Rican equivalent of a country "general store"; it also serves as the social center of the community. Drinks and snacks are sold, as neighbors congregate to exchange news and tidbits of gossip as well as purchase necessary items ranging from matches to machetes. The proprietor of the pulpería can sometimes find you a room with a local family. This is a unique opportunity to see how country folk live in Costa Rica, but don't expect luxury. A pulpería is also an excellent place to inquire about real estate. If anything is for sale or rent in the neighborhood, the proprietor will know, and she probably knows the bottom-line price as well as the asking price. ■

LEGAL **MATTERS**

In Chapter 10 we discussed the pros and cons of buying real estate in Costa Rica. The nice part is that property ownership is open to anyone, no matter what citizenship; it's fairly easy to gain a clear title; and you can feel absolutely confident about your ownership. The nasty part is that a lot of charlatans and swindlers are out there ready to take advantage of your trusting nature. Don't worry—they haven't a chance if you do things correctly and don't skip any steps in the process.

The following information comes to us courtesy of my friend Carlos Umaña, of Tacsan & Umaña law offices in San José. For those of you with connections to the World Wide Web, another source of Costa Rica legal information can be found at www.discoverypress.com/crinet.

Your first step is to cultivate a relationship with a lawyer who knows what the score is. In Costa Rica it's much easier to become an attorney than it is in the United States or Canada, so just because someone can legally assume the title *licenciado* doesn't guarantee he knows what he's doing, or even that he's ever practiced law. You'll find many people who are entitled to call themselves attorneys but actually practice law as an occasional sideline. A poor attorney isn't necessarily crooked; he could be lazy, inefficient, or incompetent, which is just as bad.

A second important point: Make certain the lawyer is working for you, exclusively for you. If you use the other person's attorney to represent both interests, you're facing the probability that the lawyer is primarily working for his first client and isn't on your side at all. Unlike the situation in the United States, this is how it can work in Costa Rica. So insist on having your attorney handle your part of the sale.

PURCHASING **COSTA RICAN PROPERTY**

To make it easy to check on land ownership, all property, with a few exceptions, must be registered at the Property Department of the Public Record Office. This office is located in Zapote and is open to the public. It's a rather easy system to research, however, it's best to have your attorney do the checking, because he knows what to look for and where.

The first step, before you hand over any money, is to run a thorough title search of the public records to see whether the property really belongs to the seller, whether the seller is who he claims to be, and whether any mortgages, liens, encumbrances, or easements come attached to the property. Mortgages and liens must be properly registered to have any effect on the buyer. So if the title is clear, you needn't worry about outstanding debts. If a lender didn't register a second deed of trust, he's out of luck. A title search should cost less than $50, and it is well worth it. If the seller was untruthful, you won't waste any more time. Actually, to get started you can research a title or plot of land yourself in the *Registro Nacional,* simply by going to the Web site and filling in a form. If you find nothing wrong with the title, you can authorize your attorney to investigate further. (For details, see the end of this chapter.)

You'll remember that all property is registered, with exceptions. These exceptions are important. Let's review the three basic categories of Costa Rican properties.

1. **Recorded land.** This includes all properties you'll find registered at the Public Record Office. The vast majority of properties for sale today fall into this category.

2. **Nonrecorded land.** This is property that could be registered at the Public Record Office but has not yet been recorded. This applies to farmland, *fincas* (ranches), or homesteads—places that haven't legally changed hands for many decades or perhaps have been

changed through a private contract. Nonrecorded land requires an attorney familiar with the procedure. It takes a judicial procedure to register land for the first time into public records. This kind of sale lacks the security granted by the Public Record Office.

3. **Nonregisterable land.** This is property that cannot be legally recorded at the Public Registry. This is the case with most beachfront property. In some instances beach properties can be possessed legally by individuals or corporations through a concession granted by the government. The lease is always through the government, but you must acquire possession from the previous possessor, if there is one.

TRANSFERRING RECORDED LAND Any individual or company, national or foreign, may legally own land sheltered by the Public Record Office system. But for legal and economic reasons, you should consider placing your property in the name of a Costa Rican corporation, or *sociedad anónima* (more about this later in this chapter).

Recorded land transfers must be granted through a public deed. That is, buyer and seller must appear before a Costa Rican notary public (to be chosen by the purchaser), who will insert the title transfer in his protocol. (A notary public is a licensed attorney who is endowed with "public trust" and the right to validate and legalize all contracts and deeds. Again, to protect your investment, you should appoint your own attorney to perform as the notary public in the transaction.)

The purchase deed, as well as any liens or mortgages agreed to by the buyer, is then presented to the Public Record Office to be registered. It's also the notary's duty to complete all recording procedures necessary to provide the title transfer with full efficacy. (This is another reason to have a good attorney working for you, someone who knows what the word *efficacy* means.)

Expenses and legal fees involved can range from 6 to 7 percent of the total amount of the transaction and on the assessed price of the property. These costs are customarily shared by buyer and seller on a fifty-fifty basis—unless agreed otherwise.

BEACHFRONT PROPERTY Because of special regulations some areas are not subject to private ownership. This is the case with most beachfront property, which is leased through concessions granted by the government. This is where things become complicated. Public Law No. 6043 of March 1977 established a restricted coastal zone called the Zona *Marítimo/Terrestre*. This law covers a strip of land, 200 meters deep, along both the Pacific Coast and the Atlantic Coast. The restricted zone is divided into two sections:

1. The Public Zone (*Zona Publica*) is that first 50-meter strip of land starting at the mean high-tide line. This is public property; the public has full access to the Public Zone.

2. The next 150-meter strip of land is called the Restricted Zone (*Zona Restringida*).

The law states that no private individual or corporation is allowed to build on or use for private purposes "any portion whatsoever" of the Public Zone. However, it's possible to obtain a lease/concession on Restricted Zone properties for private or business use. Understand that when this happens, it isn't a deed; it's a "lease concession." At first the lease is with the local municipality; later on, after a procedure, the lease is with the Costa Rica Tourism Institute. Beneficiaries of lease concessions are granted the use, occupation, and possession of the land, including the right to build.

Now comes a sticky point. The law says, "No lease concessions are granted to non–Costa Ricans who have resided in the country less than five years, nor to foreign companies, nor to national companies of which 50 percent or more of its stock is owned by non–Costa Ricans."

While that may be the law, the fact is that many if not most of the desirable Zona Restringida properties are held by Costa Rican corporations that are owned entirely by foreigners. This is, of course, difficult to verify, because ownership of a Costa Rican corporation is impossible to substantiate. (Tips on how to start a corporation are found later in this chapter.)

These lease concessions can be transferred from one person or company to another, subject to the approval of the municipality and the Costa Rican Tourism Institute. Leases are generally granted for periods that range from five to twenty years. The municipality is entitled to charge a small leasing fee. At the end of the leasing period, the lessee can apply for an extension of the lease concession, and extensions are normally granted with the previous approval of the Tourism Institute.

Beachfront land not regulated by this law can be found, but it's extremely unusual to find titled property in areas within the restricted 200-meter zone. True, some beachfront land isn't regulated, because it was in use before the beach laws were passed. These exempt parcels are so-called "grandfathered" properties. However, be cautious; many people think that their property is grandfathered when it really is not. Some claim it's grandfathered when they *know* it is not.

OFFSHORE **CORPORATIONS**

For a variety of reasons, banking secrecy laws such as those in Switzerland attract a great deal of interest among certain folks who have motives for hiding assets. As far as I know, there is no law against this as long as these accounts aren't used to defraud creditors or to evade paying taxes. Like Switzerland, Costa Rica has strict rules on nondisclosure of bank accounts.

An interesting angle of financial secrecy is the use of Costa Rican "offshore" corporations. Like bank accounts, these corporations can be started by anyone—citizen, resident, or tourist—and are supposed to be totally secret. Since there's no way of knowing just whose names are on the corporation books, it's almost impossible to discover who actually controls any of these corporations. In fact, the legal term is *sociedad anónima* or "anonymous society." That's why corporation names are appended with "S.A." instead of "Inc." or "Ltd." One common example of a legitimate use of a corporation is when buying or selling real estate. If the property belongs to a corporation, transfer of ownership is simple. You merely transfer the corporation's stock; the property belongs to whoever holds this stock.

Having stressed all of this about secrecy, I have to say that there is some uncertainty about this. Some feel that the U.S. government, using the pretext of "containing terrorism," has been pressuring the countries that allow offshore corporations to relax their rules on anonymous corporate officers. Recently the Costa Rican government insisted that all corporations file a special, one-time, year-end tax form that requested details about the officers of the corporation and how much income, if any, the corporation made. Whether any of this information will be surrendered to outsiders is questionable. For those who use their corporations for the usual purposes, such as property ownership, there is no problem. For those who have something to worry about, I would suggest a talk with your attorney and possibly changing to a new corporation.

Before we go any further, you need to understand a few crucial points. First, I am not an attorney, and even if I were, you would be foolish to accept legal advice from a book—particularly when it comes to activities as complicated as offshore corporations or foreign banking practices. Second, while most corporations and bank accounts in Costa Rica are legal, used for perfectly legitimate purposes, the ones used for illegal schemes are frequently toppled, sending overly creative schemers to jail. I suspect that what happens is that the corporation originally starts off with legal goals in mind and then branches out into a small tax fraud, which grows until it gets out of hand. Some schemes are so obvious that the IRS has little trouble spotting the smoke and flames. My final point is a reiteration of the first: I am not a lawyer, nor am I in any way urging readers to get involved in offshore corporations or secret bank accounts. I am merely reporting what Costa Rican residents and attorneys have passed along to me.

STARTING A **COSTA RICAN CORPORATION**

Costa Rica's corporate structure allows any person (Costa Rican or not) to control a company without his or her name appearing in the public records. A Costa Rican lawyer (who must be a specialist in this) sets up a corporation without the real owner's name ever appearing in the record. It is termed a *sociedad anónima con acciones al portador,* or "anonymous society with all stock owned by the bearer." This means that although there is a legal president, secretary, and treasurer (often simply employees of the attorney), the actual ownership of the corporation is invested in whoever physically has the stock certificates in his or her pocket or safe-deposit box. Even the attorney has no way of knowing whether the original client still owns the stock. This arrangement is prohibited in the United States but is perfectly legal in Costa Rica.

This corporation is free to engage in many types of business activities, both in Costa Rica and in other countries. Theoretically, because it is considered a "foreign corporation" as far as the IRS is concerned, it pays no taxes in the United States. (There's talk about changing this.) Because it's a Costa Rican corporation, it pays little or nothing on what it earns outside Costa Rica. This doesn't relieve the individual of the responsibility of reporting income and paying income taxes in his or her home country. New laws require that a yearly report of a corporation must be filed; should there be no income to report, there are no tax consequences— but not filing the report makes the corporation liable for a fine. So if you already have a corporation in Costa Rica and haven't been filing reports, see your lawyer.

Be aware that from time to time there can be arbitrary changes in tax rules for corporations. No matter that your corporation does not make money—for example: if the corporation's only asset is a house or an automobile—there could be an extra form to fill out to state that there is no income. This happened in 2003, and many people were caught unaware. The process was simple, but if you happen to be living in the United States or Canada, you might not hear about this. To avoid any fines for not filing, you need to have someone in Costa Rica watching the situation and to notify you when something like this comes up. I have my lawyer take care of things like this for me, and it is automatically taken care of. If you prefer to do it yourself, you should watch the *Tico Times* or one of the online Internet newspapers, such as *Costa Rica A.M.* or *La Nación,* or at least have a friend in Costa Rica give you a "heads-up" on the rare occasion something like this happens.

ADVANTAGES OF A CORPORATION It's always advisable for both foreigners and Costa Ricans to own land through a corporation. Among the advantages is a reduction of personal liabilities and taxes. The ownership of assets, such as real estate, boats, and automobiles, is the main purpose of most registered corporations in Costa Rica.

A corporation can be owned by a group of shareholders or fully owned by one shareholder. This way a single individual or a small group of people can operate the company in a relatively simple and inexpensive manner. The asset (your house or your car) can be sold or transferred simply by handing over the shares of the corporation, because it is owned by the corporation, not the individual, even though he or she may own all the shares. Your attorney will show you the best ways to ensure control of the company and the overall handling of corporate power.

An important point about corporations is to make sure you are getting a full-fledged corporation; there are shortened versions that have some serious drawbacks. Don't go for a cut-rate, partial incorporation, because you'll not get all the required services, and it could expire at the end of a brief period. Later you'll find you have to go back and spend more money to put the company on a par with other corporations. Most attorneys will charge from $350 to $700 to form a complete corporation.

LEGAL DETAILS There are four main stages in the process of forming a Costa Rican corporation.

1. A document called the Articles of Incorporation or Constitutive Charter of the company will need to be prepared. This document will be drawn up by your attorney. The Constitutive Charter determines the organization, administration, and bylaws of the company. This is signed by all the shareholders, the appointed members of the board of directors, the controller, and the *agente residente.*

2. Before registration in the Public Record Office, your attorney will announce the company's constitution in Costa Rica's official newspaper, *La Gaceta.* This takes about two weeks. Also, you must make a deposit of the amount of the capital stock indicated in the Constitutive Charter—usually 1,000 colones—in a national bank. The amount of shares in the corporation and their denomination are determined by the founders. All shares must have equal value and must be worth at least 1 colón, but there's no top limit to a

share's value. The money deposited can be withdrawn once the company has been duly recorded.

3. The company must be registered in the Public Record Office. This registration is essential to legally constitute a corporation in Costa Rica. The registration process is performed by the notary public (your lawyer). The whole process takes from one to three months, depending on the time it takes for the Public Registry to approve the company's bylaws, including the books.

4. You'll receive a set of three accounting books (*Diario, Mayor,* and *Inventario y Balances*) and three "legal" books (*Shareholders' Record, Shareholders' Assemblies,* and *Board of Directors' Meetings*). Your attorney will present the books to the Ministerio de Hacienda for their initial authorization. Once duly legalized, these books should register all internal affairs of the company (as well as stock transfers) and are kept privately by the shareholders. You can leave them with your attorney or place them in a secure place, such as a safe-deposit box. Remember, whoever has the books in hand also has control of the assets.

To form a Costa Rican corporation, you need a minimum of two initial shareholders. Once the company is formed and properly inscribed in the Public Record Office, the shares can be transferred to a single person, who becomes the sole shareholder of the company.

The name of the company must be in Spanish, Latin, or any native dialect. Of course a name can't be identical or equivalent to that of an existing corporation. And names with a meaning in a foreign language (such as English or German) are not allowed without special exceptions. Your attorney in charge of preparing the Articles of Incorporation will ask you for a list of names (in Spanish), and he'll research them and determine whether they will be accepted by the Public Record Office.

There must be a board of directors with at least the following officers: president, secretary, and treasurer. The president must be the principal representative of the company. Other members of the board can also be made representatives of the corporation, depending on how the founders of the company decide to do the Articles of Incorporation. The members of the board may or may not be shareholders. The directors

must be present when the company is legally formed, to personally accept their designation and sign the Corporation Charter along with the shareholders or power of attorney.

The controller cannot be a shareholder or a member of the board of directors. The person appointed as controller has to sign the Articles of Incorporation. Usually this will be someone on your lawyer's office staff.

Every Costa Rican company must designate an agente residente. The agente residente will probably be your Costa Rican attorney, who will be a formal representative for official matters. He has no powers to act on the company's behalf. The fee for this service is usually $100 a year.

BANKING **SECRECY**

Traditional tax havens—such as the Cayman Islands, Switzerland, Luxembourg, the Channel Islands, and the Netherlands Antilles—have always tempted those looking for ways to hide assets. Secret bank accounts are often used for this purpose. I've been told that medical doctors routinely hide as much of their holdings as possible in these places to avoid disaster should a multimillion-dollar malpractice suit top their insurance limits. Like the aforementioned countries, Costa Rica maintains a strict policy of banking and commercial secrecy. The amount of money you have in a bank account is supposedly sacrosanct and unavailable to curious outsiders.

One banker said, "If I disclosed information about someone's account—even to a policeman or a government official—I could go to prison." The *Tico Times* illustrated this point with a story about a suspect accused of stealing and forging checks. The crime could easily be solved if authorities could access bank records and see whether the stolen checks had been deposited to the suspect's account. But bank officials refused to help the police solve the crime because, in the process, they would become criminals themselves!

Do not think that this secrecy deters the IRS from snooping about, and I suspect not without some success. (Realize that failing to report a foreign bank account on your income tax return is a law violation.) Sometimes fraud is so transparent that all the secret bank accounts or anonymous corporations in the world wouldn't help. I suspect that the IRS has its own methods of tracking down fraud without going through the Costa Rican banking system. But there is nothing illegal about U.S. or Canadian citizens owning a bank account or majority stock in an offshore corporation, so long as profits are reported and taxes properly paid.

CHECKING PROPERTY **VIA THE WEB**

Costa Rica may be somewhat backward in some aspects, as are most developing countries, but we must admire the way the government has utilized the Internet to open the *Registro Nacional* to the public. What used to be a time-consuming and bewildering process of investigating the legal status of a piece of real estate or ownership of an automobile has now become a simple matter of calling up a Web page and entering a few numbers. Within a few seconds, you can find out if that beautiful house with a view of the valley actually belongs to the person who is trying to sell it to you. Does he have a mortgage on the property that he neglected to mention? Are there any liens against the house because of an automobile accident or a liable judgment? You can discover who were the previous owners, in case you would like to talk with them to see if they have any information for you. In some instances you can find out who the neighbors are. Before you decide to buy that bargain four-wheel-drive Toyota, you might be interested to know that it hasn't been reported stolen, or that the title is not held encumbered by a bank loan. The previous owners are also listed.

The Web site can be found at: http://196.40.22.13. Navigating the site is fairly straightforward. You'll probably need a dictionary or, better yet, an online Spanish-to-English virtual dictionary to understand some of the terms. (Go to http://wordreference.com and install the Spanish-to-English module.) Several examples are found in the help section. To look up real estate, click on *Bienes Inmuebles* and then *Catastro*. You'll find several search choices: search by name (*nombre*), by corporation number (cedula), the number on your lot plan (*número de plano*), or number of the finca or concessión (*número de finca o concesión*). To look up an automobile or an insurance policy or any number of other features, click on *Bienes Muebles,* and follow the same procedure. ■

APPENDIX

COSTA RICAN CONSULATES **IN THE UNITED STATES**

Arizona—Phoenix (area of coverage: Arizona): Andrew P. Burke, Honorary Consul, 1426 West Key Largo Court, Gilbert, AZ 85233; (602) 632–0132; fax (602) 539–0590

California—Los Angeles (areas of coverage: Arizona, Hawaii, Nevada, Southern California, and Utah): Carlos Longan, Consul, 1605 West Olympic Boulevard, Suite 400, Los Angeles, CA 90015; (213) 380–7915; fax (213) 380–5639

San Francisco (areas of coverage: Alaska, Idaho, Montana, Northern California, Oregon, and Washington): Manuel Escoto, Honorary Consul, P.O. Box 7643, Fremont, CA 94537; (510) 790–0785; fax (510) 792–5249

District of Columbia (areas of coverage: All U.S. territory): Erika Harms, Consul General, 2112 S Street, NW, Washington, DC 20008; (202) 328–6628; fax (202) 265–4795

Colorado—Denver (area of coverage: Colorado): Tito Chaverri, Honorary Consul, 3356 South Xenia Street, Denver, CO 80231-4542; (303) 696–8211; fax (303) 696–1110

Florida—Miami (area of coverage: Florida): Guillemo Jimenez, Consul, 1600 NW Le Jeune Road, Suite 102, Miami, FL 33126; (305) 871–7487 or (305) 871–7485; fax (305) 871–0860

Tampa (area of coverage: Florida): Carlos E. Odio, Consul, 2200 Barker Road, Tampa, FL 33605; (813) 248–6741; fax (813) 248–6857

Georgia—Atlanta (area of coverage: Georgia): Ana Virginia Castro, Consul, 1870 The Exchange, Suite 100, Atlanta, GA 30339; (770) 951–7025; fax (770) 951–7073

Illinois—Chicago (areas of coverage: Illinois, Indiana, Iowa, Kentucky, Michigan, Minnesota, Missouri, North Dakota, Ohio, South Dakota, and Wisconsin): Juan Salas, Consul, 185 North Wabash Avenue, Suite 1123, Chicago, IL 60601; (312) 263–2772; fax (312) 263–5807

Louisiana—New Orleans (areas of coverage: Alabama, Arkansas, Louisiana, Mississippi, New Mexico, Oklahoma, and Tennessee): Gonzalo Calderon, Consul, World Trade Center Building, 2 Canal Street, Suite 2334, New Orleans, LA 70130; (504) 581–6800; fax (504) 581–6850

Massachusetts—East Boston (area of coverage: Massachusetts): Leonard Florence, Honorary Consul, 175 McClellan Highway, East Boston, MA 02134; (617) 561–2444; fax (617) 561–2461

Minnesota—St. Paul (area of coverage: Minnesota): Anthony L. Andersen, Honorary Consul, 2424 Territorial Road, St. Paul, MN 55114; (651) 481–3616; fax (651) 645–4684

New York—New York City (areas of coverage: Connecticut, Maine, Massachusetts, New England, New Jersey, Pennsylvania, and Rhode Island): Otto Roberto Vargas, Consul, 80 Wall Street, Suite 718, New York, NY 10005; (212) 509–3066; fax (212) 509–3068

Puerto Rico—San Juan (area of coverage: Puerto Rico): Alexander Montero, Consul, Avenida Ponce de Leon, Edificio 1510, Oficina P1, Esquina Calle Pelaval, San Juan, Puerto Rico 00909; (787) 723–6227; fax (787) 723–6226

Texas—Houston (area of coverage: Texas): Eduardo Cordero, Consul, 3000 Wilcrest, Suite 112, Houston, TX 77042; (713) 266–0484; fax (713) 266–1527

San Antonio (area of coverage: Texas): Marta Rojas, Consul, 6836 San Pedro, Suite 116, San Antonio, TX 78216; (210) 824–8474; fax (210) 824–8489

COSTA RICAN CONSULATES **IN CANADA**

British Columbia—Vancouver Antonio Arreaga, Honorary Consul, Suite 430-789 West Pender Street, Vancouver, B.C. V6C 1H2 Canada; (604) 681–2152; fax (604) 688–2152

Ontario—Ottawa (areas of coverage: All Canadian territory): Carlos Miranda, Ambassador, Embassy of Costa Rica, 135 York Street, Suite 208, Ottawa, Ontario K1N 5TA Canada; (613) 562–2855; fax (613) 562–2582

Ottawa Lina Ajoy, Consul General, 135 York Street, Suite 208, Ottawa, Ontario K1N 5TA Canada; (613) 562–0842; fax (613) 562–2582

Toronto Peter Alexander Kircher, Honorary Consul, 164 Avenue Road, Toronto, Ontario M5R 2H9 Canada; (416) 961–6773; fax (416) 961–6771

Quebec—Montreal Roy Thompson, Consul General, 1425 René Levexque-West, Suite 602, Montreal, Quebec H3G 1T7 Canada; (514) 393–1057; fax (514) 393–1624

INDEX

ABOUT THE **AUTHOR**

John Howells knows Latin America well. He lived in Mexico as a youth and traveled extensively throughout America, Central America, Spain, and Portugal, publishing several guidebooks about living, retiring, and investing in foreign locations. His thirty-year love affair with Costa Rica and Central America uniquely qualifies him as an expert on what it is like to be an expatriate in this charming little country, the "Switzerland of Central America." John and his wife Sherry divide their time between Costa Rica and California, and they are in the process of building a new house on Costa Rica's Pacific Coast.